Ben Evans

The Story of a Swansea Store

Jeff Stewart MBA CMgr FCMI MIC

Print ISBN 978-1-0687077-6-6

Published by

Llyfrau Cambria Books, Wales, United Kingdom.

Cambria Books and Cambria Stories are imprints of

Cambria Publishing Ltd.

Discover our other books at: www.cambriabooks.co.uk

Dedications

With love to my mother Pat Stewart, to my late father Ken Stewart, my wife Jan, my four children Laura, Gareth, Emma and Shaun, and last but not least, my grandson Logan.

Front cover image: Author's collection
Back cover image: Author's collection

CHAPTERS

Foreword 1

Introduction 3

1 - Shopping in Swansea in the Early 1800s 7

2 - The Coming of the Department Store 13

3 - Benjamin 'Ben' Evans and B. Evans and Co. 21

4 - The Opening of the Goat Street Store 30

5 - New Stables and the Upgrade of Temple Street 40

6 - The Widening of Castle Bailey Street 1893 47

7 - Ben Evans Castle Bailey Street Opening 53

8 - B. Evans and Co. for Sale 63

9 - Ben Evans and Co. (Limited) 1895 to 1910 69

10 - Ben Evans and Co. (Limited) 1910 to 1920 105

11 - Economic and Retail Challenges 1920 to 1930 125

12 - Economic and Retail Challenges 1930 to 1940 138

13 - Economic and Retail Challenges 1940 to 1950 163

14 - Economic and Retail Challenges 1950 to 1960 185

15 - The Demise of Ben Evans & Co. Ltd. 198

REFERENCES 203

APPENDICES 206

Foreword

When I started work in West Glamorgan Archives back in the early 1990s, one of my duties was to periodically visit old people's homes and daycare centres to give slide talks on old Swansea as it was both before and after the Second World War. The conversation in the group would inevitably centre on shopping and leisure, for there were relatively few men in the audience for whom the pictures of the old town's industries and docks brought back memories of their world of work. Always, the images of the Ben Evans building would be instantly recognised and provoke expressions of regret at its loss in the Blitz. Yet I rarely ever encountered anyone in the audience who had shopped in there. "Ben Evans was where posh people shopped" was the usual response when I asked why not, "We always went to David Evans."

The old Ben Evans' Department Store contained more than one such contradiction. Instantly recognisable as one of the most iconic buildings of pre-war Swansea, yet on closer investigation the building was something of an architectural jumble: a much-loved store at the very heart of the town but one which many townspeople felt was not for the likes of them to enter. In such respect, it was somewhat akin to the Harrods of Swansea, a flagship store the town could be proud of but more of a status symbol of Swansea's prosperity than a practical place for most ordinary working people to shop in.

One wonders, had the building survived the Blitz, how long it might have survived before closure and inevitable demolition (the town elders in the 1950s and 1960s being out of love with Victorian architecture). If by chance it had survived to the twenty-first century, like the David Evans store, it would surely not have been equipped to meet the huge downturn in the city's retail business in recent years. Without a doubt, the history of Ben Evans has been a story waiting to be told in depth, and this book provides a detailed history of the store from its genesis to its ultimate demise in its much-reduced post-war premises. I commend the author, Jeff Stewart, for taking on this task and producing a clear and coherent narrative history of the store and of the man behind it, revealing that its history was much more complex and nuanced than I for one had hitherto realised. I hope that you, the reader, find the narrative as intricate and the story as fascinating as I did.

Kim Collis, West Glamorgan County Archivist 2004-2024

The Ben Evans store, viewed from Castle Square, with the Hussey Vivian statue on the left (Author's Collection)

Introduction

For over forty years, 'Ben Evans' was a symbol of architectural magnificence and was considered 'the finest store in Wales and the West of England'. However, this iconic building met a tragic end during the Three Nights' Blitz in February 1941, when enemy aircraft devastated over 41 acres of Swansea's town centre, leaving the once-grand emporium in ruins.

The legacy of the Ben Evans store endures through a poignant collection of photographs, featuring striking images of the store's impressive Castle Bailey Street frontage alongside haunting scenes of its destruction. These visual records serve as a powerful reminder of its former splendour and the devastating impact of war on the town's landscape.

While the name 'Ben Evans' has been associated with the phrase 'The Harrods of Wales,' the author has been unable to find any evidence of this term being used during the store's operational years, and it is likely a modern construct used to emphasise the store's undoubted presence and importance to Swansea.

However, whilst it drew positive comparisons to other large and impressive contemporary London stores in Victorian and Edwardian London, comprehensive information regarding the Ben Evans store and its founder is scarce despite its significance. This presents an opportunity for further investigation into this iconic establishment.

Describing itself as 'General Drapers and Complete Home Furnishers', a common misconception today is that 'Ben Evans' was one enormous store. In reality, it was a labyrinth-like structure that had successfully linked together once-individual properties on Temple Street, Goat Street, Caer Street, and Castle Bailey Street, and it continued to be a 'work-in-progress' until the building's destruction during the Swansea Blitz.

In 1866, Benjamin Evans took charge of B. Evans & Co. at No. 3 Temple Street and his business soon prospered, and for nearly 30 years he maintained a hands-on approach to what was a sales-driven, performance-oriented business. In 1895, he sold the business and retired, and the store became a publicly listed company, 'Ben Evans and Company Limited', with its board of directors based in London.

Marketed as "The Premier Fashion and Furnishing House of Wales and the West", the store's reputation for quality and variety flourished. At its peak, Ben Evans boasted an impressive 42 departments.

The store offered a range of products that included, but were not limited to, home furnishings, ladies' fashions including a fur salon, children's wear, sports equipment, travel goods, and even a full-size replica horse to allow customers to try out saddlery, harnesses, and riding attire.

In-store amenities included refreshment rooms, a restaurant and a hairdressing salon, whilst customer services included the organisation of funerals and cremations via the store's 'Mourning Department', home and commercial catering, and lawn tennis and badminton lessons.

This comprehensive array of products, services, and amenities solidified Ben Evans' status as a premier shopping destination, catering to a wide range of customer needs and preferences.

Following the destruction of the store in 1941, temporary premises were established on Walter Road, however, inaction in rebuilding Swansea's town centre after the Blitz meant that the move became a permanent one. Despite its efforts, the company could not regain its place as Swansea's premier retail outlet.

To understand the company's history, its financial performance has been reviewed. However, as intricate details of the company's balance sheet, profit and loss account, share types, debentures, and dividends can be complex to the untrained eye, much of this information has been purposely omitted from the main body of text to maintain the book's focus.

While financial details are available in the appendices for those who seek them, the primary objective of this book is to bring the store's history to life in an accessible and engaging manner.

Taking this approach, the author hopes to pique readers' interest and foster a deeper appreciation of the company's remarkable journey. To achieve this, some key financial details are necessary to provide context and structure to the story, and a timeline has been woven throughout the book using the company's annual general meeting reports as well as its annually published net profit figures, as follows:

Year	Jan 1895-- Feb 1896	Net Profit	Net Profit
1		£ 15,490	£1,701,524 (2024)

Based on a June 2024 equivalence, all inflation comparisons have been made using the Bank of England inflation calculator (1), and a year-on-year comparison of both 'actual' and 'inflation-linked' performance can be found in the Appendices.

These financial milestones, coupled with the prevailing economic conditions and the retail environment of the time, serve as guideposts that allow the reader to trace the store's journey from the initial days of Ben Evans' ownership to the sale of the business to a larger company in 1955, and its demise a few years later.

Note 1: It would not have been possible to write this book without having online access to Welsh newspapers via the excellent resources of The National Library of Wales (2) and The British Newspaper Archive. (3)

Note 2: From 1889 until 1974, the official designation of the local government in the town was 'Swansea County Borough Council and Corporation'. Unless stated otherwise, the term 'Council' is used throughout this book for consistency and brevity.

Note 3: For consistency and brevity, the term 'Annual General Meeting' is abbreviated to 'AGM' after its first use.

1 - Shopping in Swansea in the Early 1800s

At the turn of the 19th century, most British town centres were, from a retail perspective, at best functional. While general and specialist shops operated by independent craftsmen and retailers provided specific items such as shoes, clothing, and household goods, it was the daily and weekly street markets—largely unchanged for centuries—that supplied fresh produce, including meat, poultry, fish, milk, and other everyday essentials. However, the shopping experience in the UK underwent significant changes between 1800-1850, marking the transition from traditional retail practices to the emergence of modern shopping formats. In the 1820s, commercial bazaars opened in cities like Liverpool and Manchester that had set up central shopping streets, whilst Britain's largest bazaar, Grainger Market, opened in Newcastle in 1835. In London, Regent Street was built as a shopping street.

In 1800, Swansea's population was approximately 7,000, and the few streets that made up Swansea's town centre were home to numerous specialised shops, as well as several markets selling produce such as meat, fish, poultry, vegetables, flowers, and the local delicacies - cockles, oysters and laverbread. John Nixon's 1793 drawing of Market Square (4) vividly depicts a melee of customers, costermongers, street sellers and hawkers, at the shambles (meat market) regularly held there in the shadow of the castle walls.

Opposite the castle were the ruins of 'Plas House', whilst only a stone's throw away stood 'Island House', separating Market Square from Wind Street, with 'Pig Street', 'Potato Street' and 'Butter Street' (St. Mary's Street) on the other three sides of the building. By 1830, the various open-air markets had moved to a new centralised location, a purpose-built facility on Oxford St, constructed on land previously known as Rope Walk Field, a site donated by Calvert Richard Jones Esq. Market Square was cleared in 1832 and renamed Castle Square in the following year. (5)

A Paving and Lighting Commission was set up by the town's Council in 1840, whilst utilities were installed across the town centre by the Swansea Gas Company and Swansea Water Works Company, as well as in some up-market residential areas. In the same year, the ruins of the old mansion 'Plas House' were finally cleared away, and various shops, warehouses and a police station were quickly erected on the site. It would take a further forty years for Island House to be demolished as part of a road widening plan that directly adjoined Wind Street to Castle Square.

Over centuries, Swansea had grown into what had once been called a market town, built around Swansea's castle and The Strand, alongside the River Tawe. Developed out of necessity rather than designed to support the trade that a small port brings, the town was poorly laid out. Much of the land in the centre of the town was made up of burgages, plots of land that had been in the hands of some families for centuries, many of whom had migrated to Swansea from elsewhere in Britain in previous years on recognising the opportunity to make their fortune. However, the control previously enjoyed by the burgesses had been somewhat curtailed since the formation of the Swansea Council in 1835.

A considerable number of the town's burgesses were merchants and traders, responsible for the wholesaling of goods, and then selling them on to the shopkeepers, many of whom had leased their shops from the burgesses, and who focused on acquiring goods at the lowest possible cost and selling them for a profit.

The shopkeeper constantly adjusted his inventory to stay relevant, and manage his business within tight profit margins; success or failure depended greatly upon his understanding of market trends and his adeptness in accurately assessing price shifts.

Shopkeepers and their families often lived above or behind their shop premises, renting spare rooms to their shop assistants or apprentices. Most shops were poorly lit and ventilated, so it was not uncommon for their business to be conducted from a wooden counter extending onto the road or pavement outside. Most shops were owned or leased by men, with some exceptions, including widows of shop owners; indeed, in the early part of the century, women were not permitted to own property or sign contracts. Despite constraints on ownership, women did manage stores such as millinery shops, seamstress shops, and dressmaking establishments, whilst others worked as street vendors, selling items from a basket or operating shop stalls where they sold goods they either purchased wholesale or made themselves.

Fishmongers, butchers, bakers, milk sellers and the like represented a dwindling number of independent retailers who sold their goods and services. It was not unknown for traders to engage in deceptive practices to stretch their profits. Sulphuric acid was added to beer, sawdust from ash and elder trees was added to tea, ground-up alum, peas, and beans were used to bulk up what was sold as 'pure flour', whilst used tea leaves were 'recovered' by generously sprinkling them with black lead before being resold, all in attempts to maximise their gains. Customers buying milk brought their jugs to the shop, where they would be served directly from a churn, and took their chances on whether or not it had been diluted.

It was not until after the second Swansea Cholera epidemic in 1849 (the first was in 1830), and the passing of the Public Health Act of 1849, that Swansea Council set up a Local Board of Health (in 1850). From that time, local newspapers often reported on traders being fined for misrepresenting their products to the public.

At the beginning of the 1800s, goods were typically not priced at all, so customers had to enquire about the cost, allowing room for negotiation, and shopkeepers would adjust prices upwards or downwards based on the perceived affluence of the customer to secure a sale. Furthermore, customers were not allowed to handle the merchandise without assistance from the shop's clerk. All items were kept behind the counter, in drawers, or cases, out of the customer's reach, for fear of theft.

By the 1830s, significant changes began to occur as more shop owners displayed items on counters and shelves, with clearly marked individual prices, and by the 1850s, this was the norm.

As a direct consequence of the Industrial Revolution, a flood of affordable, mass-produced goods poured forth from workshops and factories throughout Britain, Europe, and beyond. The opening of Swansea's North and South Docks meant that, in addition to receiving copper barques, the town was regularly visited by vessels laden with tea, coffee, silks, spices, oil, preserved meats and manufactured products. Goods made elsewhere in Britain were abundant in the local market, and stock could be quickly renewed thanks to the ever-growing rail links.

In Swansea, various emporiums with a plethora of offerings populated Castle Street, Castle Square, Wind Street, Goat Street, Oxford Street and other adjoining streets (the following examples are from 1835-1845):

'**The Golden Harp**' was trying to sell 'Linen and Woollen Draper, Haberdashery, Hosiery, Silk Mercery, Hats and Gloves at a 'full 25% under the usual prices'.

'**H. I. Jones**' offered 'Shawls and handkerchiefs of every description, printed muslins, ginghams, silks, parasols, veils etc as well as West of England Cloths and Cassimeres, and London hats of the best quality'

'**The Emporium**' offered 'Carpeting, Moreens, Irish Linens, Sheeting, Woollen Clothes and Trousering, as well as London and Paris Hats, Caps etc

'**The Golden Key**' offered 'Brussels, Kidderminster, Venetian, and Victoria Felt Carpets, plus West of England Cloth, Gossamer and Felt Hats'.

The neighbouring '**China and Glass Rooms**' shop offered 'A good assortment of Breakfast, Tea, Dinner and Dessert Services.'

'**The Foreign Wine Vaults**' was trying hard to sell French Wines from what appears to be a dubious source, and apologising for the taste of the previous stock!

'**Walton and Company's New Tea Shop**' on Castle St, opposite the Wheatsheaf Inn, offered a 'huge choice of Black Teas, Green Tea, Mixed Teas and Coffees'

'**J. Lyon, Clock and Watchmaker**' of 'St. Mary (or Butter) Street - 'Working Jeweller and Engraver, Musical Boxes repaired, Door and Coffin Plates engraved, Sword Blades and Steel Articles of every description embossed with Arms, Crests, Ciphers, etc.'

'**Eli James**' of Island House, 'respectfully informed his Friends and the Public' that the stock of his 'Declining Drapery Business' - 'the whole of his extensive and well-assorted stock' will be sold at 'Very Reduced Prices'. A month later he was advertising his 'new stock'!

At the '**The Lounge and Promenade**', a fancy title temporarily given to No.3 Temple Street, 'Licensed Hawker No.2105' Mr Barras Mier was offering 'Rosewood Desks and Workboxes, Musical Clocks and Boxes, Old and Modern Paintings, China and Opal Ornaments, Sheffield Plated

Articles, Jewellery - Foreign and English, Berlin Iron Jewellery, Bronze and Lava Ornaments, besides hundreds of other articles.'

The Great Exhibition at Crystal Palace in Hyde Park, London, held in 1851, further fuelled Britain's thirst for new and often exotic goods, with thousands of new products on show but not on sale. Whilst plate glass had been available for some years, following the 300,000 panes of plate glass showcased as part of the main structure of Crystal Palace, the now cheaper and more available product was swiftly introduced into the marketplace, and soon most local shops featured plate glass windows that brightened interiors and showed off the merchandise prominently displayed within the store. In addition, nicely painted shop fronts appeared, often with an alluring shop window designed to draw in passers-by. These changes marked a shift towards a more modern and customer-friendly shopping experience.

Many shops moved from singular offerings or services towards a more general nature, often with a peculiar assortment of products gathered under one roof, and catered to every social class. Shops had distinct layouts, yet they shared common features. Typically, a 'modern' shop would have a glass door or window to attract customers. Inside, there would be a well-lit counter area where transactions took place, surrounded by racks filled with merchandise. A staff member would be on hand to assist customers, ensuring they found what they needed in the shop's offerings. Despite differences in appearance and ambience, these shops served as vital hubs of commerce, catering to the diverse needs of society.

'By the 1850s, Britain had changed. It was now a more industrialised and urbanised society. The middle class, larger, richer, and more powerful than thirty years earlier, sought to establish itself culturally. Mass production made goods more affordable to the middle class, who forged and performed their identities partly through consumption and display. Literacy was much higher, and books and magazines were more plentiful and cheaper, thanks to the development of machine-made paper, the rotary steam press, and power-binding. Britain was now a middle-class nation.' Susie L. Steinbach (6)

Wales had become the first industrialised nation in the world, and few British towns experienced such rapid growth in population, significance, and commercial activity as Swansea did in the first half of the 19th century, transitioning from a quaint seaside resort to a bustling hub of industry.

As its importance as a leading centre of industry in Victorian Britain became ever more apparent, the town's population (including its outlying areas) rose to approximately 20,000 by 1850. To further enhance its position, the Great Western Railway Station at High Street was inaugurated in the same year, whilst the North Dock was officially opened in 1852, followed by the South Dock in 1857.

To accommodate the increased growth in both business and population, the town saw an influx of companies setting up or relocating to the area. This also led to a considerable increase in new shops, hotels and inns. All these establishments needed staff, and for the first time on such a large scale, many of those employed were women.

Teeming with a diverse array of industrial works, Swansea had rightly earned its reputation as the 'metallurgical centre of the world' or Copperopolis. Yet despite the town's remarkable progress, it lagged behind other thriving towns and cities when it came to the development of the town itself, and in particular, its main thoroughfares that, in contrast to its booming industrial sector, remained stuck in the early 1800s.

By the 1870s, there were nearly 300,000 shops in the UK, a figure that would double over the next thirty years, fuelled by a combination of factors, including the rise of the middle class, improved transportation networks, and the insatiable appetite of consumers for a wider array of goods and services.

2 - The Coming of the Department Store

Many of today's department stores have evolved into cultural institutions, but their origins are far more modest and rooted in a time when shopping bore little resemblance to today's experience.

By the end of the 1700s, clear retail markets had emerged in the larger cities of Britain and Europe. With shopping swiftly evolving into a fashionable pastime among the affluent, high-end goods were in demand. Rather than being sent from places like London or Bristol, where these establishments enjoyed regular business from a wealthy clientele that indulged in leisurely browsing for luxury items, the well-to-do were asking for such emporiums to be opened across the provinces, resulting in the opening of shops by jewellers, tailors, milliners, furniture-makers, and many others.

By the middle of the 19th century, many budding entrepreneurs recognised that their rapidly developing female customer base was interested in a wider array of goods. Keen to expand their retail empires, they acquired adjacent properties and connected them internally. This approach inevitably allowed for individual sections to be created within the premises, enabling more efficient use of existing space that often facilitated further business growth. This initiative created a completely novel retail concept: the department store.

Unlike some traditional shops that still bartered on prices, in these emporiums prices were marked clearly to provide transparency. Additionally, customers could request refunds, adding to the convenience and appeal of this new shopping experience. With the emergence of a wider array of products, including disposable goods and mass-produced clothing, stores experienced a surge in diversity and availability, however, by the 1870s they accounted for only 1% of Britain's shops. Nevertheless, this expansion prompted the need for more consumers to sustain the burgeoning consumer economy, and Britain's newly affluent middle class fitted the bill.

The owners of some of the larger shops opted to repurpose their storage and accommodation areas into additional selling spaces to offer a diverse array of goods under one roof. They often featured separate areas for ladies and gentlemen to better focus on the customers' wants and needs, allowing for discretion while browsing. As the significance of displaying goods from outside the building became clearer, "purpose-built" department stores emerged.

Often vast in comparison to traditional stores, the new department stores offered a diverse range of goods all under one roof, organised into distinct departments, in a safe, well-lit, and welcoming environment. The Bon Marché in Brixton, established in 1877 on Ferndale Road, London SW9, is regarded as the first purpose-built department store, which included in its design 50 staff bedrooms, reflecting awareness of the requirement for staff to live on the premises.

As the number of shops in each town grew, so did the requirement for female shop assistants, and as many young women opted for shop work, by 1890, there were over 200,000 'shop girls' employed in Britain. Perceived as more glamorous than rural, service or factory work, the pay was low and hours were long, with staff expected to work 6 days a week from early morning until late evening.

A typical department store operated with a rigid, regimental-like hierarchy. Department managers, senior supervisors, floorwalkers and buyers were at the top, salespeople and clerks in the middle, and junior assistants and apprentices at the bottom. Male staff were prevalent in the furniture and hardware departments, as well as in management roles. Young and unmarried women were employed in the clothing and accessories departments that catered to the rising middle-class female shoppers. Promotion opportunities were limited, especially for female staff, who were expected to leave upon marriage. While staff did not wear uniforms as such, they were expected to dress in black or dark blue.

The use of first names between staff members was frowned upon, and many department stores used a naming system to reflect the store's hierarchy. Senior staff would use more formal titles like 'Mr' or 'Mrs', and junior staff were often addressed just by their surname, e.g. 'Thomas' rather than 'Mr Thomas'. Female staff were commonly referred to as 'young ladies' regardless of age, whilst male staff in junior roles were called 'young men'.

Many stores used alternative 'store surnames' as part of their system. For example, during working hours Mr Williams (the person's real name) may well have been known within the store as 'Mr Wallace', the name prominently seen via the badge on his jacket. In contrast, Harrods staff were known by their number rather than name when dealing with customers. The impersonal numbering system helped to maintain a professional distance between staff and customers.

Most retail jobs were 'live in', and, according to Christopher P. Hosgood (7) shop assistants were 'absolutely powerless and helpless' as young employees that lived on the premises, often in dormitory-style accommodation, could be monitored closely.

Numerous early department stores, including iconic establishments like Charles Jenner (1838) in Scotland, John Lewis (1864), Whiteleys (1867) and Arthur Liberty (1875) in London, as well as Lewis Lewis in Swansea (1866) were established by drapers, textile merchants who possessed a deep understanding of the tastes and purchasing power of middle-class women, a demographic that would ultimately drive the department store to unprecedented levels of luxury and success across Europe and the United States.

Fortnum & Mason, established in 1707, and Harrods, founded in 1849, began as grocery stores, although before entering the grocery market, Charles Henry Harrod ran a draper's shop for 25 years.

Amidst the predominantly male ownership of the early department stores, there was one notable exception. In 1850, Elizabeth Harvey inherited her late husband Benjamin's linen shop and entered into a partnership with store manager James Nichols, who had married Benjamin Harvey's niece some years before. They aimed to sell luxury goods via their store Harvey Nichols, which occupied the entire block between Seville Street and Sloane Street. In 1889, the existing space was demolished to make way for a new, purpose-built department store, before it relocated to its present location on Knightsbridge in 1904.

In 1866, Lewis Lewis, a draper from Llanegwad in Carmarthen, took on the lease of 27 High Street in Swansea. By 1873, he had rebuilt no. 27, which he had extended by buying nos. 28 and 29. Together, these properties shared a 75-foot-long shop frontage of what in the 20th century became better known as the Lewis Lewis Department Store. To ensure his showrooms were spacious, he also leased nos. 9-15 on King Street (now Upper Kings Lane). After his death, additional space continued to be added to the store via the purchase of 90 and 91 Orchard Street.

One of the first stores in Swansea to utilise fixed pricing, Lewis Lewis introduced a 'store to door' delivery service to the houses of its Swansea customers, and a service to the Railway Station for those customers who had travelled to the store from outside Swansea.

Thought to have had the first escalator installed in a Welsh store it is also fondly remembered for its overhead 'cash railway', a system of rails, balls and canisters that moved orders, cash and receipts between departments, accounts and customers. In 'Under Milk Wood', Swansea poet Dylan Thomas's 'play for voices', he evokes his childhood memories of the cash railways used in Swansea stores, perhaps those he had heard in both the Lewis Lewis and Ben Evans stores when describing 'Mog Edwards' drapery store, 'where the change hums on wires.'

Divided into four departments, Harding, Howell & Co's Grand Fashionable Magazine, established in 1796 at 89 Pall Mall in St James's, London holds a strong claim to the title of the world's first department store, it was 'Whiteleys' department store that first claimed to be the biggest in the world.

Founded by Yorkshireman William Whiteley, who launched a drapery shop at 31 Westbourne Grove in 1863, the business had rapidly expanded to occupy an entire row of shops within four years. His new department store featured 17 distinct departments, and his motto was 'Everything from a Pin to an Elephant.' Dressmaking operations commenced in 1868, marking the expansion of the store's offerings beyond drapery.

In 1872, the premises employed 622 individuals, with an additional 1,000 workers engaged outside the store, and the company ventured into new territory adding a housing agency and refreshment room, marking their first ventures outside traditional retail. Whiteley further diversified by introducing food sales in 1875, and in 1876, a building and decorating department was added to the store's repertoire, a profitable move as local properties needed regular repainting.

Despite facing staunch opposition from smaller tradesmen as well as local authorities regarding his ambitious plans, William Whiteley, the self-styled 'Universal Provider', persevered and his business continued to thrive, bolstered by a delivery service that extended up to 25 miles from the store. Acclaimed as 'an immense symposium of the arts and industries of the nation and of the world', in 1887 it fell victim to a catastrophic fire and was destroyed in what is regarded as one of the most significant blazes in London's history. Allegedly caused by disgruntled competitors and tradesmen, this incident marked the culmination of a series of four previous fires that had plagued the business since 1882.

A new store was soon rebuilt, and by 1890, it had expanded significantly employing over 6,000 staff members. Many of these employees resided in company-owned dormitories and were segregated by gender. They worked long hours from 7 am to 11 pm, six days a week, and were subject to strict adherence to 176 company rules. Although live-in staff had access to reading rooms and various company social groups, Whiteley's regimented work methods ensured that his business was continually in the crosshairs of the new trade union groups that had sprung up to protect workers' rights, as were the other department stores of that time. In 1899, the business went public on the London Stock Exchange, and at the turn of the century, 'Whiteleys' was recognised as the leading department store in London.

In a tragic turn of events, in 1907, William Whiteley was shot and killed in his own office by Horace George Rayner (8) who had asserted to be his illegitimate son under the alias 'Cecil Whiteley'.

Following his death the board, which included two of his real sons, made significant changes to the company's direction, allowing the leases on the various Westbourne Grove properties to expire and moving the business into a newly constructed, purpose-built store on Queens Road (now Queensway). At the grand opening of the new Whiteleys store on November 21, 1911, the Lord Mayor of London officiated an event that attracted thousands of attendees, during which it was proclaimed that Whiteleys was 'the largest shop in the world'

Today, Harrods occupies a 5-acre site with 330 departments that cover 1.1 million sq. ft (100,000 m2) of retail space. With the motto 'Omnia Omnibus Ubique', Latin for 'All things for all people, everywhere', it is styled as 'The World's Leading Luxury Department Store & Food Emporium' and is one of the largest and most famous department stores in the world.

In 1824, Charles Henry Harrod began his entrepreneurial journey at the age of 25, founding a business at No. 228 Borough High Street in Southwark. Operating under various descriptions such as a draper, mercer, and haberdasher, he managed this enterprise until at least 1831. In 1834, he ventured into the wholesale grocery business in London's East End, establishing a presence in Stepney at No. 4 Cable Street, with a particular focus on tea. In 1849, he assumed control of a small shop in the district of Brompton, situated on the site of the current Harrods store. After seeing the opportunities presented by the Great Exhibition of 1851 in nearby Hyde Park, Harrod seized the opportunity to expand his business.

Initially operating out of a single room with just two assistants and a messenger boy, Harrod's son, Charles Digby Harrod, played a pivotal role in transforming the business into a thriving retail operation. Their store diversified its offerings, selling products such as medicines, perfumes, stationery, fruits, and vegetables. By 1881, it had experienced significant growth, acquiring adjacent buildings and employing over one hundred individuals.

The store's fortunes took a catastrophic turn in early December 1883 when it was consumed by flames and reduced to ashes. Nevertheless, Charles Harrod fulfilled all his Christmas delivery commitments and achieved record profits during that period. A new building was soon erected on the same site, and he began extending credit to the stores' most valued customers for the first time, reflecting the store's commitment to customer satisfaction and loyalty.

Following a chance meeting in London with businessman Edgar Cohen, Charles Harrod sold his interest in the store for £120,000 (equivalent to £14,110,759 in 2021) via a stock market flotation in 1889. The new entity was named Harrod's Stores Limited, marking a significant milestone in the company's evolution. Sir Alfred James Newton assumed the role of Chairman, with Richard Burbidge serving as Managing Director.

On 16th November 1898, Harrods unveiled England's first 'moving staircase,' known as an escalator, at their Brompton Road stores. This innovative device consisted of a woven leather conveyor belt-like unit, adorned with a mahogany, silver and plate-glass balustrade. Those customers brave enough to experience this novel mode of transportation were offered brandy at the top of the escalator 'to revive them after their ordeal.'

Financier William Mendel, who joined the board in 1891, was instrumental in securing funds to support the company's expansion efforts. By 1905, Harrods had become the largest department store in Europe, employing 3,000 staff and achieving an annual turnover of £2 million. In 1917, Richard Burbidge was succeeded by his son Woodman Burbidge as Managing Director. Woodman Burbidge, in turn, passed the mantle to his son Richard in 1935, ensuring a legacy of leadership continuity within the Burbidge family.

The store experienced several changes in ownership over the ensuing years, with House of Fraser acquiring it in 1959. Later, in 1985, the Fayed brothers purchased House of Fraser, thereby gaining control of Harrods. In May 2010, the store was sold to Qatar Holdings, the sovereign wealth fund of the State of Qatar, which remains its current owner as of this writing.

From 1909 onwards, Harrods faced competition from a formidable rival---Selfridges. Founded by American Harry Gordon Selfridge, Selfridges quickly became a prominent fixture on Oxford Street, boasting a magnificent baroque-style department store bearing its founder's name. Selfridges' store featured 100 departments, amenities such as restaurants, reading and writing rooms, refreshment areas, and even a rooftop garden. Selfridges also distinguished itself with its highly trained staff, whose selling and product demonstration skills further enhanced the store's appeal and reputation. In 1927, Selfridge purchased Whiteleys for £10 million.

However, it is a lesser-known department store in London—William Tarn & Co.—that will lead us to the main subject of this book.

William Tarn & Co. was a prominent department store located at Nos. 165, 167, 169, 171 & 173 Newington Causeway & New Kent Road, in the Elephant and Castle district of Southwark, London. The business traces its origins back to a drapery shop established by William Tarn around 1799.

By 1841, Tarn & Co. had evolved into a multifaceted enterprise, listed in various London trade directories as 'cabinet makers, bedstead manufacturers, upholsterers, furniture dealers, silk mercers, linen drapers, and general house furnishers.'

The expansion solidified its position as the largest retailer in Elephant and Castle, a bustling shopping area often referred to as 'The Piccadilly of South London.' (9):

'In the eighties and nineties of the last century, [it] was regarded as a centre of fashion. Well-to-do residents of the South London suburbs used to drive in their carriages and pairs to shop at Messrs Tarns', but about 1910 this store closed down.'

Postcard - Author's collection

At William Tarn & Co., the young Ben Evans acquired valuable experience in the department store business, as did two of his most trusted associates and future Managing Directors of Ben Evans & Co., John White and Meredith Thomas.

3 - Benjamin 'Ben' Evans and B. Evans and Co.

Benjamin Evans was born in 1838, the third son of the late Mr Thomas Evans, a farmer from Maesyrhiw, Llansadwrn, Carmarthenshire, from a family of freeholders. Following his father's untimely passing in 1842, leaving a widow and four young children, Ben attributed much of his subsequent success to the invaluable lessons imparted by his mother Margaret during his upbringing, and she remained his most trusted adviser until her passing in 1874. While he received some education from the local district, he primarily relied on self-education to forge his path forward.

He left home at the age of 12 and moved to the small village of Reynoldston on the Gower Peninsula near Swansea, where he gained his first exposure to the general drapery trade whilst apprenticed at the small store of his uncle Mr John Rees, his mother's brother. At the age of 16, he sought to gain experience working in an urban environment, and his next move was to work for his father's brother, Mr Benjamin Evans, who owned and managed 'London House' in Newport and was considered to be the largest drapery concern in South Wales.

Another move followed within two or three years, when eager to broaden his knowledge, he ventured to London and secured a position at William Tarn & Co., a notable South London retail establishment. The 1861 census documents show that Benjamin Evans from Llangadog in Carmarthenshire, aged 22, was 'living in' on the premises of W. Tarn & Co. in Newington Causeway.

During his two years at Tarn & Co., he dedicated himself to mastering the business, refining his skills and enhancing his knowledge of the trade. While there, he developed a strong interest in the French language. Eager to further his expertise in drapery, he relocated to Paris, where he secured a position with Messrs Arbelot, one of France's prestigious silk firms. His commitment and skill earned him the admiration of his colleagues and superiors. After returning to Britain as a representative for one of Lyon's prominent silk houses, Monsieur Arbelot continued to inquire about his welfare through British visitors to his store.

In early April 1861, Benjamin Evans of Newport established a branch of his business at 'Swansea House', No. 2 Temple Street, having taken over the business of 'Mr King.' The store was to 'be entrusted to experienced managers, and the showrooms, as before, will be under the superintendence of Mr King and Miss Baskerville'. The store reopened on April 16th 1861, trading as 'Ben Evans & Co.', a partnership made up of Benjamin Evans, Henry David John, and Ben Evans. Mr Evan Evans, the brother of the young Ben Evans, was also employed in the new enterprise. The announcement of this partnership was encapsulated in a circular issued by Mr Benjamin Evans (the uncle) which heralded the beginning of a new era for the business. (10) It stated:

'I take this opportunity of announcing my having taken into partnership Mr H. D. John and my nephew Mr Benjamin Evans, by whom the business will henceforth be managed under the style of Ben Evans and Co.'

However, the business did not run as planned. A formal Dissolution of Partnership occurred on 3rd July 1863 (11) with all outstanding claims on the business to be sent to and settled by H. D. John, who remained at No. 2 Temple Street and traded as (or at least advertised as) 'H. D. John, late B. Evans & Co.'

It is unclear if the ownership of 'Swansea House' was retained by B. Evans & Co. and the shop then leased to Mr John, or if Benjamin Evans (the elder) retained a financial stake in the business with 'young' Ben Evans. Nevertheless, the Lewis Bros. & Co. drapers shop at 'Sydenham House', No. 3 Temple Street was purchased and Evan Evans took over the day-to-day running of the store.

A Fire in Temple Street

Tragedy struck on Thursday 10th May 1866 when a devastating fire ravaged No. 2 Temple Street, claiming the lives of several individuals including Mr John, and damaging the properties on either side, namely the Queen Insurance Company at No. 1 Temple Street, managed by Watkin T. Hurndall a 'Valuer of Draper's Stock', and the B. Evans & Co. store at No. 3 Temple Street, managed by Evan Evans.

Mr John's drapery store was staffed by six female assistants, four male assistants, and two apprentices, whilst he also employed two servants. Mr John, his wife and children, four female assistants, and two servants stayed overnight at the premises, while the other staff members slept elsewhere. John Wareham, the store's cashier, mentioned that around 10:30 p.m. on

Wednesday he handed over approximately £30 to Mr John, turned off the gas in the shop at the meter, and then left.

Two of the female assistants, Miss Annie Wooton and Miss Sarah Deakin, shared a bedroom at the top of the house. Annie Wooton later stated that they went to bed around 11 p.m. on Wednesday, and she noticed Mr John at his bedroom door. She fell asleep but was awakened by Miss Deakin, who informed her that the house was on fire. She rushed downstairs until she reached the shop door, but couldn't exit the premises due to the dense smoke. Peering through the skylight at the back of the building, she noticed flames below, blocking her escape in that direction.

She then hurried into the sitting room, where Mr John appeared holding the cashbox. Mr John opened the window and called out to bystanders to bring the fire escape, subsequently brought by Police Constable Owen John, Sergeant Wilson, and Inspector Ball after 'about five minutes'. During this time, Mr John dashed up and down the stairs several times, and passed a small child to Inspector Ball, whilst Miss Wooton was rescued using the fire escape. Miss Wooton said she was unaware of any escape route via the roof.

Witness Mr David Hopkins, who lived opposite No. 2 Temple St, recounted that he could see Mr and Mrs John at the window, or at least 'I presumed the figure to be Mr John as he was in his shirt sleeves'. He heard Mrs John cry out 'For God's sake, bring the fire escape to save my child' while holding a child in her arms. After Miss Wooton and an infant were rescued, he said that he did not see anyone else at the windows, expressing surprise that no ladder was brought to the second-floor window adjacent to the one from which individuals were rescued.

He believed that if prompt action had been taken, Mr and Mrs John might have been saved. Specifically, he suggested that if the inspector had entered the room upon his initial ascent and another person had followed to assist with the rescue, the outcome might have been different.

On the street outside, there had been some discussion as to whether Mr and Mrs John had escaped the fire, as one bystander stated to the police that she knew the couple well and had seen them outside the property at the time of the blaze. confusing as to who was or was not still inside the building.

After the store was razed to the ground, it was discovered that eight souls had perished along with the shop and premises: Henry David John, together with Louisa John his wife, Esther John his young daughter, Sarah Deakin, Fanny Smith, Margaret Esther Davies, Catherine Howells, and Annie Edwards.

Whilst the source of the fire was undetermined, such was the ferocity of the blaze that in the inquest held on May 18th (12) the Coroner stated: '…the said Henry David John, together with the said other portions, were then and there suffocated and burnt, but the remains thereof, having been inspected by the said Jurors, cannot be individually distinguished or identified, and so the Jurors say that by the means aforesaid the said Henry David John came to his death by misfortune.'

The incident was so serious that in addition to the verdict of 'Accidental Death', the Jury recommended:

1. That in future the escape in this town shall be so placed that it may at once be used by the public or by the police. That a second escape should be provided, and a catch sheet, as well as a small crowbar and a speaking trumpet.
2. That the fire bell has been, and is liable to be, mistaken for other bells in frequent use in the town, and therefore a special toned bell should be substituted.
3: That every exertion was used by the members of the police force and that the water supply was ample; lastly, that Inspector Ball performed his duties to the entire satisfaction of the jury.

In the days before the inquest, the Swansea and Glamorgan Herald (13) noted that, due to spectator interest, the site was still guarded by the police.

Whilst the properties of Messrs Hurndall and Evans had received 'considerable damage', Mr Hurndall placed an advert stating that his shop, although 'damaged by fire and water', had reopened for business.

It also reported that Swansea's Head Constable Allison received the following letter from Mr Evans Evans, whose premises were next to those destroyed by the fire:

3, Temple Street, Swansea,
17th May, 1866

Dear Sir,
Under a sense of deep obligation to yourself and every member of the
police force on duty in Temple Street, on the unfortunate morning of
Thursday last, I beg to forward you a cheque for £10, for distribution
amongst your men—not for a moment deeming such a sum anything like
a sufficient reward for their valuable services in saving my property from
utter destruction (which 1 cannot but attribute to your prompt and
judicious arrangements, and to the zeal and activity displayed by your men
in carrying them out,) but merely as a mark of my gratitude and
appreciation of your and their conduct.

I am Dear Sir, yours faithfully and obliged,

EVAN EVANS —To Mr Allison, Head Constable.

In the days following the fire, the following appeared in the local press
(14):

THE GOLD FINDERS - A PROLIFIC HEAP OF RUBBISH:
The old axiom that 'It's an ill will that blows nobody good' has again been
verified in our town. On Saturday last, a quantity of rubbish -the remains
of the fire in Temple St - was carted away from the street by order of the
police authorities, onto the beach, near the Infirmary, and early on Sunday
morning, and during several following days, hundreds of people have
been busy searching the debris for anything they might find, and search,
in many instances was not without reward, for during Sunday, nearly £20
in coins of different value, was recovered, besides a large quantity of
valuable articles in jewellery, and other small trinkets - such as are
generally sold in a draper's establishment. At the time we write the search
has not entirely given up.'

Ben Evans returned from France to Swansea in 1866 and assumed full
control of 'Evans & Co,', soon trading out of both Nos. 2 and 3 Temple
Street. In the aftermath of the fire, Evan Evans' health was profoundly
affected, and at only 30 yr. old, he succumbed to his illness in 1867.

The block of properties in the diagram (between Temple Street, Goat Street, Caer Street, and Castle Bailey Street) shows at least 25 street-facing properties and a similar number of internal workshops and warehouses, with numerous different leaseholders and freeholders.

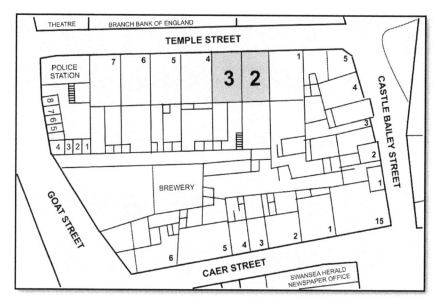

Ben Evans & Company - Nos. 2 and 3 Temple St

By 1869 Ben Evans had purchased substantial warehouse facilities behind his premises.

Early evidence of Ben Evans' understanding of the importance of staff welfare and morale was demonstrated in an article in the Cambrian newspaper on the 8th of July 1870, which described his employee's annual outing:

ANNUAL OUTING.-The whole of the assistants of Messrs B. Evans, and Co., the well-known drapers of No. 2 and 3, Temple Street, Swansea, yesterday (Thursday) afternoon enjoyed their annual picnic at Park Mill. Etc

The party, consisting of about twenty-five ladies and gentlemen started from the establishment in Temple Street in a large break and three horses, which had been supplied by Mr Williams, livery stable keeper, and under an experienced Jehu the party arrived safely at their destination, the lovely scenery on the route being much enjoyed.

After an excellent tea at the pleasant hostelry, the Gower Inn, the whole party enjoyed the remainder of the day in true picnic style, some really good vocal harmony adding much to the pleasures of the day. Mr Benjamin Evans was present, and it was evident that the most kind and cordial feelings exist between the employer and the employed. Mr Evans has since his establishment in Swansea, annually given a treat of this character to the whole of his assistants, and we can only say generally on behalf of those who are so closely pent-up in establishments of this kind that we wish the example of Mr Evans was more universally adopted. Such treats are thoroughly appreciated by the employees, as it proves to them that the principal takes a deep interest in their welfare, and where this is seen and felt, good practical results are sure to follow. During the evening Mr Evans was sincerely thanked by his assistants for the treat which he had so kindly afforded them.

A report in the Cambrian in July 1881 describing the B. Evans & Co. annual outing offered clues as to the company's growth, with six large vehicles needed to transport the staff.

'For some years past it has been the thoughtfully kind practice of the Squire of Penllergare to throw open his grounds in the summer months to holidaymakers, and to place at their disposal the resources of woods and water and gardens. The members of the Working Men's Club have more than once availed themselves of this liberality, and yesterday the same courtesy was extended to the large number of employees of B. Evans and Co., drapers, etc., Temple and Caer Streets, Swansea, who were accompanied by the chief of the firm, Mr Benjamin Evans, and the heads of departments, Messrs White, Blanchard, etc.

A very large party left town soon after mid-day in six large breaks, and arrived at Penllergare Grounds in good time, where they were welcomed by Mr and Mrs Llewelyn, who considerately provided what was lacking in the way of tables, etc. In the course of the afternoon, Mr and Mrs Llewelyn placed themselves at the head of an interested group to make a peregrination to the points of greatest attraction, and to explain what otherwise would have been less enjoyed because less understood.

Before Mr and Mrs Llewelyn left the ground, Mr B. Evans proposed a hearty vote of thanks to them for their courteous reception. Into a few sentences the speaker crowded references to the scientific, the socially administrative, and the philanthropic services rendered to the country by the Penllergare family, and the cheers of the picnickers echoed their thanks for permission to see so lovely a place.'

The centre of Swansea town witnessed a high turnover of drapers' shops, cabinet makers, and furnishers, most of whom were based in or around Goat Street, Castle Street, and Temple Street, and amidst the many fake 'closing down sales' was genuine hardship. Keen to establish themselves as reputable vendors, traders relied heavily on offering credit. However, due to the terms demanded, this practice threatened to put many of them out of business within one or two years, with some shops closing within months, not even making it to the end of their lease agreements.

Falling into debt was viewed as a moral failing, and the origins of credit reporting in the United Kingdom can be traced back to 1803 when a group of London tailors began sharing information about customers who failed to settle their debts. During the harsh economic conditions of the Victorian era, many people resorted to using credit or pawning personal belongings like clothing to obtain funds for necessities such as food. These loans would then have to be repaid with interest.

Indebtedness was treated as a criminal offence, and those unable to pay their debts could end up incarcerated in debtors' prisons, where they were required to work and pay for their upkeep until the debt was cleared, either by themselves or their families. Imprisoning debtors was eventually abolished in 1869, marking the end of an era where debt was criminalised and seen as a moral transgression rather than a financial issue. This shift in attitudes towards debt and credit paved the way for more modern approaches to lending and borrowing in the UK.

In 1872, Ben Evans introduced the 'Ready-Money Principle' to his business, abandoning the traditional credit method used for many years. Neighbouring businesses doubted his logic, and his friends strongly advised him against it, believing that customers would prefer to buy from outlets that offered credit.

Within months he managed to eliminate all the debt associated with his business. This enabled him to pay his creditors more quickly and increased his cash flow, allowing him to negotiate more favourable purchasing terms. He often bought up stock from traders forced out of, or exiting, the market at very competitive rates, while offering his stock at 'low prices with an acceptable profit margin' at a level that customers were willing to pay in cash. Seven years later, he thanked his customers for their ongoing patronage in an open letter featured in The Cambrian. (15)

In 1874, a warehouse behind the stores at Nos. 2 and 3 was added, accessed via 'Temple Lane', an internal alleyway previously accessed via Goat Street. After some internal changes, they were opened as part of the larger store. In the following year, the company purchased the lease and stock of Cook, Son and Co. at No. 1 Temple Street, while in 1878, No. 4 Temple Street was acquired from Mrs Roberts, mantle maker, milliner, and costumier.

In July 1882, the firm purchased the stock and premises of Messrs Morgan William & Company at No. 6 Temple Street. Mrs Hughes' 'Millinery, Silk and Shawl Establishment', at No. 4 Castle Street (aka Castle Bailey St) was also purchased later the same year, and in 1883, Ben Evans bought 'The Sporting Depot Company' at No. 1/2 Castle Bailey St, although the store was inaccessible from the front of the building.

No. 1 Caer Street was acquired in the same year and transformed into the 'travelling requisites and fancy leather goods department'. Ben Evans continued his ambitious expansion plans by purchasing the adjacent property at 15/15A Castle Square in 1884, although this acquisition did not offer direct access to the rest of the store from the front of the building, it was a vital part of Ben Evans' plans.

On the afternoon of 17th January 1884, Temple Street was the scene of much interest, as a 'great crowd' gathered to witness the trial of 'an ingenious and simple escape' where people utilised a rope to let themselves down quickly and safely from the upper windows of Messrs B. Evans and Co. establishment into the street. A reporter for the Cambrian newspaper observed that 'if such simple means had been at hand when the great Temple Street fatal fire occurred some years ago, eight lives might have been saved.'

4 - The Opening of the Goat Street Store

On the 4th of September 1886, Nos. 36, 37 and 38 Goat Street were officially opened, enabling the firm to add a substantial extension to its growing Cabinet Furniture business. Linking internally to No. 6 Temple Street and No. 5 Caer Street on the ground floor, the First floor on Goat Street was utilised solely for home furnishings.

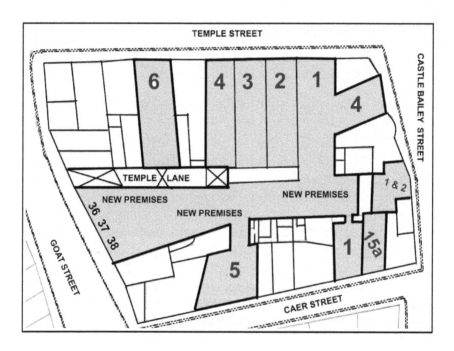

Ben Evans Store - 1886 Opening

The following description is one researched, compiled, and rewritten by the author from various reports of the day, as they included some contradictions and errors. Sketches and diagrams are added by the author for further explanation. (16) (17) (18)

The site of what was once 'The Plas' now hosts Swansea's finest business edifice. Once the palatial residence of the esteemed Cradock family, this location has been transformed into the premier business establishment in the town. During the construction of Messrs B. Evans and Co.'s new premises in Goat Street, a portion of a wall that remained from 'The Plas' had to be dismantled, a reminder of the historical significance of the ground upon which now stands the largest drapery emporium in Wales.

Designed by the architectural firm of Messrs. Seward and Thomas of Swansea and Cardiff, the grand and imposing Goat Street store frontage dwarfs the neighbouring houses. Standing at a height of 60 feet from the pavement below, the building's silhouette is punctuated by three intricately designed freestone gables, with the central one bearing a distinctive oval panel inscribed with the building's erection date of 1885. The façade is supported by six imposing pillars crafted from Portland stone, with the same material extending to the fascia and cornice above the shop front. An ingenious touch is the inclusion of a spring sunblind, strategically placed to shield the shop windows from the sun's glare. Above, the upper section of the front showcases buff Ebbw Vale bricks, tastefully accented with red brick bands and window arches. The keystones, cornices, and window sills are meticulously crafted from face stone, enhancing the overall aesthetic.

Upon entering the building from the street, the interior lives up to the promise of its exterior grandeur, ensuring a seamless blend of form and function throughout the structure.

The Ground Floor: This newly constructed space is bathed in natural light streaming through expansive plate glass windows, showcasing an array of meticulously arranged and enticing furniture pieces. The ground floor boasts an impressive entrance framed in moulded and polished teak, complemented by plate glass panels. What was once a workshop now houses a vast array of furniture, catering to every taste and budget, from modest to opulent.

Upon entry from the street, the first shop is spacious, lofty, and well-lit. The furniture on display provides a striking contrast against the French grey hue of the match-boarding adorning the walls. Adjacent to this shop, connected by a large, lofty opening, is a space formerly utilised as a packing room but now transformed into an elegant showroom. Accessible from this area is the current Lace Shop via a well-designed pitch pine staircase. Beyond lies the expansive Show Room, now seamlessly linked to the Goat Street establishment, an integral part of the furnishing department, showcasing a curated selection of brass and iron bedsteads.

An opening in the side wall provides direct access to the Carpet Shop in Caer Street. Previously disconnected from the rest of the emporium, it now allows for a continuous stretch of Show Rooms extending over 200 feet in total depth, running from Goat Street to Castle Bailey Street. On returning to the front shop on Goat Street, one descends via a wide flight of stairs to the Basement level.

The Basement: The basement floor has been meticulously outfitted as a Packing and Receiving Room, complete with a counter, shelves, and other essentials, providing ample space for these vital aspects of the business. The floor is uniformly boarded, while the walls are clad in Portland cement, ensuring durability and practicality, and fortified against dampness.

Despite its subterranean location, lighting presents no challenge in this era of innovation. Illumination is provided via Hayward's patent prismatic lights, ingeniously installed within the pavements, and the expansive space is bathed in brilliant illumination. These lights, cleverly set within an iron frame on rollers, glide back beneath the window, facilitating the seamless conveyance of goods below. The system is self-locking and impervious to external tampering, thus ensuring security.

Goods slated for delivery are transported from the Show Rooms via a large lift, where they are expertly packed before being conveyed back up to the loading platform in the cartway, accessible from Goat Street. Incoming shipments from manufacturers are smoothly guided down a rolling way into the Receiving Room, where they undergo unpacking, sorting, and subsequent distribution to their respective departments via the lift, which aids the swift and seamless flow of business operations.

A brief passage leads to the lift, which spans from the basement floor to the pinnacle of the building. A ladder and trap are strategically positioned to enable the loading of goods onto delivery vans. We ascend a wide staircase and return to the Ground Floor retail area, where a polished pitch pine staircase provides access to the First Floor.

The First Floor: Dedicated to fine furniture, this floor is arguably the pinnacle of elegance within the entire building. Positioned at the same level as the ground floor of the Upper Temple Street establishment, it is dedicated to displaying a variety of top-tier furniture pieces. The space is flooded with natural light via eight large plate glass windows facing Goat Street, enhancing the showcase of furniture on display.

Continuity with the old premises is maintained through a brief flight of stairs to the present Carpet Room. This staircase is ingeniously designed with a well-hole that offers a view down to the ground floor. A sizable Wenham Lantern Light positioned directly above the stairs ensures ample illumination on the first floor and through the well-hole onto the ground floor.

Accessible from the carpet room, a bridge spans Temple Lane, providing direct connectivity to the first floor of the furniture shop on Temple Street. To ensure safety, a fireproof door stands at the end of the bridge. One of the most aesthetically pleasing and functional features of the entire building, the design of the stairs and balustrades leaves a lasting impression, their grandeur truly remarkable.

From the vantage point of the first floor, peering through the expansive opening onto the floor below, one gains a sense, albeit incomplete, of the scale of the recent additions. The view extends along a lengthy corridor lined with an array of valuable and exquisite goods, hinting at the vastness of the space. The floor space allocated to the furnishing department alone now approaches nearly half an acre.

Stepping back from the stairs, one gains a sense of the premises' vastness, though words may fall short of capturing its entirety. Particularly enchanting is the night-time ambience, when the space is bathed in the warm glow of the new Wenham light, offering a captivating alternative to electric illumination. Every mirror and gleaming surface reflects this light, casting a spellbinding scene.

Ascending another handsomely carpeted staircase, reminiscent of the robustness found in ancient manor houses, we climb to the Second Floor.

The Second Floor: The Second Floor welcomes visitors with a refreshment room and adjacent ladies' retiring and cloakrooms. The interior is tastefully decorated and appointed, exuding an air of luxury and charm.

The rooms are lavishly furnished to create a welcoming atmosphere. The walls and ceiling are adorned in a light cream hue, complemented by woodwork painted in a slightly darker shade of cream, accented with touches of light blue, perfectly complementing the subtle hues of the woodwork and doors. The focal point of the room is a polished walnut chimney piece, adorned with bevelled mirror panels. A charming touch is the cosy recess, designed as an alcove shaded by a screen, housing a lift that connects to the kitchen above.

Adorning the walls are oil paintings, ingeniously hung using a simple mechanism that allows for easy adjustment. The room is impeccably appointed, offering a sanctuary where ladies can relax and rejuvenate themselves during their shopping excursions, or after a lengthy journey from the countryside. Equipped with a light dinner lift from the kitchen above, this room caters to the needs of shoppers, offering a delightful respite from the rigours of a busy day.

On the same floor is the dining room for the use of the employees, accessible from a staff-only stairway that ascends from the cartway below up to the staff dining room as well as offering access to the third floor where the store's impressive Kitchen is located. The employee's dining area is a spacious room designed to accommodate the numerous assistants employed on the premises.

The walls of the dining room feature a warm and inviting terracotta tint, whilst the two fireplaces, equipped with slow-combustion stoves, are complemented by handsome 'Rouge Royal' chimneypieces, that lend a cosy ambience to the space. A portrait of Napoleon I adorns one of the chimneypieces, while a well-curated selection of books stands on one side of the room. The comfort of the employees is a priority, and the overall atmosphere radiates warmth and brightness, a testament to Messrs B. Evans & Co.'s dedication to the well-being and comfort of their staff.

The Third Floor: As we ascend to the third floor via the staff stairway, the front windows offer a breathtaking panorama of Mumbles Head and the Bay. Positioned above St. Mary's Tower, this part of the building commands a vista over the entirety of the structures between Goat Street and the sea. The standout feature of this floor is undoubtedly the kitchen, showcasing ample provision for this crucial aspect of operations. The antiquated notion of situating the kitchen at the lowest level of a building has long been debunked, giving way to a more sensible approach of placing it as high as possible. This strategic placement aims to prevent the dissemination of cooking odours throughout the rest of the building, something particularly objectionable in large establishments, and a common issue faced under the old arrangement.

Equipped with two cooking ranges, one functioning as a standard cooking furnace, the other serving as a backup in case of emergencies, this kitchen boasts remarkable capabilities. The primary range, an impressive fourteen-foot creation crafted by Messrs Benham of London, is installed on a fireproof platform. It operates using both gas and coal fires and features a large boiler whose tubes pass through the furnace, providing steam to a hermetically sealed oven ideal for cooking vegetables, plus a coal fire oven, and gas jets for boiling saucepans. With the capacity to cater to up to 500 individuals simultaneously, this range ensures culinary excellence on a grand scale. Situated in the roof space directly above the range, a spacious lantern light maintains a consistent temperature around the food. A smaller range is positioned against the opposite wall, providing flexibility as needed.

Excellent ventilation is ensured in the kitchen, as it is throughout the rest of the building, given that the ventilation system has been meticulously planned. Tobin's Tubes are installed on each floor to facilitate the intake and circulation of fresh air throughout the building. In addition, extraction flues are integrated into the walls and positioned just below the ceiling line to remove stale air, thus maintaining a healthy and comfortable environment for occupants throughout the building.

Continuing on the same level, a passage leads to several servants' bedrooms, a housekeeper's room, and a storage area, conveniently avoiding extensive stair climbing. This centralised placement of the administrative department ensures operational efficiency without interfering with the business functions of the premises. The previously mentioned lifts. offer easy access to other parts of the building.

The building contractors on the project were local company Messrs Thomas, Watkins, and Jenkins, whilst the building utilities, including the gas arrangements and the Wenham light, were installed by Mr John Legg, gas and electrical engineer, of Nelson Street.

The Quest for Shorter Working Hours

In the same month, a meeting was held at The Albert Hall, called by members of 'The Shorter Hours Movement', consisting mostly of shop assistants. In previous decades, several groups had been set up in Britain to challenge the working hours expected by employers, such as The Nine Hours Movement, as well as those specific to shop workers, with names like the Early Closing Association and The Shop Hours Labour League hoping to get shop owners to reduce staff working hours voluntarily.

The standard workweek spanned from Monday through Saturday, closing at 9:00 pm, with a half-day off on Sunday. However, Christian reformers had advocated for the complete cessation of Sunday business activities. In practice, it was not uncommon for assistants to be expected to stay for an hour or more after closing to organise goods and ensure the shop was tidy.

In 1884 Mr Thomas Sutherst, president of the Shop Hours Labour League, wrote: (19)

'I believe I am within the mark in stating that the majority of shop assistants in this country work from 75 to 90 hours in every week. Of that majority one-fourth work the full 90 hours per week, two-fourths 80 hours, and the remaining fourth 75 hours. ... I do not wish to make it appear that shop-keeping is an unpleasant occupation, but that which is healthy and agreeable for a reasonable time becomes irksome and injurious if continued for a too long period. . . . Stuffs, calicos, and silk cannot be continually torn, cut, or moved without throwing off clouds of minute particles which necessarily impregnate the air of the whole shop. In the evening long rows of gas-burners help to use up what little freshness is left in the air.'

Ten Factory Acts had been introduced since 1800, however, none had considered the work of the shop assistant. Then in 1873, the Liberal MP Sir John Lubbock proposed that shops be included in the next Factory Act, alas, his bill was rejected by his peers in Parliament. In 1886, he proposed a bill that restricted the working hours of children and young persons employed in shops, and this time the committee that reviewed his proposal agreed with his sentiments, stating: (20)

'Your committee, being satisfied that the hours of shop assistants range in many places as high as from eighty-four to eighty-five hours per week, are convinced that such long hours must be generally injurious and often ruinous to health and that the same amount of business might be compressed into a shorter space of time.'

Lubbock's Bill became law under the title of the Shop Hours Regulation Act 1886, however, it was impractical as it did not cover adult female shop workers, protecting only apprentices and child workers. The cap set on hours allowed was unreasonably high at seventy-four hours per week, and there were no mechanisms in place to effectively enforce the law, resulting in few prosecutions initiated by private individuals, as obtaining evidence to support these cases proved to be extremely challenging.

The committee's comment that '...such long hours must be generally injurious and often ruinous to health' was a small but important recognition of what was to be a key driver to the reduction of working hours, the poor health of shop workers, and a celebrated physician of the day, Dr Benjamin Ward Richardson FRS FRCP wrote: (21)

'The effects of shop labour of the kind named on females under twenty-one, or on males under twenty-one, is of necessity injurious, as impeding their growth and the natural development of the organs of the body. To the female, the mischief is of a kind calculated to extend to the offspring she may bear. ... In my opinion, eight hours daily is the maximum time during which labour ought to be carried on in shops.'

Whilst Mr Lawson Tait, a leading specialist in women's diseases, and regarded as one of the fathers of gynaecology, stated: (22)

'I can speak of women only, and from a large hospital experience can say that the prolonged hours of labour to which young women are subjected in such operations as millinery and shop work generally are extremely detrimental to their health. ... A great many cases have come under my observation of women suffering from uterine displacements, chronic inflammatory diseases of the ovaries and tubes.'

The Shorter Hours Movement Meeting held on 19th August at The Albert Hall in Swansea (23) was chaired by The Mayor of Swansea, Mr W. J. Rees, and supported by the Rev. Canon Richards, Councillor R. D. Burnie, Dr Griffiths, and Benjamin Evans, amongst others. The subject matter at hand was why it was felt necessary to keep shops open so late in the evening, given that Swansea shops were often open until 9.00 pm and later, allowing no time for an individual to have recreation time, while at the same time being detrimental to a person's health.

One of the speakers, Mr D. C. Jones, said it had been calculated that there were 2,000 assistants in Swansea who, with public support, would be in a position to get shorter daily working hours. He hoped, 'for the sake of the young ladies employed behind the counters, that they would, ere long, attain the object they desired. It was hard for ladies to have to work as they did—they could not stand it like men.'

After various other guests had spoken to the crowd, all endorsing the need for shorter working days, Dr Griffiths took the floor and expressed wholehearted support for the early closing movement, a cause he opined that had captured his attention for many years, dating back to his early days as a medical practitioner in Swansea. It became evident to him that a significant number of drapers' assistants, both male and female, were suffering from various ailments directly linked to excessive work hours and confinement. Through his inquiries, Dr Griffiths discovered an alarming trend: a disproportionate number of young men succumbed to consumption annually—a trend he attributed to their demanding work conditions.

Driven by concern, Dr Griffiths engaged with the drapers of Swansea to understand why their establishments remained open late into the evening. Their unanimous response was one of helplessness—they felt compelled to keep their shops open due to public demand and fierce competition but expressed a genuine desire to close at more reasonable hours. He firmly believed that the majority of Swansea's residents shared this sentiment, arguing that the earlier closure of shops was for the benefit of both workers and the community at large, and emphasised that successful competition did not require keeping shops open from dawn till dusk. He asserted that 'if all tradesmen were to unite and agree to shorter working hours, they would not only accomplish their tasks more efficiently but also thrive in their endeavours.' He vividly outlined the detrimental effects of long working hours, deploring them from social, moral, intellectual, and physical standpoints. The bleak picture he painted was a shameful reflection of the nineteenth century, an era that should have long abandoned such practices.

The remedy, Dr Griffiths contended, lay in adopting shorter working hours. What was needed, he stressed, was organisation and persistent advocacy. Only by organising and advocating for change could they effectively address this pressing issue and usher in a more equitable and sustainable approach to work. Finally, he proposed that 'this meeting agrees with the shorter hours movement committee in endeavouring to secure the privileges enjoyed by the artisans of this country and agrees to help by every means to obtain this object, and by doing their shopping at an earlier hour.'

Amidst resounding applause, Mr Benjamin Evans took the floor, acknowledging the insightful comments made by Dr Griffiths, which he recognised were grounded in his medical expertise and experience. Mr Evans confessed to feeling somewhat conflicted as the seconder of the resolution, given that his store did not adhere to early closing. However, he clarified that whilst he may be guilty in practice he wholeheartedly supported the spirit of early closing and was honoured to second the resolution. He proceeded to explain the challenges he faced in implementing earlier closing times. With a sizeable business, he relied on a steady flow of customers and could not afford to turn them away.

Disagreeing with Dr Griffiths on the matter of late shopping, Mr Evans noted that many respectable customers frequented shops later in the day simply because they were open. He suggested that the real solution lay in legislation—a parliamentary act that would mandate early closing for all shops. Reflecting on past unsuccessful attempts to achieve early closing in Swansea, Mr Evans publicly declared his willingness to lead by example. He pledged that if just three or four other tradesmen were to join him, he would commit to closing his shop at 7.00 pm, starting from October and lasting through to February. This gesture demonstrated his genuine commitment to the cause and his willingness to take proactive steps towards achieving it.

The following month, B. Evans and Co. was one of only four local establishments to take part in a new 'Early Closing' scheme whereby their shops would be closed four days a week at 7.00 pm. The Shorter Hour Association Committee stated that 'whilst taking part in this initiative is voluntary, it is hoped that other local companies will also follow suit in furtherance of the welfare of those employed by them.' (24)

The movement to reduce working hours continued at pace over the following years, the endorsement of the town's biggest store helping to grow the movement locally, and in September 1890, the Swansea and Glamorgan Herald commented: (25)

'We are pleased to learn that some of the leading tradesmen of Swansea, following the good example of Mr Benjamin Evans, are making arrangements for the early closing of their shops during the winter months. It is to be hoped that all the tradesmen of the town will join in this movement and that the public will give them every support, by making their purchases early.'

5 - New Stables and the Upgrade of Temple Street

Despite an authorisation in place to demolish properties in several streets surrounding the old Parish Church as part of the Town Improvement Scheme, limited progress had been made. However, in April 1890, the Cambrian newspaper advised its readers that Ben Evans and Co. had begun construction work on this 'prime area for development' where it was building new company stables. Five months later, an article by Peter Clare in The Cambrian on 12th September 1890 described B. Evans and Co.'s new buildings and stables. (26)

B. EVANS AND CO.'S MODEL STABLES. A SUBSTANTIAL ADDITION TO SWANSEA'S SIGHTS. KINDNESS TO ANIMALS INCULCATED BY PRECEPT AND EXAMPLE. By PETER CLARE

'Mr B. Evans. the founder and head of the great firm of Messrs B. Evans and Co. whose premises are known as the 'Whiteleys of Wales ' — is himself an excellent judge and true lover of the horse. He is pardonably proud of his stud of light van and other horses, which are engaged in despatching goods to and from the Temple Block to all parts of the neighbourhood.

That two of his animals took the first and second prizes at the Swansea Horse Show a fortnight ago, says something for their quality, there having been a hot competition at the show all round, some of the best animals in the country in many classes having been brought to the show-yard for the occasion. But, apart from prize-taking, no one can see the horses and vehicles of B. Evans and Co., standing at their doors or speeding about the streets, without being struck by their handsome appearance and the evident care with which they are chosen and treated.'

The firm's main stables were previously situated at the rear of Northampton Place, however, as the business expanded and the number of horses increased, the accommodation proved insufficient, necessitating a relocation to a larger site capable of housing the entire equine establishment. The site previously occupied by Penrice Court on Frog Street and the Hope and Anchor Inn on Fisher Street presented itself as an ideal option, and following the closure of both the tavern and the court,

Mr Evans seized the opportunity and acquired the property.

He wanted his company to have the premier stables in Wales, and whilst he enlisted the expertise of Mr H. C. Portsmouth to design the new facilities, Ben Evans had direct involvement in the planning and construction processes.

The construction contract was entrusted to Messrs Jenkins Bros., the sons of Mr David Jenkins from the esteemed firm of Messrs Thomas, Watkins, and Jenkins. Mr Evans left no room for compromise, insisting on the utilisation of top-notch materials and craftsmanship, and placed particular emphasis on the quality of the mortar, ensuring meticulous attention to detail throughout the construction process. One of the contractors expressed to the Cambrian: 'It is a pleasure to be involved in such a project for such a man. He demands nothing but the best, yet he truly appreciates our efforts when we deliver our finest work.'

The keen eye of Mr Fowler, the foreman of works, led to the discovery of several mullions from the older St. Mary's Church windows on the site, as well as the unearthing of a label carving, believed to depict the likeness of Alina de Mowbray, Swansea's esteemed benefactress. The artefacts were removed from the site and were carefully preserved in the Royal Institution of South Wales.

Mr Clare believed that the new stables with their exceptional design, superior craftsmanship, and attention to detail, would leave a lasting impression on all who have the opportunity to experience them first-hand, and was poised to become a prominent attraction for visitors to Swansea, 'much like the renowned stables of the 'Magasin du Louvre' and the 'Bon Marché' are to visitors in Paris.'

A Description of the Stables: The front section facing Frog Street features a spacious residence for Mr Reed, the foreman, who has been employed by the firm for over 17 years. The house comprises seven rooms and a scullery, offering a spacious, bright, and exceedingly comfortable living space. Adorning the apex of the front gable is a striking Red Dragon crafted in terracotta. This emblem, whether by design or happenstance, beautifully symbolises Mr Evans's allegiance to the contemporary resurgence of Welsh aspirations among his compatriots. Beneath the scullery of the stable house lies an ancient cellar spanning approximately eight square feet, now sealed off.

This house was formerly the location of St. Mary's Parsonage, where, on one fateful Sunday morning, the parson was unexpectedly delayed during his shaving routine. Remarkably, this minor delay proved providential, as it inadvertently spared many lives. While the congregation patiently awaited the parson's appearance in the churchyard, tragedy struck - the roof and side walls of the church collapsed, narrowly avoiding what could have been a devastating loss of life.

To the left of this residence stands the entrance gateway, adorned with an elegant archway. Both structures boast a construction of red Ebbw Vale brick, complemented by Bridgend stone cornices and accents. The gable of the house is adorned with tile hanging, adding a distinctive touch to the façade.

Upon passing through the archway, one is greeted by a sizeable open yard, paved with blue Staffordshire chequered paving bricks that ensure efficient drainage, with careful attention given to the design of falls to swiftly divert rainwater during heavy storms. On the left-hand side of the yard, visitors access a covered area through a lofty archway standing over 120 feet tall, providing ample space and shelter for various activities. This yard serves as a space for horse grooming and other related activities while also providing a dry passage between the stables which occupy two sides of the covered area, with the harness rooms and washing facilities situated on the third side.

Access to the stable proper is provided through two doors from the covered way, where meticulous attention has been given to achieving optimal sanitary conditions. The stable layout accommodates twelve stalls and two loose boxes, with ample room behind the horses for passage. The flooring of the stalls and passages consists of buff adamantine clinkers set in cement, atop a cement concrete foundation. Rigorous consideration has been given to drainage, with pipes of sufficient diameter installed to ensure swift removal of water, thus maintaining a clean and hygienic environment.

Great care has been given to ventilation, and in addition to the fanlights installed in the windows, a continuous supply of fresh air is ensured through inter-tubes integrated into the walls, delivering a steady flow of fresh air into the stable. Large gratings are positioned 13 feet above the floor, through which the stale air is drawn out through the ceiling using three Boyle's large-size air pump ventilators mounted on the roof.

All stall divisions, mangers, and other components were provided by Messrs Musgrave and Co of London and Belfast, known for their superior quality. The stall divisions are constructed from iron, featuring a ventilating panel in the upper section consisting of upright bars, whilst the lower part is filled with polished pitch pine, measuring two inches thick. Musgrave's patent tying arrangements are utilised, significantly minimising the risk of injury to horses. The mangers are crafted from iron and are complemented by a wall lining of glazed tiles sporting a delicate green tint, adding both functionality and aesthetic appeal to the stable environment.

Adjacent to the main door of the stable, enclosed shafts are situated on either side, connecting to the floor above and serving as channels for the delivery of hay and straw. A spacious chaff room is located at one end of the stable, supplied directly from the floor above, facilitating convenient access to feed for the horses.

On the opposite side of the covered yard lie the harness rooms. The smaller room houses the steel yard in connection with the weighbridge, positioned just outside, and serves as storage for harnesses not in constant use. The larger room accommodates the regular van harness and boasts a spacious, lofty interior, with walls and ceilings lined with match boarding. Both rooms are equipped with hot-water pipes for heating.

Adjacent to the harness rooms is the washing room. Designated for cleaning harnesses and small articles, it features a sink with hot and cold water supply, along with a boiler for preparing mashes and other necessities. To prevent direct exposure to stable fumes, which can taint fodder, the stairs to the loft are located in the washing room, ensuring a separate access point. The loft spans the entirety of the stable and offers ample storage space for hay, straw, and other essentials.

At one end of the loft, a spacious lock-up corn room is provided, offering ample storage for grain. The corn bins are situated on the floor, each equipped with a chute at the bottom to convey the corn directly into the stable below. Ingeniously designed, this arrangement ensures that only one feed can be drawn at a time, reminiscent of the mechanism of an old-fashioned gunpowder flask.

On the same floor, positioned above the harness rooms, are two additional lock-up rooms. These versatile spaces can serve as storage areas or, if necessary, be converted into bedrooms for the stable men. Notably, provisions have been made for water storage during times of scarcity, with two large iron cisterns installed in the roof, capable of holding a total of 13,000 gallons. Such foresight ensures that stable operations can continue smoothly even during periods of limited water availability.

Returning once more to the open yard, directly opposite the stable building, we encounter a sizeable detached loose box, intended for use when a horse requires isolation due to illness or other circumstances. Adjacent to this is the manure pit, strategically positioned for efficient waste disposal. Facing the entrance from the street stands a large and lofty van shed, featuring an arched front three spans wide. With a generous floor space measuring approximately 40 feet by 30 feet, this shed can accommodate up to 20 vans.

Above the van shed is a spacious upper storey designated for use as a workshop, boasting a separate entrance and staircase accessible from Fisher Street. Adjacent to the workshop entrance, ample space is allocated for an engine house, intended for powering chaff-cutters and other machinery utilised within the workshops. The entirety of the buildings, except for the street-facing front, are clad in buff Ebbw Vale pressed bricks, with chamfered bricks accentuating all angles, adding a touch of elegance to the exterior.

Mr. Ben Evans.
(From a photograph by H. A. Chapman, High-street, Swansea.)

Mr Benjamin 'Ben' Evans - Copyright Status Unknown

Temple Street Refurbishment and Re-Opening

After over three months of work, Ben Evans's Temple Street store frontage was re-opened to the public on Saturday 29th November 1890 with a Grand Winter Show offering 'all kinds of goods, including fashions and novelties of the most attractive description'. Mr Evans had a natural affection for No. 3, given that it was the nucleus of his business, and he had hesitated for a long time before making any changes.

However, the wear and tear of the old structure and the increased convenience that could be achieved through re-arrangement eventually became too significant to ignore. Consequently, the premises were handed over to architect Mr H. C. Portsmouth and the building contractors for renovation.

The following description is one researched, compiled, and rewritten by the author from various reports of the day, as they included some contradictions and errors: (27) (28)

Significant alterations were made at the back of Nos. 3 and 4 Temple Street. The No. 4 shop, which previously was not very long, was extended, along with No. 3, to the full length of shops No. 1 and 2. The rear section is then lit by ornamental and balustraded well-holes, as termed by the architect. Further back, the ceiling opens up to the roof, featuring several large and effective skylights.

The former counting house and lace curtain room were combined into one large room dedicated entirely to lace and other curtains. This room features a staircase and balustrade that overlooks shops No. 3 and 4, while another staircase leads to the enlarged showrooms. The showrooms now extend over the entire first floors of shops Nos. 1, 2, 3, and 4, forming a splendid suite of light and airy apartments. Part of the first floor over No. 4 is designated for fitting rooms. From showroom No. 2, there is access to a convenient ladies' cloakroom, lavatories, offices, and more.

Another part of the building features a long, entirely new passage connecting the workrooms on the upper floors with the Goat Street block, providing airy and convenient lavatories and offices for the female assistants. The Carpet Room remains as it was before but is now lighter and has better access. Previously used as a library, an assembly room, and later converted into a dormitory, the Counting House was relocated to the first floor of the Caer Street block and is now conveniently accessible from all the shops on the Temple Street level. All the balustrading used throughout the altered sections is made of bright and varnished pitch pine with an elegant design. The walls are painted in a pale pea green, accented by complementary hues.

The artificial lighting is 'entirely novel and interesting', combining both gas light and ventilation. The burners, known as Clapton Lamps, are triple and arranged beneath a pendant. Above the group of lights is a large reflector, or cowl, made of white porcelain. The heated air from the gas combustion is carried up through a broad tube to the pendant, then through pipes into the walls of the building, and finally to the outer air. This new principle of combined lighting and ventilation is said to have greatly improved the ventilation of the premises.

B. Evans & Co. Employees Join Artillery Volunteers

In June 1892, with the full support of Mr Ben Evans, Captain Logan approached the store's staff to propose joining the Artillery Volunteers. Mr Evans, known for encouraging reasonable outdoor recreation among his employees, readily endorsed the idea, given that this development not only provided an avenue for physical fitness and discipline but also fostered a sense of camaraderie and civic responsibility among the store's male employees, offering them a new opportunity for personal and professional growth.

The suggestion was met with overwhelming enthusiasm, resulting in 67 young men enrolling as members of the Artillery Volunteers that very evening. A meeting was subsequently held, presided over by Mr B. Evans himself. Addressing the gathering Captain Logan elucidated the benefits of joining a volunteer corps. The initiative sparked such interest among the Temple Street employees that forecasts suggested the number of recruits could exceed 80 by the following week.

Within days, the recruits had been measured for their uniforms, and plans were made for the 'shop' volunteers to join the Corps in their regular parade to the Parish Church on the upcoming Sunday. There were ongoing discussions about appointing dedicated officers for this particular section of the Artillery Volunteers, ensuring focused attention to their specific interests and needs.

6 - The Widening of Castle Bailey Street 1893

Island House, an obstruction that separated Castle Square from Wind Street, was removed in 1879/80, transforming a location that bottlenecked access from Wind Street with two perilously narrow passages into an expansive main thoroughfare. However, rather than continue the road-widening programme to extend the entire main artery between the Guildhall and the upper reaches of the town, the road-widening activities came to an abrupt halt, leaving Castle Bailey and Castle Streets unchanged, and retaining their narrow and unwieldy conditions prohibiting safe access to nearly all forms of traffic.

The Council's hesitance may have been influenced by the costly lesson learned from the Alexandra Road improvement project that was initially estimated to cost tens of thousands of pounds, the endeavour ultimately incurred expenses amounting to hundreds of thousands of pounds. Despite this significant investment, the project yielded limited tangible benefits, aside from the removal of many notorious establishments, and was deemed by some as a vanity project that offered little to accommodate the actual growth of the town.

As the population of Swansea continued to expand and traffic volumes rapidly increased, the inherent dangers of Castle Bailey and Castle Streets' perpetually narrow thoroughfares became increasingly apparent. For two decades or more, the Council had recognised the imperative need to widen these streets; however, despite ongoing discussions and the formulation of various plans, the implementation of these schemes was repeatedly delayed due to concerns over the associated costs. After a member of the Council identified what he thought was a potential solution to address the most perilous section of the remaining narrow gateway in the town centre, the Council agreed to include a provision in an Omnibus Bill to be presented to Parliament that sought the authority to compulsorily acquire the necessary properties along Castle Bailey Street to widen the thoroughfare.

Despite successfully obtaining the necessary powers, and whilst the path forward seemed straightforward, the Council continued to hesitate and delay, primarily due to concerns regarding the associated costs. With the losses incurred over the Alexandra Road project no doubt still fresh in their minds, the Council was faced with the prospect of property owners inflating their asking prices for compulsory purchase, and this was indeed the case. Repeatedly, the Council initiated negotiations with property holders to facilitate street widening, however, prohibitive prices were consistently demanded by one or more of the landlords, resulting in the negotiations stalling at the preliminary stage.

In early 1890, property owners on Castle Bailey Street were asked to state the price at which they would be willing to sell their interests. The total demand from the property owners amounted to £19,000, broken down as - Mr Hancorne, for his shop on the corner of Temple Street and Castle Bailey Street, £6,000; Mr Grose, for his leasehold interest in the same property, £2,000; the Osborne family, for the Wheat Sheaf Hotel, £6,000; and Messrs B. Evans and Co. £5,000 for the remaining four shops, plus the entire frontage to be created on the new street.

Following a Council meeting to discuss matters, the Mayor, Aldermen, and most of the Councillors considered these prices exorbitant especially since, while Parliament had only sanctioned a loan of £13,000, Mr Bell, the Borough Surveyor had estimated the total cost of widening to be £12,000.

There was a misapprehension as to what the improvement would finally cost, and it was unlikely that the town would pay whatever the private owners chose to demand. It was argued that scarcely any such work as this had ever been carried out by private arrangement, but always through arbitrating valuers or else by a jury called by the Sheriff under the powers of the new Swansea Council Act. It was pointed out that most of the Castle Bailey Street property in the hands of Messrs B Evans and Co. had been acquired by private purchase within a comparatively recent date, so any examination before arbitrators or before a jury would reveal these figures, and something like a fair estimate of the real value would be attained. Discussions were further complicated by the revival of an old plan to create a central and joint Railway Station in Worcester Place, and the meeting ended in a deadlock.

B. Evans and Co. was the chief property owner in the immediate area of Castle Bailey Street and had continued to profitably develop their property by rebuilding and enlarging their existing shops. Should the road-widening issue not be resolved, and the company develop its Castle Bailey Street frontage, then it would spell the end of the Council's plans to widen the street, for the price would then be unaffordable.

This procrastination persisted until the time limit for action was nearly exhausted. Then in 1892, Ben Evans stepped forward to address the Council as to the challenge of widening Castle Bailey Street. At that time, he owned four shops along that thoroughfare, and all of the property immediately behind the buildings slated for removal in the event of street widening also belonged to him.

Mr Evans made a generous offer to the Council, proposing to sell his holdings to them at a price determined by an appraiser of their choosing, rather than at the enhanced value he had paid for them. His offer was accepted, but his proposal had a condition attached: they would have to successfully negotiate with the other landlords for the agreement to proceed. If they were unsuccessful, then it would be nullified.

Unfortunately, negotiations with the other property owners proved unsuccessful, and the deal collapsed. Once again, the matter was postponed and set aside by the Council Committee. Undeterred, Mr Evans remained steadfast in his determination to see the street widened, and one by one, he acquired possession of the properties.

While the prices paid were more than market value, Ben Evans persevered, securing five of the seven shops. The two remaining premises were the Wheat Sheaf Tavern and the premises located on the north-east corner. Mr Evans returned to the Council once more and proposed that they assess the fair value of the entire property, including the two outstanding properties, pay him the determined amount, and accept his guarantee that he would carry out the necessary clearance work.

After deliberation, the Council agreed to this proposal, and a sum of £16,000 was agreed upon, acknowledging that this amount would only compensate Mr Evans for the setback of his existing properties. He chose to accept it rather than further delay the matter. Subsequently, he purchased the two remaining properties and signalled his intent to the Council to proceed with the improvement project.

On the 15th of February 1893, following a monthly Council meeting, the entire body of the Council assembled in Castle Bailey Street to witness the initial steps towards the street's transformation. Whilst technically a private initiative, it was also openly acknowledged as a noteworthy public improvement, and the occasion quickly took on the character of a civic ritual, drawing a sizeable crowd to the street's vicinity.

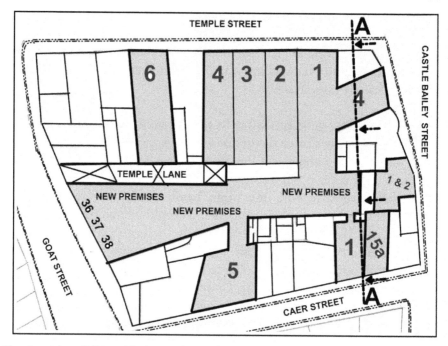

To the right of 'Line A' above shows the property purchased by Ben Evans and subsequently demolished to construct (a) the new Castle Bailey Street building, and (b) provide space for part of the Council's Castle Bailey Street Widening Plan.

The mayor, Alderman Chapman, agreed to remove the first pile of masonry and leveraged a plank beneath one of the old Wheat Sheaf's window sills, causing a gable to cascade onto the roadway below.

Ben Evans was prompted to say a few words to those in attendance. He noted that the widening of Castle Bailey Street had been something everyone in Swansea supported, or at least he had never heard a dissenting voice against the proposal. However, he understood that the cost of such a project was a major obstacle for the Council. (29)

'Terms were settled between myself and the Council, and it was agreed by the unanimous wisdom of the Council, that the powers vested in them should be placed in my hands and that I should-- if I could - be allowed to carry through this work, which would be both a private and a public improvement. I can tell you, however, that though backed by compulsory powers, it did not prove to me that properties could be purchased cheaply, or that owners of properties wanted for public improvements could be more easily dealt with as far as money matters were concerned.

That I found to my cost; the deeper I went into the negotiations of the purchase of the properties not already in my hands, the more I was made to feel the magnitude of the burden I had taken upon myself, and the more clearly I saw how well the chosen representatives had done for all their constituents—at least all excepting one. All those difficulties, however, have been overcome, as the ceremony of today is sufficient evidence. I have endeavoured to take fully into account the question— What sort of a structure ought to be built here, for the sake of the appearance and reputation of the borough, as well as for the special requirements of my business? With this public aspect of the matter in view. I have every reason to believe that, when the buildings are erected and properly exposed to one and all of the burgesses will feel that they will not be unworthy of Swansea.

I thank the Mayor for his kindness in coming here and taking part in the little ceremony which we have seen him perform so well. and I thank you all here for your presence, which I take as a token of your sympathy with me and with the town in efforts at local street improvement, and I trust that, about this time next year. I may again venture to invite you to be present to witness the public opening of the new premises, which are to take the place of the old Wheat Sheaf and of the other old houses whose final demolition will date from this day.'

Within a month, the entire area had been cleared, and work began to replace the hazardous, cramped street that measured only 18 feet across, with a thoroughfare nearly 50 feet wide. Mr Evans had commissioned the architects' firm, Messrs J. P. Jones and Rowlands, of Swansea and Cardiff, to design the new B. Evans & Co. building. Mr David Jenkins, who had successfully built the B. Evans and Co. Stables facility nearby, was engaged as the building contractor, and a team of workers were soon diligently laying the foundations for the new structure that would tower over Castle Bailey Street.

On 21 April 1893, following a few days as a guest of his nephew Ben Evans, the proprietor of London House in Newport, Mr Benjamin Evans passed away at his home in Caerleon, aged 74.

Problems in Caer Street

Things did not progress as smoothly as was hoped. In August of that year, Sir John T. D. Llewelyn of Penllergare, the owner of the property on the opposite side of Caer Street, gave notice of an injunction to restrain the erection of the new buildings to a height of eighty feet, and claimed damages for 'interference by the defendant with the access of light and air to the plaintiff's messuages'. Given that Sir John's legal representatives had not acted until the 10th of August, thousands of pounds had already been expended on the basements and uprights of the Caer Street frontage. (30)

An out-of-court resolution was finally reached between Sir John and Ben Evans. Upon the expansion of Caer Street's southern side, spanning from the corner of Castle Square to Goat Street, both men would contribute £2,000 each to the Council. This contribution would serve as public recognition of the enhancement to their properties resulting from the street widening, whilst noting that these payments only partially covered the expenses incurred for the road expansion, which would be widened to a minimum of 31 feet. Ben Evans also agreed to act as guarantor for the rental payments of Sir John's properties on the southern side of Caer Street. This arrangement was designed to prevent any potential loss of income for Sir John due to concerns about diminished light resulting from the height of Mr Evans's new buildings. Both Ben Evans and Sir John knew that the widening of Castle Bailey Street, aligning its new west side with Castle Square's west side, would significantly enhance the value of Sir John's properties in Castle Square and on the corner of Caer Street.

Furthermore, an agreement was reached that future buildings along Caer Street, be they on the current north side or any future south side, may be constructed to reasonable heights. This would avert the need for costly and unpleasant legal actions such as writs and injunctions, as seen in the present situation. In a gesture of goodwill and to avoid future legal disputes among influential local figures, Ben Evans also committed to covering half of Sir John's legal expenses.

In June 1894, the Ben Evans Employees Rugby XV played their first match, losing in a spirited encounter against the Young Man's Christian Association (aka the YMCA) at the Recreation Ground on Oystermouth Road. (31)

7 - Ben Evans Castle Bailey Street Opening

On Saturday 24th November 1894, the Mayor and Council of Swansea officially inaugurated the new thoroughfare that was Castle Bailey Street. The event was advertised in the local press as a joint celebration, together with the opening of the new and magnificent commercial building of B. Evans and Co.; formally recognising what was a public and private success.

The Mayor and Council convened at the Guildhall, where they were joined by Lord and Lady Swansea, their son the Honourable Aubrey Vivian, and two of their daughters, the Honourable Violet Vivian and the Honourable Averil Vivian, all of whom attended to pay tribute to Mr B. Evans for his outstanding achievement in executing this grand project. Proceeding to Castle Bailey Street, they were joined by several other Swansea dignitaries.

The crowd present erupted into cheers as Mr Ben Evans, accompanied by Mr John White (General Manager of B. Evans and Co.), approached to greet the Mayor and Council. Mr Evans, amidst the fervent applause, proudly presented his worship with a beautifully crafted gold key, symbolising the opening of the splendid new premises. With the ceremony concluded, Mr Evans guided his guests through the entire building which captivated and delighted all who participated and took nearly an hour to complete. Subsequently, everyone adjourned to the exquisite refreshment room, where 'wine and delectable treats' were enjoyed, and speeches were made.

In his speech, Mr Evans stated that, although securing all the required land demanded a significant investment of his time, patience, and financial resources, he did so without resorting to any legal dispute or litigation. He stated that he had pledged his new building would meet the standards and earn the commendation of the town's civic leaders and had entrusted Mr J. P. Rowlands with the task of designing both the exterior elevation and interior layout, prioritising architectural beauty and impact within the constraints of the project. He confidently asserted that this objective had been achieved splendidly.

Continuing his address, he praised the contractor, Mr David Jenkins, for his exemplary execution of the work, and extended general commendation to all involved, with special gratitude to his good friend, Mr John White, for his invaluable assistance and collaboration.

After the Mayor of Swansea toasted the health of Mr Evans, The Right Hon. Lord Swansea, Henry Hussey Vivian, was asked to speak, and in response to calls, Lord Swansea proclaimed: (32)

'Mr Mayor, Mr B. Evans, and gentlemen—I ventured to come here today because I earnestly desired to do as much honour as I possibly could to our most deserving and energetic fellow citizen, Mr B. Evans.

I occupy no official position in the borough now, but at the same time, as a Swansea man born and bred, having lived among you all my life, and having represented you in different capacities, both as a county member of Parliament and also as a member for the Swansea district, I could not refrain from being present amongst you today. I regard this as a very joyful and honourable day for Swansea.'

Lord Swansea commended Mr Evans not only for his commercial achievements but also for his selfless contributions to Swansea's overall development. He highlighted that Mr Evans' endeavours were driven by a desire to enhance the town's prosperity rather than solely for personal profit.

'This grand building in the centre of the town will be a monument to the constant energy and prominent business talent of our friend Mr Evans, whose difficulties in acquiring the site we can all understand. It has been a Herculean task to sweep away the old buildings and erect such a magnificent block, and then Mr Evans has spared no expense in the design he has carried out, which is worthy of himself and of the town of Swansea. Mr Evans has not looked at it from a mere utilitarian point of view, but he has kept his eye on the artistic necessities, and so the result is the magnificent structure you see today, which I can truly say is the most beautiful building in the town.

I hope that Mr Evans's efforts will induce others to follow his example and that this will be regarded as a monument of the success which attends the individual effort of the citizen who likes to attend to his own business and to push it forward vigorously. And I join with you most heartily in wishing every possible success and blessing may attend the efforts of this great arm and I only trust Mr Evans's health may be fully re-established, and that he may for a long life prove a blessing and ornament to our neighbourhood.'

This event marked Lord Swansea's final public appearance, as he tragically passed away just four days later at the age of 73.

A Description of the New Castle Bailey Street Building

The following description is one researched, compiled, and rewritten by the author from various reports of the day, as they included some contradictions and errors: (33) (34)

Rising majestically, an immense palatial structure commands attention, crowned at its centre by a towering mansard roof and adorned at its corners with lofty circular turrets. Facing Castle Bailey Street, the shops boast a frontage spanning 135 feet, while towards Caer Street, it extends for 93 feet, and towards Temple Street, it covers 43 feet. The average elevation of the building stands at 60 feet, with the central feature being the mansard rising to 102 feet at its peak.

The exterior is adorned with intricate carvings, a testament to the craftsmanship of Mr Houghton, the talented carver. Atop the central entrance, two figures symbolise Time bestowing Fame upon Swansea, whilst a section of the façade showcases maps depicting Europe, Asia, Africa, and America, interspersed with whimsical figures adorned in various styles of headgear representing each continent, side panels feature representations of Science and Art, as well as leading operatic characters. Above, the town's coat of arms proudly adorns the shield, as does the motto, 'Floreat Swansea'.

The generously proportioned windows are illuminated by numerous ornate cast iron lamp pillars crafted by Messrs McFarlane and Company of Glasgow. Each pillar supports three lanterns provided by the Gas Company of London. An expansive balcony, spanning nearly the length of the building, graces the third floor, offering a grand vantage point. The balcony railings are also supplied by MacFarlane and Company.

The balcony is designed to enhance the safety of occupants in the event of a fire emergency and is entirely fireproof. In such a dire situation, individuals could seek refuge on the balcony until assistance arrives, significantly improving their chances of survival.

The primary entrance to the new premises is situated centrally along Castle Bailey Street, featuring two spacious arches supported by elegant classical pillars, adorned with a panelled ceiling and mosaic flooring. Each porch floor boasts Patterson's adamant mosaic, a luxurious and visually stunning feature that comprises pieces of red and white marble meticulously set in adamant. Prominently displayed at the centre are the words 'Evans and Company', meticulously crafted and polished to perfection. The ceiling of the main entrance is designed in the style of the French Renaissance, and lit by three large incandescent lamps, illuminating the ceiling both day and night, further accentuating its elegance and charm.

In addition to the main entrance, the premises boast three other entrances - one at the corner facing Castle Square, one at the junction of Temple Street and Castle Bailey Street, and one on Caer Street. Similar grandeur characterises all other entrances throughout the building.

Exiting through the swing door from this vestibule, one encounters the main staircase, which descends to the men's mercery shop below and ascends to a showroom above. Directly upon leaving the vestibule is an area dedicated to fancy goods, which is also accessible via the Temple Street entrance. Adorning each side are fixtures, with a double fixture positioned at the centre. This shop is situated at the base of a sizeable well, from which natural light illuminates the central area and provides a view of the showrooms above.

The four imposing pillars supporting the superstructure are seamlessly integrated into the central fixtures, with the ironwork and joinery throughout the premises adorned in three shades of green, accented with touches of gilding. Richly coloured cornices crafted from plaster add to the opulence of the interior. Above the counter, polished brass gas pendants hang from the ceiling, strategically positioned to illuminate the display of light goods.

The gentlemen's mercery department, located on the left, boasts a separate entrance from Castle Square. The fittings here and elsewhere in the establishment are crafted from a blend of teak, walnut, and mahogany, meticulously polished to perfection.

The Basement: Ascending to the right and entering the basement shops, visitors will find a room on the lower level, currently prepared for use in the upcoming Christmas bazaar but intended for bedsteads in the future. The walls in this area are lined with Edwards's glazed 'Ruabon' bricks in shades of blue, chocolate, and white, creating a visually striking ambience. Despite being below street level, natural light floods the space through Hayward's semi-prismatic lights and stall-boards. This area is situated on the same level as the carpet room in Caer Street, and the establishment has an entrance that connects directly to it. Beneath the mercery department, there is a similarly spacious basement area. The staircases linking the floors are constructed from solid teak, featuring pitch-pine balusters and intricately pierced panels, each at a width of six feet. The basement floors, laid by the Woodblock Flooring Company, exhibit an oak-laid herringbone pattern on a concrete base.

Ground Floor: Ascending the main staircase, situated to the left of the central entrance, visitors encounter the first of several expansive showrooms, designated for use as the ladies' outfitting department. Conveniently, the trying-on rooms are equipped with large pier mirrors, allowing customers to view themselves from all angles without straining their necks unnecessarily. A short flight of stairs leads to another sizeable showroom, dedicated to mantles.

First Floor: This area is illuminated by large windows facing Castle Street and Temple Street, supplemented by lantern lights that are positioned overhead. Additionally, there are more trying-on rooms available in this section. Ascending again, we arrive at the new refreshment rooms.

Second Floor - The New Refreshment Rooms: The new refreshment rooms offer the finest culinary delights while enjoying a picturesque view of Castle Square, Wind Street, and Castle Bailey Street. The ceilings and walls are adorned in vibrant colours, and a dado of 'Lincrusta Walton' (an embossed wallpaper) encircles the room at a height of approximately four feet, adding a touch of sophistication. Throughout this space, elegant fittings abound, and the mantelpiece, crafted from Caen stone according to the architect's design, features a sizeable dog grate, flanked by charming tiles in warm brown hues. Adjacent to the refreshment rooms is the new cloakroom for ladies, equipped with the latest lavatories for convenience. Across the passage, a serving room houses a lift from the kitchen above.

Further up the stairs, additional showrooms await, offering splendid views of Swansea Castle opposite, although they are not yet fully furnished. On the next floor, spacious workrooms, bathed in natural light and an airy ambience, await. Each of these rooms is connected to the premises on Caer Street.

Third Floor: Continuing upward, we arrive at the kitchen and adjoining larders, equipped with modern culinary amenities including an American stove and grill, ensuring the preparation of delectable dishes with both efficiency and precision. On the same floor are several staff bedrooms. Indeed, the staff bedrooms occupy nearly all of the upper floors and have been meticulously crafted.

Mansard and Rooftop: Continuing along the main staircase, we arrive at the chambers nestled within the central mansard, and reach the leaded rooftop of the building. Situated atop the highest terrain in the town centre, the new premises' mansard roof towers a full hundred feet above street level.

Ascending from the mansard roof is a towering flagstaff, standing fifty feet tall and anchored by a sturdy crown-like arch. On ceremonial days, a flag measuring thirty feet long will unfurl from its mast. Lightning conductors are affixed to the flagstaff, as well as to the peaks of other turrets protruding from the building.

The views of Swansea from the roof are magnificent; from this vantage point, not only does the sweeping bay come into view, with occasional glimpses of the Devon coast, but also the hills rising behind the town and stretching towards the Mumbles. The expansive panorama extends to the Swansea Valley, the open expanse of Kilvey, and offers a bird's-eye view of the town's most notable buildings and winding streets, appearing minuscule from such an elevation.

Moving from the kitchen to the Caer Street block, one catches a glimpse of the top of the lift descending through the rooms previously described, including the carpet room. Descending on our journey, we cross a bridge into the Temple Street block, from where one can behold a view of the reconstructed cross-shop. The roof of this area takes on a circular form, constructed with a combination of glass and wood adorned with ornate ironwork, skilfully crafted by Messrs Lloyd Brothers. Adjacent to the entrance on Caer Street, we arrive at the new carpet room. This space boasts oak flooring and is decorated consistent with the aesthetic found throughout the rest of the building, and it is here that we encounter the new passenger lift.

Author's collection

Swansea's First Passenger Lift: A hydraulic lift has been installed, providing a convenient and comfortable way of getting from one floor to another. This lift, crafted and supplied by the Otis Elevator Company of London, represents the latest in elevator technology and is the first of its kind in Swansea. The elevator car and machinery boast polished mahogany construction.

The lift is fitted with comfortably upholstered seats that line both sides, complemented by two large mirrors strategically positioned to reflect each other. This clever arrangement creates the illusion of a more expansive compartment, enhancing the cosy ambience of the carriage. The car's floor features parquet work, while its sides are adorned with mahogany and bevelled mirrors, with a fancy glass top that provides natural light during the day and gas illumination at night.

Beneath the car, a spacious luggage box is fixed for transporting carpets and other items to the upper floors. The architect-designed casing surrounding the lift is executed in deal (pine) embellished with colourful accents and brass wire panels.

The elevator car can accommodate six passengers in addition to the attendant, at a rate of motion of 30 seconds upwards and 15 seconds downwards for the entire five-floor distance, while 'Electrobell' communication allows customers to summon the lift to any floor by pressing a button beside the entrance.

The lift is designed with multiple fail-safe mechanisms to ensure passengers' security. Firstly, it operates on four sturdy wire-rope cables, each individually guaranteed to bear three times the maximum strain anticipated. This alone provides a twelve-fold assurance of safety. In addition, the car's cables are arranged to function under a patented lever system. In the unlikely event that one cable was to snap, the lever would automatically engage a powerful brake, immediately halting the car's descent, a redundant safety measure that ensures passengers can ride with confidence, knowing that every precaution has been taken to mitigate any potential risks.

The elevator operates through hydraulic pressure, with large 2,500-gallon water tanks fixed at both its top and bottom, and is equipped with a cylinder fitted with a double valve system that allows one rope's action to move the lift either upwards or downwards. When water descends from the upper tank into the lower part of the cylinder, it pushes the piston upward, raising the car. If the process is reversed, water flows from the lower part of the cylinder to a tank below, exerting downward pressure on the piston and lowering the car. This continuous circulation of water minimises wastage. Mr Legg of Swansea supplied and installed the tanks, gas engines, and all connections, as well as the gas and water supply fixtures.

Beneath the carpet room is the basement, housing the gas engine and other machinery, as well as clean and well-appointed lavatories for the employees.

Ben Evans Store, Castle Bailey Street Frontage - Author's collection

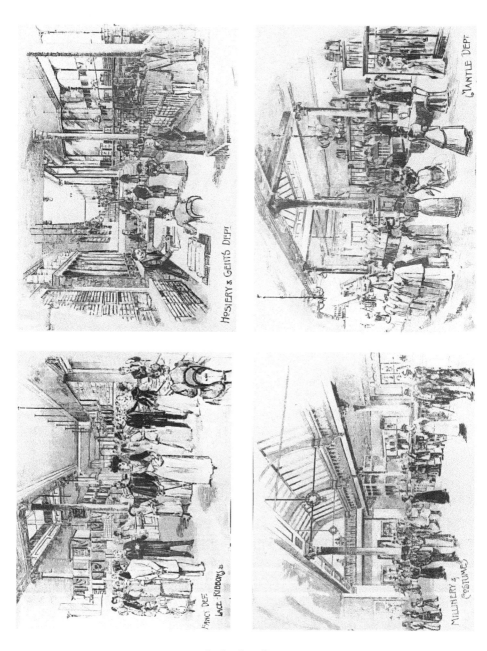

Author's collection

8 - B. Evans and Co. for Sale

In early July 1891, it was reported that Ben Evans had been taken ill with a severe attack of rheumatism, and after an initial period of three weeks, he suffered a serious relapse, during which time he was bedridden. (35) Following the improvement in his health, it was decided that together with his wife he would take a vacation; however, he was taken ill whilst visiting Egypt.

Reports suggested that the illness was a fleeting one. However, a report in The Cambrian on 4th March 1892 made it clear that this was not the case at all. Whilst Mr & Mrs Evans had departed Alexandria bound for Marseilles a few days before, 'It must be clarified that the recent paragraph circulated in a local publication, asserting Mr Evans' communication to a friend in Swansea about his improving health, is entirely baseless. Mr Evans did not send such a letter, and unfortunately, the optimistic depiction of his health recovery is largely inaccurate.'

After returning to his home 'Corrymore' on Gower Road, Sketty a few weeks later, Mr Evans' poor health would be the deciding factor in the decision to sell the business.

In January of 1895, a rumour in the City of London that a large retail business in Wales was soon to become a limited company forced Messrs Howell and Co. of Cardiff to ask The Sketch newspaper to issue an official statement confirming that their business was not to be turned into a company. In the same report, it was stated that the rumour, albeit circumstantial, may have developed due to 'the fact that a large Swansea business of a like kind is about to be issued.'

A month later, on February 13th, The Sketch reported the following: (36)

BEN EVANS AND CO. LIMITED.-This Swansea drapery business is being offered to the public and with a moderate capital. Both the shares and debentures- which, by the way, yield 5 per cent- are a good investment, and the whole concern is both a good home investment and comes from an honest quarter.

About two years' purchase is asked for the goodwill, and the debentures seem to us a very tempting security, being amply secured on freehold and leasehold premises, besides having a floating charge on the assets of a flourishing business. We have no doubt the public subscription will be very large.

The following month, the Llanelli Mercury confirmed that B. Evans & Co. Ltd was soon to become a public company. (37)

'Seldom has a local business been floated under conditions so favourable for permanent success as that of Messrs B. Evans & Co. The full prospectus will be found on our sixth page, but we may remark here that the business has for many years been universally recognised as one of the best in Wales and the Western of England. This colossal business is a household word. The share capital, it will be seen, is £103,000, and the debenture stock £75,000.

The £75,000 of 5%, first mortgage debentures are offered at 105% and are redeemable at 110%. Of this amount, £32,100 has been already taken by the directors, etc., and of the ordinary shares £46,700 has also been taken the same way. As a joint-stock concern, the business is transferred from the vendors at a most reasonable price, £133,730 only being paid for freehold and leasehold properties and fixtures valued at £101,260; and the balance,£32,481, for good-will--practically two years' purchase; in point of fact one of the cheapest properties that has been offered for a long time, if ever a good, sound property like this has been let go at such a bargain. We received a telegram from London yesterday stating that pound shares are being dealt with in 5s. premium, the debentures at £107.'

On the 13th of February, The Western Mail (38) noted that Mr Ben Evans had relinquished the business from 1st January 1895 with the following assets, in addition to the goodwill, stock, etc., included in the sale:

Freehold Properties:

No. 15 Castle Square
Nos. 2, 3. 4. and 5, Castle Bailey Street
No. 1, Temple Street
Nos. 1. 2, 3, 4. and 5, Caer Street
Nos. 36. 37 and 38. Goat Street
A warehouse in Temple Lane
Stables and a dwelling-house in Frog Street

Leasehold Properties:

Nos. 2, 3, 4, 6, and 7 Temple Street
No. 46. Castle Bailey Street

The newspaper noted that considering the moderate capital required for a well-established business such as Ben Evans and Company, 'there will be no need to tout for investors in such a concern as this, and there is little question that the share capital will be subscribed several times over'. It was intended to allocate a liberal share of the capital to the over 350 Ben Evans employees, as well as to the store's customers and the residents of Swansea.

The South Wales Daily Post also covered the sale and described the business as 'established upwards of 25 years ago in Swansea by Mr Benjamin Evans, a business described as 'The Shoolbred of Wales', (39) the report explaining that Mr Evans was selling the business owing to his failing health and that Mr White, who had been the store's General Manager for sixteen years, would be the Managing Director of the new company. Mr White had entered into a five-year agreement with the Company to continue his service 'under which his additional income, compared with that received at present, will depend on the continued growth of the Company's prosperity'. It was also intended to continue the existing arrangements with the experienced staff of buyers and assistants.

The share capital of 'Ben Evans and Co., Limited', the report said, would be 'largely over-subscribed', noting that a substantial portion 'will be taken by employees and customers of the firm'.

A few weeks later, it was confirmed that shares had 'been applied for between five and six times over, and the directors had a big weeding-out process to go through, the idea being to allot to such persons — chiefly local — that will be likely to benefit the company.' (40)

Following the offering, on February 20th The Sketch reported: (41)
'The Ben Evans issue has gone very well, with various estimates making the public subscriptions from three to five times the required amount. Just now the public temper is very uncertain, but it is a healthy sign that when a really sound home industrial concern is offered, it is eagerly snapped up.'

The List of Applications will be closed at or before 4 p.m. on Friday, the 15th day of February, 1895, for Town; and the following Morning for the Country.

BEN EVANS & CO., Ltd.

Incorporated under the Companies Acts, 1862 to 1893, whereby the liability of the Shareholders is limited to the amount of their Shares.

SHARE CAPITAL - - £103,000,

DIVIDED INTO

100,000 ORDINARY SHARES OF £1 EACH.   3000 FOUNDERS' SHARES OF £1 EACH.

DEBENTURE STOCK:

75,000 FIVE PER CENT. FIRST MORTGAGE DEBENTURE STOCK.

A few days later, it was reported that, following B. Evans and Co.'s successful move, other companies in the same line of business were looking to do the same: (42)

'Anent the recent conversion of the firm of Messrs B. Evans & Co. into a limited liability company, a Cardiff contemporary states that several big drapery establishments in London contemplate following in the wake of the local Whiteleys.'

Ben Evans in Retirement

Soon after the sale of his company, Benjamin Evans retired. His reputation was beyond reproach, both as a man and as a businessman, and he remained a 'wanted man' in the eyes of those who felt he could be an agent for further positive change in Swansea.

Despite turning down offers of mayoralty in both Swansea and Llandovery, as well as several invitations to run as a parliamentary candidate for the Conservative Party, in an interview with a representative of The Cambrian on Friday 23rd September 1898, he directly addressed the suggestion of his candidacy for the upcoming mayoralty. He began by expressing his unfamiliarity with the individuals behind the letters advocating for his nomination, highlighting that, had they consulted him beforehand, such letters might have been unnecessary.

Mr Evans stated that the esteemed position should be earned through substantial contributions to the welfare of the ratepayers, rather than being casually offered or accepted. He pointed out that there were still diligent, capable, and deserving members of the Council who had not yet been recognised with the mayoralty, and he suggested that these individuals would be admirable successors to the current Mayor rather than him. As a significant shareholder in the newly formed company, he remained committed to its continued prosperity.

He also maintained an active interest in Swansea's development, pledging to uphold his dedication to public service and charitable endeavours, and expressed his intention to support community initiatives whenever possible.

In March 1894, Mr Evans accepted the role of Justice of the Peace for Glamorgan, and later in Carmarthenshire, his appointment to the magisterial bench underscored his reputation within the community. In 1900, he acted as High Sheriff of Carmarthen. His philanthropic endeavours were, although often unnoticed, extensive and greatly impactful. Amongst his many contributions, he funded the construction of a state-of-the-art operating theatre at Swansea Hospital, amounting to over £2,000. He also made significant donations to several religious and educational initiatives.

His acts of benevolence were discreet, guided by the principle of not seeking recognition, as he believed in the biblical admonition of maintaining discretion when carrying out charitable acts.

In retirement, he and his wife left Swansea and settled in Llandovery, where he took on the role of warden at Llanfair Church. There, he financed the renovation/rebuilding of the tower. He actively participated in establishing Llandingat Church House, contributing £100 towards its construction and additionally lending £150 without interest. The Church House was repurposed into reading rooms, a billiard room, and a smoke room. Previously, he had generously supported a related institution known as Llandingat Young Men's Guild, which became redundant upon the acquisition of new premises.

In 1911, he succeeded the late Earl Cawdor as trustee of Llandovery College, where his generous contributions are said to have revitalised the institution, exemplified by his substantial £1,000 donation to the building fund during the college's expansion phase. In addition, he gifted a science school to the institution at a cost exceeding £2,000, which at the time of his death was under construction, officially opening in July of the following year.

Two of Ben Evans' most trusted lieutenants would go on to succeed him as Managing Director of the company: first John White (from 1895 to 1907) and later Meredith Thomas (from 1907 to 1912). Like Ben Evans before them, both men had spent time learning the department store business at William Tarn & Co. in London.

9 - Ben Evans and Co. (Limited) 1895 to 1910

Economic Conditions

The late Victorian and early Edwardian eras saw overall economic growth and prosperity; however, there was an increasing sense that Britain's competitive edge was slipping compared to its industrial rivals. This sparked concerns about economic inefficiency, the need for state reform, and a drive for imperial expansion to find new markets and resources.

The late Victorian era saw a growing sense of national decline and limits to the liberal, free-market economic model compared to rising industrial powers like Germany and the United States. Military failures in the Boer War (1899-1902) exposed weaknesses in Britain's 'free enterprise' system and fuelled concerns about 'national efficiency'. There was increasing anxiety about social problems like urban poverty that raised questions about the adequacy of the state's role. However, the economy was still prospering overall, with rising incomes and living standards for many. The early Edwardian era was viewed as a period of widespread peace and economic prosperity, with no severe country-wide depressions. Britain's growth rate, manufacturing output, and productivity remained strong. However, there were signs of relative industrial decline compared to rivals, with older industries like textiles and clothing shedding workers while new growth sectors lagged.

Concerns grew about maintaining economic competitiveness, especially after the economic shocks of the 1873 'Long Depression' highlighted overproduction issues. This fuelled calls for greater state intervention and imperial expansion to find new markets for excess British industrial capacity through the 'Scramble for Africa': the invasion and colonisation of most of Africa by seven Western European powers between 1833 and 1914.

Retail Environment

Despite the dominance of independent, family-run shops on British high streets, the early 20th century was a transformative period for the UK retail landscape, due to the rise of many iconic retail chains. Notable examples include Home and Colonial for groceries, Freeman Hardy & Willis for shoes, and the American-owned Woolworth store, all of which had begun as small, independent retailers. During this period, innovative department stores also emerged, revolutionising the shopping experience.

These stores offered a diverse range of goods under one roof in an exciting and sensory environment. Elaborate and theatrical window displays featuring headless wax mannequins in staged scenes became a common strategy to draw shoppers inside. Additionally, neon signs first appeared on shopfronts, attracting attention during the night.

Marketing techniques also evolved significantly. Advertising expanded beyond simple leaflets, with retailers adopting more sophisticated tactics such as billboards to promote their stores. Despite these advancements, a steady rise in retail prices gradually eroded consumers' purchasing power, impacting their ability to buy goods over time.

The first meeting of the new directors of Messrs B. Evans and Co. (Limited) was held at Swansea on Saturday 6th July 1895 (43), the new Chairman, Sir Joseph Renals, Bart. and the current Lord Mayor of London presided.

In carrying out the necessary due diligence on the business before its flotation, the limited company's appointed accountants, Messrs Percy Mason and Co. of London, had certified that the average annual net profit for the previous four years (1890-1894 inclusive) was £13,036 18s 10d (£1,431,961 in 2024).

The London-based directors were very impressed by the 'extent and magnificence of the premises', whilst Sir Joseph commented that the business was 'of routine character'. Under new management but with the same mantra of being the best, the board of directors of the limited company continued to upgrade the store with the latest and best utilities.

Electric Light at the New Premises, January 1895

In early January 1895, electric lighting was introduced to the store for the first time. (44) The company commissioned Messrs J. C. Howell (Limited) of London and Llanelli to install the 'new light', and the impressive façade of Castle Bailey Street was illuminated for the first time by ten large electric lamps suspended from the lower balcony, 'casting a soft, pure glow that accentuated the grandeur of the building'. The installation was subsequently extended to the windows.

A generator housed in the store's basement, featuring an Otto Crossley gas engine, delivered the power. The store used Crompton-Pochin lamps, 'celebrated for their unmatched stability of burning—a testament to the significant strides made in achieving the desired consistency, particularly in large-scale lighting such as that produced by arc lamps'. Contractors Messrs J. C. Howell utilised mostly local electrical technicians on the contract, under the guidance of electrical engineer Mr Henry Coles.

Ben Evans was not, however, the first Swansea store to be illuminated; that honour belonged to John S. Brown - ironmonger, bicycle salesman and engineer - who, using a Victoria Dynamo Set, lit his Oxford Street store in 1886. The store's conversion to electricity appeared to have been good for Mr Brown's business, as in 1894 he opened new and substantial three-storey premises on Oxford Street.

Swansea would first see electric lighting on its streets on 9th November 1900, when Alexandra Road and St Helen's Road were illuminated, and a general supply was made available to the town on 10th December the same year. The town's new power station was located on the Strand, a few hundred yards away from the Ben Evans store. (45)

Ben Evans Performance 1895-1910

Year	Jan 1895- Feb 1896	Net Profit	Net Profit
1		£ 15,490***	£1,701,524 *** Based on 2024 Equivalence

*** The company's first Balance Sheet and P&L covered a 14-month trading period. The accompanying notes stating the financial information provided cover the period from January 1st 1895 (the date at which the business was taken over as a going concern) to 27th February 1896, viz., 11 months (see (d) in Appendices).

At the company's first Annual General Meeting, (AGM) Alderman Gwilym Evans chaired the proceedings in the absence of Sir Joseph Renals, who was convalescing in Europe due to ill health. Alderman Evans also noted that the company's founder, Mr Ben Evans, was out of the country and unable to attend the meeting. He explained that, although it might not be widely known, Ben Evans had sold the business and no longer had direct involvement.

However, Mr Evans had applied for a substantial number of shares based on the prospectus and remained the largest shareholder and debenture-holder in the company. Additionally, the company's new Managing Director, Mr John White, was the second-largest shareholder.

Whilst Alderman Evans further elucidated that the fortunes of a company such as Ben Evans relied heavily on the performance of the local industries, notwithstanding the great depression of trade in the staple industries of the district, viz. the coal and tin-plate trades, sales in the limited company's first trading period had exceeded any previous year, the result could not be considered as other than satisfactory. Considering the existing depression, the company had made a good start. He added that as soon as trade brightened, there was no doubt their business would increase further, though in that respect they must not expect great things.

New Heating System Fitted, March 1896

In late March 1896, the Cambrian newspaper reported that a new heating system had been successfully installed at Ben Evans and Co. Ltd using technology from the American Radiator Company. (46)

'On Wednesday afternoon, a significant gathering of gentlemen convened to witness first-hand the impeccable execution of the heating arrangements and the efficiency with which the apparatus fulfils its intended purpose.'

Present that day was Mr Henry S. Downe, the manager of the European branch of the radiator company, and he readily took on the task of explaining the entire installation process and the underlying principle behind it, which involves 'the radiation of heat through hot water.'

Author's collection

Mr Downe demonstrated that the fuel consumption necessary to keep the boiler operational was minimal and the entire apparatus, installed by Mr Legg of Swansea, required little maintenance. He explained that within the basement of the store, a portable boiler has been installed with the capacity to heat six thousand feet of 4-inch pipes, nearly double the current requirements of the establishment. The water is circulated from the boiler to the highest point of the building through a flow pipe, connecting to other pipes on each floor, which are then linked to 'aesthetically pleasing' heat radiators. With the aid of stop-cocks, heat distribution can be controlled independently on each floor without affecting others. Upon completing its circuit through the pipes, the water returns to the boiler for reheating, having only lost 10 per cent of its initial heat after traversing the entire 3,500 feet of piping installed. To minimise friction, the main pipes are constructed of wrought iron.

The American Radiator Company's system was widely used in America, and several prominent institutions in Great Britain had already adopted it. He was pleased to announce that the most extensive installation in a business establishment thus far is the one at Messrs Ben Evans and Company.

Year	March 1896-- Feb 1897	Net Profit	Net Profit
2		£ 13,992	£1,555,056 (2024)

In April 1897, at the 2nd AGM, Chairman Sir Joseph Renals addressed the shareholders. 'The financial report for the past year is satisfactory for several reasons,' he said. 'Despite the ongoing depression in the coal and tinplate trades within the district, sales have increased significantly, surpassing those of any previous year. This positive outcome is reflected in a proportionally lower stock, increased sales, and consequently, increased profits.'

'The continued depression in Swansea's staple trade has negatively impacted both the town and the surrounding areas, making these results even more noteworthy. This remarkable achievement can be attributed not only to the popularity and appeal of Ben Evans and Co. but also to their consistent provision of excellent value to customers for cash purchases. Furthermore, the dedication, attention, and courtesy of the employees have played a crucial role in achieving this success.'

The Chairman pointed out that the shareholders had a splendid property, 'there was none to compare with it in Wales and the West,' and proclaimed that with the present excellent management, there was no reason why the prosperity which had marked it for so many years should not be extended for long years to come. Shareholders had received notice that an extraordinary general meeting was to be held upon the conclusion of the annual general meeting. Having assessed the business over the previous two years, the board proposed to expand the current building further by the purchase and conversion of 'Cave's Corner', a property on the corner of Caer Street and Goat Street that formed an important angle in the block largely owned by Ben Evans and Co.

Following the annual gathering, an extraordinary meeting was convened to discuss the approval of utilising company funds to purchase Cave's Corner and to modernise and adapt it to match the purposes and standards of the rest of the premises. The directors believed that acquiring Cave's Corner would significantly increase business, and they emphasised that the expected profit margin would be substantial, large enough to cover the interest seven times over, making it a highly recommended investment. The directors hoped that the current shareholders would see this as a safe and highly desirable opportunity. The proposal was approved, and the meeting concluded.

The contract for rebuilding the Goat and Caer Street corner of Messrs Ben Evans and Co.'s premises was awarded within weeks of its approval. The work was to be carried out by Messrs Lloyd Bros of Swansea, at £6,100, with completion scheduled in 'about six months'.

When completed, the company planned to utilise the improved structural changes to increase the comfort and security of their large staff of assistants, providing bathrooms, lavatories, a library, and other amenities, further demonstrating their commitment to making the establishment one of the best conducted in the country. The board reasoned that the alterations would not only enhance the current structure but would also result in a highly desirable street improvement.

Messrs Ben Evans and Co. agreed, for a consideration from the Council, to relinquish approximately 100 square feet of land covered by the buildings to be demolished, to allow the Council to substantially widen the roadway on Caer Street as part of its street improvement plans.

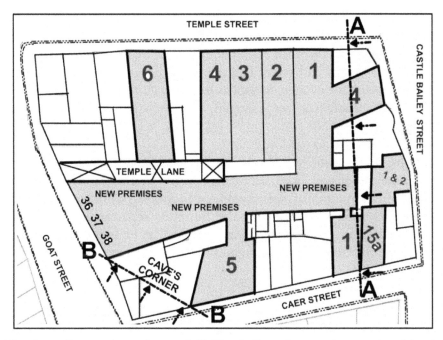

The above diagram shows (bottom left) 'Cave's Corner', a premises purchased by the company. The buildings above 'Line B' were integrated into the store, whilst the buildings below the line were demolished as part of the Council's Caer Street Widening Plan.

Year 3	March 1897-- Feb 1898	Net Profit £15,285	Net Profit £1,659,702 (2024)

In April 1898, Chairman Sir Joseph Renals addressed the shareholders at the 3rd AGM and proclaimed that, notwithstanding the absence of any marked revival in the staple trades of Swansea and the surrounding districts, sales for the past year had increased, amounting to more than any previous year. This was particularly satisfactory given that the new premises, which were to be shortly opened, had not yet yielded any material benefit.

The buildings on the freehold site at the corner of Goat Street and Caer Street were nearly completed and were expected to open shortly after Easter. The new premises were needed to accommodate expanding trade, including the introduction of one or two new departments which management believed were needed to explore previously identified but still untapped markets, intending to significantly increase profits through new trade.

One of the new departments was a tailoring department, particularly desirable because as women ventured into areas traditionally occupied by men, it was crucial to have skilled personnel capable of creating tailor-made garments for women, as well as handling all aspects of men's attire. Additionally, there was an enlarged and improved extension of the furniture department.

The Chairman mentioned that these new departments, although planned for future expansion, were already in active operation. The tailoring department, in particular, was capable of producing work comparable to the best London houses, whilst the furniture department had already made significant strides in the ornamental line, and it was now proposed to increase the stock of practical and serviceable furniture.

Year	March 1898-- Feb 1899	Net Profit	Net Profit
4		£15,297	£1,661,010 (2024)

The company's fourth AGM of the shareholders was held at the company's registered offices in Swansea, with Chairman Sir Joseph Renals presiding. 'We are very thankful to present such a report for the fourth year of our existence as a limited liability company, and we earnestly believe that the business of Ben Evans and Company has never been in a sounder or better position than it is today.'

The new buildings on the freehold site at the corner of Goat Street and Caer Street had been completed, and the results already obtained fully justified the actions taken in making the extensions. Whilst the board were pleased with the alterations, the Council had not yet acted on its plan to widen Caer Street. The Chairman hoped that they would soon act, 'although we understand that, as shareholders, we will have to contribute towards the cost. We will be glad to do this, for it will allow our premises to stand out properly, and people will be able to appreciate the magnificent buildings we have.'

The Development of Caer Street and Goat Street Corner

On 18th May 1898, the company launched the reopening of its western frontage in tandem with its 'Grand Spring and Summer Show of Fashions'. The reopening of the store followed a significant expansion to the premises, specifically the complete revamp of the block of buildings nestled on and around the corner of Caer Street and Goat Street, the ageing structures demolished to pave the way for the new development. The architect was Mr Rowlands, of Wind Street, and the contractors were Messrs Lloyd Brothers.

The following description is one researched, compiled, and rewritten by the author from various reports of the day, as they included some contradictions and errors: (47) (48)

The new wing addressed a longstanding need for additional floor space to accommodate the growing demand for soft furnishings. In addition, a Ladies' & Gentlemen's Tailoring Department has also been added and is located within the new facilities. Nestled within the basement of the new department on Goat Street and Caer Street is a spacious Polishing Department measuring 90 feet by 30 feet, whilst on the ground floor, aligned with Caer Street, the area is dedicated to cabinet furniture. The Cabinet Furniture department is enhanced by the ample natural light streaming in through extensive side windows and has a sense of openness and ventilation enhanced by strategically positioned wells in the floor above.

Accessible from this department is the Temple Street ground floor via a meticulously crafted central staircase, adjacent to the Counting House. On the right side of the Counting House lies the Soft Furnishing Department, offering picturesque views overlooking Goat Street and Caer Street. Within this well-ventilated and spacious room is a telephone for the convenience of visitors, and directly across from the telephone is a lift ready to transport the Counting House books to the Strong Room located in the basement.

Ascending to the next floor reveals an even more remarkable transformation, where a soft furnishings showroom spanning 130 feet in length and 55 feet in width awaits. Undoubtedly, it stands as one of the most exquisite showrooms in the entire kingdom. While the previous showroom, dedicated to costumes and mantles, garnered admiration from all who beheld it, the recent alterations have elevated it to new heights. From a balcony bridge connected with the showroom, a view is afforded of the Mantle and Costume Department.

The changes made to the building have not been limited to the retail departments. Recognising the importance of their staff's wellbeing to their success, one of the most striking and gratifying aspects of the new premises lies in the accommodation provided on the upper floors for their assistants. The bedrooms are as spacious as they are well-ventilated, boasting a modern and airy feel. In addition, an excellent suite of bathrooms and lavatories has been installed, equipped with Twyford's glazed fire-clay bricks and every conceivable modern convenience.

Rather than the elaborate ceremonies of previous B. Evans and Co. openings, events that were faithfully followed by wordy descriptions in the local press, the new corporate owners opted instead for a four-page supplement in The Cambrian newspaper, which offered an overview of the various departments along with layout drawings of the ground, first and second floors.

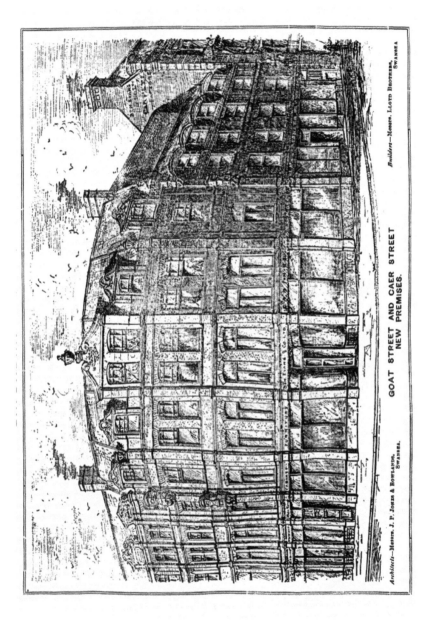

Ben Evans store, Goat Street-Caer Street Corner - Copyright Status Unknown

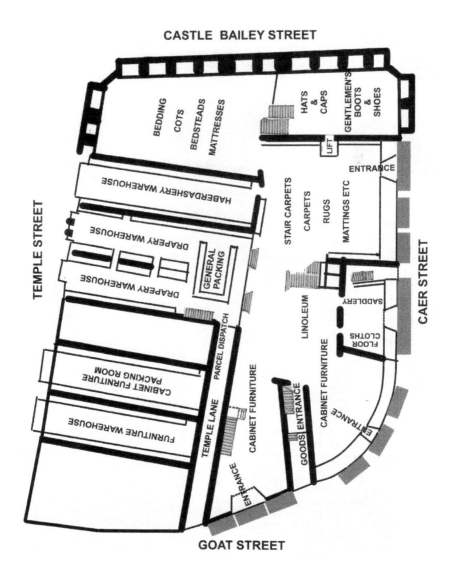

Ground Floor- Goat Street and Caer Street Entrances - May 1898

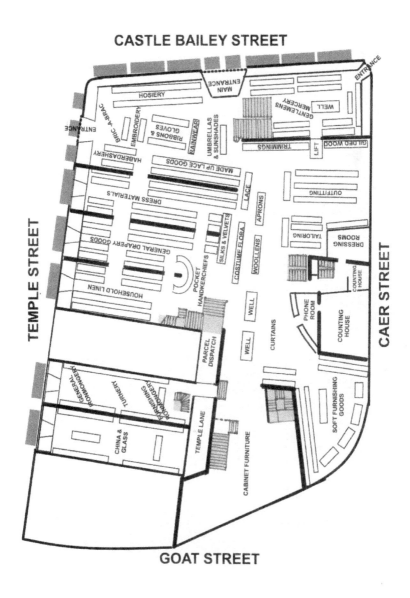

First Floor of Goat Street with the Main Entrance on the Ground Floor
on Castle Bailey Street - May 1898

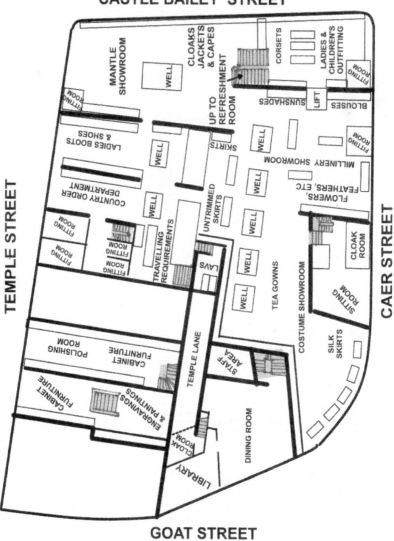

Second Floor of Goat Street - May 1898

A New Competitor

In 1899, S. Andrews & Son of Cardiff constructed a new building in Swansea on the site of the old Theatre Royal, at the corner of Temple Street and Goat Street.

Solomon Andrews, originally from Wiltshire, was a notable entrepreneur and the head of Solomon Andrews and Son, a prominent Cardiff-based bus and tram-operating company. His business interests extended across Britain, encompassing various bus and tram ventures across multiple cities, alongside engagements in construction, hospitality, and retail.

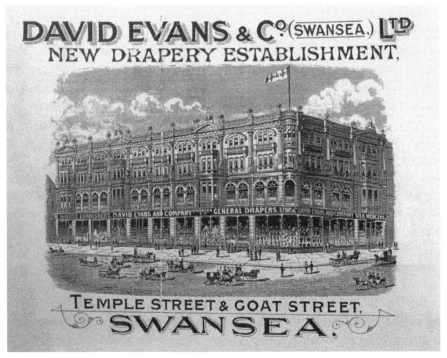

From author's collection

Andrews established David Evans & Co (Swansea) Ltd in 1900, partnering with two other individuals: his son Francis Emile Andrews, who assumed the role of the inaugural Chairman, and David Evans, a respected local draper, who took on the position of the company's first Managing Director and who lent his name to the store.

Year 5	March 1899-- Feb 1900	Net Profit £16,129	Net Profit £1,731,450 (2024)

Chairman Sir Joseph Renals presided over the fifth AGM of the shareholders held in Swansea and praised the performance of the Managing Director and his staff in producing another solid twelve months of trading, with profits at their highest level since the limited company's formation.

Very likely with new neighbours David Evans & Co. in mind, the Chairman rallied the shareholders. He had, he said, heard the word 'competition' spoken frequently in recent times. However, he confessed that he was not afraid of that word, as honest and honourable competition was always welcome. He believed that the same word, perhaps with even greater emphasis, was used when the founder of the business began his career. The Chairman did not doubt that it was 'competition' that led to the increased wealth of gentlemen like Mr Ben Evans.

Addressing the local shareholders present, the Chairman said that in commercial circles, particularly in London, nearly all manufacturers of a certain kind could be found clustered in specific districts. As a result, people knew where to go when they wanted to do business. Similarly, in Swansea, people would be as likely to come to Ben Evans and Co. as to anyone else.

Competition sharpened their intellect, made them more vigilant, and pushed them to do their very best. Therefore, he had no reservations in saying that he did not fear competition, but rather preferred it. Ben Evans & Co. Ltd, 'with its past experience, beautifully displayed windows, ability to pay cash for everything, and the keen intelligence of their departmental buyers' had little to fear from competition.

The Chairman informed the shareholders that they had agreed on new contract terms with Managing Director John White; 'arrangements had been made by which his services would be retained for the benefit of the company for a long number of years to come'. He added that shareholders would agree with him that 'this was an item, all others left unconsidered, which was sufficient almost to guarantee the prosperity of Ben Evans and Co.' He also took the opportunity to remark on how pleased both the board and the shareholders were at Mr Ben Evans' recent appointment as

High Sheriff of Carmarthenshire.

Year	March 1900-- Feb 1901	Net Profit	Net Profit
6		£15,583	£1,600,105 (2024)

At the sixth AGM of the company's shareholders, Chairman Renals congratulated the Managing Director and his staff on the previous year's trading performance, given the adverse circumstances with which they had to deal, the results were most satisfactory. 'The prosperity of the company was never greater than it was at the present moment, the outlook for the future was never brighter, and the reputation of the firm, with the clients and everyone associated with it, was of the very best and most desirable order.'

The Chairman highlighted several factors that mitigated against what could have been a much more successful year; but, considering everything, they had no cause for complaint. Very few similar institutions could show better results, even though they had faced disappointments with the weather and local trade disturbances—circumstances that did not affect similar establishments in London. Another adverse circumstance that mitigated greater prosperity was the disastrous war in South Africa. All wars have detrimental effects on trade; some may be justifiable, particularly in times of national danger or imperial necessity, but they invariably bring harmful consequences in their wake.

Taxation had increased considerably, leading to economic retrenchment at home. However, regardless of taxation, the necessities of life must be provided, and institutions like theirs were the first to suffer. Despite restraints on expenditure, they managed to show an increased return, although this increase was accompanied by a slight decrease in profit.

That was easily explained, and he thought it was only right to explain it to the shareholders. During the year, certain conditions led to manufacturers increasing the selling prices of their goods. However, instead of raising the Company's prices proportionately to the increase in cost, the directors, in perfect agreement with the Managing Director, had decided to pass the advantage on to their clients, many of whom were shareholders.

This decision meant that while the profits could have been larger, it was deemed better to ensure customer satisfaction by not raising prices. He believed the shareholders would agree that it was more beneficial to keep their customers happy than to risk dissatisfaction.

The Chairman stated that he would like to see future balance sheets reflect a change in the figures represented by outstanding debts. He reminded shareholders that to provide clients with the best value for their money, the company must continue to pay cash. To achieve this, they must secure the necessary funds, and if these do not come from their customers, there is no other resource available.

Year	March 1901-- Feb 1902	Net Profit	Net Profit
7		£15,351	£1,576,282 (2024)

The seventh AGM of the shareholders of Messrs Ben Evans and Company, Limited, was held at the company's registered offices in Swansea, with Chairman Sir Joseph Renals presiding.

Although profits were on par with the previous year, the Chairman said he thought shareholders would agree with him that they had no right to complain about their year's trading. He stated that, despite the plateau in profits, 'it was the most successful balance sheet, the most promising as representing the most successful year in the history of Ben Evans and Co., Ltd., and what was very satisfactory from a shareholder's point of view, they had the largest balance to their credit at the bank that the history of the concern had known.'

The Chairman said that the company had always faced, and likely always would face some drawbacks, but the business had flourished despite the disastrous effects of the war in South Africa on trade and commerce. On this point, he expressed hope that the prospects for peace would soon herald the dawn of more prosperous times.

Year	March 1902-- Feb 1903	Net Profit	Net Profit
8		£15,360	£1,577,206 (2024)

At the eighth AGM held in April 1903, the Chairman took great pride in presenting a report on behalf of the directors that mirrored the robust and substantial reports of the past seven years. It was a testament to the company's unwavering strength and stability as a thriving enterprise that they derived immense satisfaction from the continued loyalty of their esteemed clientele, to whom they owed a profound debt of gratitude. It remained the firm's steadfast commitment to extend the utmost courtesy and exceptional service to these valued customers, and the directors pledged to consistently demonstrate that the company offered unparalleled value across its diverse range of products and markets. This ethos had been the cornerstone of their success, and they vowed to uphold these principles with renewed vigour in the years ahead.

The company could boast of having 'the finest premises in the West of England—perhaps he might say in the Principality because what the West of England would be without gallant little Wales he really did not know'. The directors had contemplated that during the coming year, they would make alterations to the premises, not only to improve their attractiveness but also to add greatly to the comfort and convenience of the customers. The Chairman stated that he hoped the Council's planned alterations to Caer Street would be completed soon, with the knowledge that Sir John Llewelyn and Ben Evans and Co. would contribute largely to the alterations. He suggested they should be advocated and made by the Council at once.

The company had consistently achieved year-over-year sales growth, and the upward trajectory was undoubtedly encouraging, yet it was the expected norm – a necessity, as it represented the sole avenue for driving increased profitability. Under no circumstances could they contemplate burdening their valued clients with higher prices, as the current profit margins were fair and reasonable. In an era of escalating operational costs, the imperative was to identify alternative means of sustaining dividends rather than curtailing them. The solution, he said, lay in augmenting returns, thereby amplifying the aggregate profits.

Addressing the burden of rising costs, the Chairman stated that one significant contributor to escalating expenses was the Poor Rate, something inextricably linked to the plight of the underprivileged. It was a cause for concern not only in Swansea but across the nation, as the ever-growing Poor Rates placed an increasing strain on taxpayers. Perhaps forgetting he was in Wales, he pontificated: 'No true Englishman would ever begrudge providing relief to their fellow countrymen who found themselves in honest and deserving circumstances of poverty... the Poor

Rates would continue to soar until the overburdened taxpayer rose in righteous indignation, protesting against their hard-earned money being squandered on maintaining a burgeoning population of pauper aliens – the outcasts from every land.'

The Chairman's comments were motivated by concerns at that time over the perceived rising immigration of Jews and other 'undesirable aliens' from Eastern Europe.

'This invading army of foreigners, detrimental to England's interests, was swelling at an alarming rate of 20,000 per month, contributing substantially to the growth of the criminal underclass. Whether housed in prisons, lunatic asylums, workhouses, or receiving direct relief, their presence imposed an unjustifiable burden upon the already overburdened ratepayers. This travesty unfolded while brave Englishmen, who had fought valiantly for their country, returned to dwellings that could scarcely be called homes, condemned by a grateful nation to eke out a miserable existence in poverty and despair.'

The Chairman said that the directors believed that when those in positions of wisdom and authority realised 'the terrible toll this influx of aliens, with their ability to subsist on meagre means, was inflicting upon the working classes – quite literally taking the bread from their mouths', they would inevitably legislate measures to provide relief to enterprises such as theirs, thereby reducing the unjustly imposed rates under which they currently suffered. It was high time, they asserted, to protest against the misdirection of these funds.

The proposed legislation aimed to curb this tide and alleviate the strain on local communities and resources. In March 1902, a report was presented to the House of Commons regarding immigration into Britain. While not proving any serious displacement of skilled British labour, the report noted some impact on native shopkeepers and potentially female workers. The commissioners did not recommend excluding immigrant aliens. However, they advocated regulating the entrance of certain immigrant classes, especially those from Eastern Europe. They also proposed provisions for deporting 'undesirable aliens'.

The greatest problem attributed to immigrants was the overcrowding they caused in parts of London. To address this, the report proposed preventing aliens from entering already overcrowded districts. Under the recommendations, if an immigrant was reasonably suspected of criminality, notorious misconduct, or lacked visible means of support after two years, authorities could bring them before a court. The court could then order the immigrant to leave the country, with the ship owner who brought them being required to return them to the port of embarkation.

The May 1902 YMCA newsletter 'The Record' mentions that the Ben Evans Employees team was one of several teams including Baycliffe, St. Mary's and the YMCA took part in a 'ping-pong' competition held at the Midland Café. (49)

Year	March 1903-- Feb 1904	Net Profit	Net Profit
9		£14,534	£1,476,343 (2024)

Chairing the ninth AGM, Sir Joseph Renals extended his heartfelt congratulations to the town of Swansea on the 'esteemed privilege' of an upcoming visit from 'our great King and his consort' to cut the first sod of what would later be called 'The King's Dock'. He affirmed that it was an understatement to say that King Edward VII would find unwavering loyalty in the Principality, equal to any other part of His Majesty's dominions. He congratulated the Mayor on the honour of receiving the sovereign, and the town on the forthcoming Bath and West of England Show, as well as the magnificent gift of an art gallery bestowed to the town by Mr Glynn Vivian. These auspicious events, he declared, were clear indications of Swansea's remarkable progress and ascendancy.

Lastly, Sir Joseph extended his congratulations to the shareholders on the balance sheet presented to them, even though the profits in 1903 did not quite match the heights of previous years. Nevertheless, he commended the company's continued advancement and prosperity. The chief cause, he explained, was the miserable climatic conditions; the weather made all the difference for the drapery trade and was as sensitive as any barometer. Complaints of bad trade had been general throughout the country except London, which had 'the world as its clientele'.

Sir Joseph said that although everything was sunshine and attractive inside Messrs Ben Evans' establishment, 'the weather outside was so wet that one would not have sent out a dog in it to buy a collar unless actuated by the benevolent wish that he might get drowned in the attempt'.

The advent of 1904 was welcomed, he said, not only because they had already had a considerable amount of sunshine, but because, as a consequence, he was able to make the gratifying announcement that the first month of the present financial year showed a larger increase of business than in any other month preceding in the company's history.

A year prior, Sir Joseph had spoken passionately about the immense burden of rates weighing heavily upon their shoulders – rates that were substantially increased due to the necessity of maintaining a vast number of 'pauper aliens'. This situation, he said, not only disadvantaged the ratepayers but also prejudiced the working classes at large.

Driven largely by concerns over Jewish immigration from Eastern Europe, an Act had been proposed in Parliament that, while ostensibly aimed at controlling immigration, evoked debate that revealed widespread anti-Semitic prejudices and fears about foreign labour and perceived threats to British culture and society.

He expressed gratitude that the Government had since introduced a Bill to regulate the influx of nearly a quarter of a million aliens to Britain's shores, most of whom gravitated towards the country's industrial centres. However, he said, he would have welcomed an extension of the Bill's provisions to address criminal aliens retrospectively, as 'no one could object to the deportation of such an undesirable crew back to their respective fatherlands, where they could be dealt with by their compatriots, receiving the sympathy that habitual criminals undoubtedly deserved'.

Sir Joseph's stance highlighted the growing concerns in some circles over the economic and societal impacts of unchecked alien immigration, particularly from a criminal element. Regulating inflows and enabling deportations were among the proposed solutions.

Year	March 1904 - Feb 1905	Net Profit	Net Profit
10		£13,893	£1,411,231 (2024)

Chairman Sir Joseph Renals presided over the tenth AGM held in Swansea. When moving the adoption of the report, said he was sure he interpreted the feelings of everyone present when he expressed how deeply they regretted the ill health of the founder of this successful business, Mr Benjamin Evans. He thought they would agree that they should send a telegram expressing their regret, and sincere hope that he might be spared for long years to come.

Despite a drop in profit in the last trading period, they had a successful and progressive business; they had a faithful Managing Director and staff, and they knew that everything that was done was in the interests of the shareholders. During the last year, they had had the largest turnover in any previous year, and considering some of the best London houses had done distinctly badly, he thought the company had had a remarkably good year.

Akin to numerous kindred institutions in London and throughout the country, they had grappled with disheartening influences. However, Sir Joseph expressed confidence that the recent alterations to the premises would enhance the convenience for their clients and prove attractive in drawing many new customers, which they eagerly anticipated. Notably, the entire cost of these alterations had been defrayed from revenue, ensuring that it would not recur as an expense in the future. The board had thought it advisable in the interests of the company to renew several of the leases, and that had been done on what they thought were advantageous terms to the company. The level of rates paid was a bone of contention, as they had been increased and would be increasing again, something that was a 'concern to all who have to pay parochial rates in whatever borough they live'.

The Chairman suggested that on any future lease agreement, it would be 'very desirable to add a safety clause, stating that the rates must be paid first and that if happily anything should be left in the poor tenant's pockets he will hand it over to the unfortunate landlord'.

In July 1904, the King and Queen visited Swansea to attend the sod-cutting ceremony of the town's new 'King's Dock'. Two days before the King's scheduled arrival, twelve of his horses were dispatched to the town, where they were accommodated at Ben Evans & Co.'s stables on Frog Street. Sir Joseph underscored the company's commitment to progress and modernisation while upholding the cherished values of patriotism and loyalty to the Crown. Despite the expenditure incurred accommodating the visit of the King and Queen to Swansea, the town's unwavering patriotism and undoubted loyalty would not permit even an iota of regret in this regard. The honour of hosting the royal couple was a source of immense pride, transcending any financial considerations.

Enacted in August 1905, The Aliens Act 1905 was a landmark piece of legislation passed by the Parliament of the United Kingdom that, giving the Home Secretary overall responsibility for immigration and nationality matters, for the first time in British history, introduced immigration controls and registration. While not explicitly targeting any particular group, the Act was largely motivated by the significant increase in Jewish immigration from Eastern Europe after 1880, which had raised concerns among some in Britain.

The Act required immigrants to disembark only at designated ports where they could be inspected, and allowed for their exclusion on medical grounds or if they were deemed a threat to national security. Immigration officers could deny entry to those deemed 'undesirable immigrants' who appeared unable to support themselves or were likely to become a public charge. The Act marked the end of an open-door policy for immigration to Britain and paved the way for more restrictive legislation such as the Aliens Restriction Act of 1914 during World War I.

Year	March 1905-- Feb 1906	Net Profit	Net Profit
11		£14,275	£1,450,034 (2024)

Whilst the company remained on a sound footing and turnover had increased, profits had remained relatively static for the third consecutive year. That said, shareholders at the eleventh AGM should be pleased to know that the first month's trading of the new financial year was considerably more than that of the previous year.

Sir Joseph expressed his fervent anticipation for the future of the important town of Swansea, a town of significance, he said, not only to the Principality but to the Empire as a whole. He eagerly looked forward to Swansea making rapid strides in its progress and development. The opening of the new King's Dock, he declared, held immense significance for the town. It represented a vast expansion of facilities for trade and commerce, paving the way for thousands of new houses to be constructed.

These new dwellings would inevitably require inhabitants, who would in turn seek goods and services from esteemed establishments such as Ben Evans and Co. Moreover, the new dock would attract new trades and manufacturers to the area, indirectly benefiting enterprises like Ben Evans and Co. through increased economic activity and demand for their offerings. Sir Joseph's remarks painted a vivid picture of what he felt was Swansea's promising future, and he felt that everyone present would agree with him that all things pointed to better times.

The Chairman noted that peace reigned, and he was pleased to see the prominent part played by America and England in bringing about this restful condition. Sometimes 'he permitted himself to dream of the federation of the great English-speaking races, and if that time should ever come, he thought it would, then war and rumours of wars would be hushed and forever growing still.'

Year 12	March 1906-- Feb 1907	Net Profit £14,685	Net Profit £1,491,682 (2024)

Despite the profits of the company remaining static for the fourth consecutive year, the Chairman spoke of the very excellent and satisfactory accounts and suggested an even more progressive future. Expenses had increased during the past year, the money being spent to improve the comforts of both male and female staff, something the Chairman said 'ought to receive very favourable consideration at the hands of a firm of the high standing of Ben Evans and Co.'. Debts were very carefully reviewed every month, and a very liberal allowance had been made in the amount scheduled for bad and doubtful debts.

Revisiting comments he made a year earlier, Sir Joseph said the construction of the new King's Dock at Swansea would not only increase the population but also bring new industries and new trade to the town, from which Ben Evans would undoubtedly benefit.

He believed that Swansea deserved a better railway approach, and he did not think it reflected well on the authorities that passengers, after a long journey, should have to change at Landore just outside the town. They were forced to pause in this suburban retreat, ostensibly to take in the beautiful surroundings of the picturesque Landore region. However, he failed to appreciate those supposed beauties, finding Swansea itself far more attractive. Yet even Landore had its compensating advantages in the form of the marked courtesy extended by the railway officials during the stopover at that dreary-looking place.

On 30th August 1907, John White passed away at his home, Windsor Lodge, Mount Pleasant, aged 56 years.

John White (Managing Director from 1895 to 1907)

Born in Llanon, Carmarthenshire, in 1850, after completing his schooling, John White apprenticed with the firm of Lewis, a draper's shop located on Castle Street. Following this, he gained experience working for Mr Llewelyn Richards before venturing to London to work at Messrs W. Tarn & Co. store. He returned to Swansea in 1873 and joined Messrs Ben Evans at Nos. 2 and 3 Temple Street, at which time 'they employed around 30 individuals'.

Ben Evans recognised Mr White as a prudent, capable, and industrious manager, who meticulously oversaw and safeguarded the fortunes of the firm, and demonstrated a thorough understanding of every aspect of the drapery and related industries that Mr Evans wanted to integrate into his company. Mr White was made the General Manager of the growing enterprise.

In 1895, when B. Evans and Co. became a Limited Company, Mr White's exemplary service led to his appointment as Managing Director. Under Mr White's leadership, the store met all targets set by its new owners, paying dividends to shareholders in their first year of business.

After ten years of growth and continually surpassing company financial targets, John White's health began to deteriorate in early February 1906, at which time he took time away from his work to recover. Despite taking a prolonged break, his respite did not yield significant improvement, and he resumed his duties. Unfortunately, Mr White was soon compelled to take to his bed where he was cared for by his wife, Mrs Harriett Latimer White, and his doctor, T. D. Griffiths, at his home. He endured considerable suffering for several weeks, attributed to heart and kidney ailments, and after recognising that he was in the later stages of his illness, it became evident that recovery was beyond reach. Following a prolonged and agonising illness, he passed away on 30th August 1907, aged 56 years old.

Following his death, the company's board met the following month to appoint a new Managing Director. Mr E. Meredith Thomas, a senior manager at Ben Evans, was asked to attend the meeting during which it was unanimously agreed to offer him the position of Managing Director, a position he subsequently accepted.

In November of that year, Sir Joseph Renals, Bart, passed away at his residence in Bickley, Kent. He was 64 years old. Born in Nottingham, he was Lord Mayor of London in 1894-95 and was a partner in the firm of merchants Renals and Co. in London. He had been Chairman of Messrs Ben Evans and Co. (Limited) Swansea, since the formation of the company in 1895.

Year	March 1907-- Feb 1908	Net Profit	Net Profit
13		£14,967	£1,505,153 (2024)

The 13th AGM was presided over by new Chairman James Jackson J.P. D.L., whose opening remarks were to lament the loss of both the company's first Chairman as well as its highly respected Managing Director. The loss of either man was a blow to the company, but the Chairman felt he could hardly find adequate words to describe the sense of misfortune that they had suffered with the passing of John White who had trained from his early youth under the direct guidance and influence of the founder of the business, Ben Evans, and who was well-versed in every detail of the drapery trade, particularly the methods and features unique to their establishment.

When the question arose as to who should succeed John White, they had a man ready who possessed all the necessary qualifications. This individual had extensive and intimate knowledge of the business, having held a responsible position and performed his duties with credit to himself and profit to the company. Furthermore, Meredith Thomas had effectively taken the helm during the last few months when John White was unable to manage affairs.

The Chairman then addressed the business environment and the performance of the company and remarked that while the drapery trade is generally seen as having its ups and downs, the business of Ben Evans and Co. was a notable exception. The accounts presented that day, along with those from previous years, highlighted the stability of the figures and the remarkable consistency of the trade. The variations in their business had been kept within strictly modest limits, demonstrating a steady and reliable performance. That said, last year was challenging for the drapery trade, and in various parts of the country, the business struggled. A gentleman at a shareholders' meeting in London mentioned that, despite his years of experience, he had never encountered a more depressing time than in 1907. This year saw the downfall of several previously prosperous concerns in London and elsewhere.

Several factors contributed to these difficulties. The country had moved from the 'fat years' of the trade cycle to the 'lean years', while the aftermath of the South African War, with its £250 million expenditure, still lingered, resulting in an income tax burden of about £50,000 higher than before the war. There was also uncertainty about the potential impact of upcoming legislation on property, which dampened the spending inclination of the well-to-do, while lack of employment similarly affected the working classes. There had been a substantial rise in wholesale prices, but it was impossible to implement a corresponding increase in retail charges. Finally, adverse weather conditions in April, May, and June severely hampered even the most diligent salesmen's efforts to boost business.

Despite these conditions, sales transactions were higher than the previous year, although margins were lower, whilst profits were on par with those of the previous trading period. While there was nothing 'particularly heroic' in their accounts, they were better than they appeared on the surface. This was because they had covered the costs of outside painting and redecorating workrooms and living quarters out of their revenue to promote the comfort of their employees and a writing room was opened within the store, something that has already been much used by customers. Shareholders voiced their concern over the rise in outstanding debt owed, a subject that resulted in a robust exchange with the Chairman and board members.

Year	March 1908-- Feb 1909	Net Profit	Net Profit
14		£16,667	£1,675,000 (2024)

A large volume of trade had been done by the company during 1907-8, and with the increased turnover, goods were able to be sold cheaper and customers were attracted in larger numbers. A comparison of the two years showed improvement in almost every entry in the balance sheet and profits had increased again. Many of the conveniences available to customers were unknown a generation earlier, and now writing rooms, refreshment rooms, telephones, and various other amenities were provided for their use. Although no special additions had been made in the past year, attention and expenditure were focused on providing a new carpet, which greatly enhanced the appearance and comfort of the departments.

When addressing shareholders at the 14th AGM, Chairman James Jackson offered a vision of darker times for Britain. While the company financial accounts showed quite clearly that Swansea, along with Ben Evans, had largely managed to rise above the depressing commercial influences affecting other districts, the causes affecting the general trade of the country, which he had mentioned in the previous meeting, were still largely in effect, and unfortunately, additional detrimental elements had emerged. The commercial recovery in America, almost unparalleled given the severe financial crisis it had faced, was still incomplete.

The effects of the immense £250 million expenditure on the South African War lingered and would continue to do so for many years, and there was the looming shadow of a potential future war that could shake the British Empire to its foundations. From a business perspective, there was growing distrust as to the direction of modern democratic legislation, and uncertainty about the surprises the upcoming Budget might hold.

As evidenced by the poor reports and unprofitable operations of major shipping companies, which served as a rough yet effective barometer, world trade was sluggish, and official figures showed that British trade was distinctly languishing. Confidence had largely disappeared, and enterprise was so stagnant that money was being hoarded instead of used. Demand for trade purposes was so low that bank rates were deplorably low, with prospects of further decline. These factors combined to cripple public spending power. Although perhaps not quite as severe as 1907, especially for the drapery trade, the year 1908 had been generally disappointing. All these factors combined to undermine confidence.

The welfare of Ben Evans was inseparably linked with Swansea's prosperity, and fortunately, Swansea maintained a better record than many less-favoured localities. The variety of industries operated within a mile or two of the town helped to ensure the town's economic diversity. While some industries were depressed, others thrived, resulting in a profitable balance overall. Imports and exports had more than doubled over the previous 14 years (the lifespan of Ben Evans and Co. Ltd) reaching nearly six million tons. The Chairman commented that although the operations of the Harbour Trust had not shown the steady uniformity of Ben Evans, they had, like Ben Evans, seldom regressed, adding, 'Judged by the rapidly increasing business at the port, the future of Swansea should leave little cause for anxiety.'

The Chairman spoke of what he called 'the event of the year in the drapery world', the establishment of a gigantic business in the West End of London by an American firm, achieved through lavish expenditure of capital and a flood of advertisements. This marked a complete reversal of the recognised methods and practices previously existing in the trade.

The histories of businesses like Ben Evans, William Whiteley, Sir John Barker, Mr D.H. Evans, and others had been characterised by gradual progress. 'These businesses started from small, modest beginnings, gradually adding departments and shops. Each new addition was carefully established before moving on to the next, with every rung of the ladder tested before scaling higher. Any rush or rash move was equivalent to disaster, and their success was achieved only through skill, patience, and indomitable perseverance.'

In contrast, the new venture by the American firm ignored these old methods. Gradual progress was replaced by a sudden leap, and step-by-step advancement was bypassed in favour of one significant jump. The Chairman quipped, 'It would be interesting to observe the outcome of this bold approach. If proved to be successful, it would be one of the greatest triumphs of hope over experience seen for many a day.'

He did not mention the store by name but was referring to Selfridges, founded by American Harry Gordon Selfridge, a business that quickly became a prominent fixture on Oxford Street, in the West End of London.

Year 15	March 1909-- Feb 1910	Net Profit £16,588	Net Profit £1,649,512 (2024)

At the 15th AGM held in April 1910, Chairman James Jackson was pleased to welcome the company's founder and largest shareholder, Mr Ben Evans J.P.

Chairman Jackson commented that whilst locally the year had been characterised as a red-letter one by the opening of the new King's Dock, an event pregnant with possibilities and enormous benefit and widespread prosperity for the town, the tinplate trade was 'in a flourishing state', and the coal trade had been rescued from threatened paralysis, the same influences from the previous year continued to hamper the prosperity of the country.

The lingering effects of the South African War persisted, and there was still anxiety regarding the upcoming legislation, as although the character of the Budget had been clarified, its impact on the country's welfare remained uncertain until its effects were experienced first-hand.

Fortunately, Ben Evans & Co had surpassed not only these external challenges but also the perennial issue plaguing the drapery trade—the uncertainty and fickleness of the weather, which had characterised many months of the year. Once again, the company presented a singularly consistent record of figures, and profit matched that of the previous trading period.

The company had extended the area of their activities by starting a second motor vehicle and offering house-to-house delivery to purchasers within a radius of thirty miles or more of Swansea, to the evident satisfaction of their outlying customers and increasing their sales. In addition, further development was made to the store's telephone system, 'with a significant amount of experience and ingenuity applied to ensure maximum convenience for customers.'

The Chairman moved the adoption of the report and statement of accounts for the year, which was carried unanimously, and then invited Mr Ben Evans to speak to shareholders. Ben Evans was warmly received and expressed his pleasure that the business which carried his name was doing so well.

Referring to the results achieved since Meredith Thomas had been appointed Managing Director, he said that results clearly showed that he was worthy of the confidence of the directorate. He added that the only advice he could offer the board of directors was to 'keep down the book debts and owe as little as possible to their creditors', something the shareholders present.

Ben Evans & Co. Ltd in Court

In July 1909, Messrs Ben Evans and Co., Ltd., were summoned for employing women on Thursday afternoon after 4 p.m. Mr A. Andrews, representing the company, admitted to a technical offence. Mr Timothy, H.M.I., said he had taken statements from 32 girls. (50)

Upon Mr Andrews' inquiry, it was revealed that the work was a mourning order for the funeral of the late High Sheriff, Mr Walter Rice Evans, and had to be sent off by Friday. The girls were to have another day's holiday and did not complain about any sweating practices.

Everything possible was done for the comfort and convenience of the employees. Mr Andrews stated that his clients were victims of circumstances and had no option but to comply with the order, as it could not be prevented due to the unfortunate loss of Mr Evans. The order was received late on Wednesday night, and the funeral was scheduled for Saturday, making it physically impossible to complete the work within the ordinary time frame.

The magnitude of the order was such that four porters had to be sent on Friday night to deliver it by Saturday morning. Mr Andrews emphasised that there was no desire to take advantage of the staff, who all had a holiday later, nor any intention to impose on them. He requested a nominal penalty, even if they could not be treated under the First Offenders Act. The Chairman stated that they would be dealt with a fine of 10 shillings, inclusive, imposed.

Ben Evans Delivery Horse & Trap (Author's collection)

Ben Evans Millinery showroom to the left with the customer's Reading and Writing Room in the background. (Author's collection)

Ladies & Children's Outfitting Department. (Author's collection)

*The Ben Evans Glass and China showroom in the Furniture Department.
(Author's collection)*

The *Ben Evans Ladies Blouse Department* (*(Author's collection)*

The *Ben Evans General Drapery Department* (*Author's collection)*

The Ben Evans Costume Showroom (Author's collection)

The Ben Evans Saddlery & Horse Clothing Workshops (Author's collection)

10 - Ben Evans and Co. (Limited) 1910 to 1920

Economic Conditions

By 1910, Britain's share of world industrial capacity stood at 15%, behind Germany's 16% and less than half of the United States' 35%; however, Britain still led the world in trade, finance and shipping, and had strong manufacturing and mining bases. Although there were signs of sluggishness in shifting resources from old industries like coal, iron, steel, and cotton to new growth industries like chemicals and motor vehicles, the coal industry still played a significant role as the focus of the global energy market.

Several progressive reforms had been introduced to improve the welfare of the worker, notably the 1908 Pensions Act and the National Insurance Act of 1911, often regarded as early steps toward the welfare state, however, these measures proved inadequate in addressing the growing tensions between social classes. Workers experienced conflict with their trade unions as the conciliation strategy adopted by the unions in dealing with employers regularly conflicted with their members' inclination to pursue direct industrial action.

In the period between 1911 and 1914, later termed 'The Great Unrest', there were more than 3,000 strikes, predominantly unofficial. Among the notable strikes of the period was the August 1911 Llanelli Railway strike where, whilst protesting low wages, the striking workers were met with severe police repression that resulted in two deaths. Similarly, on 31st August 1913 in Dublin, on 'Bloody Sunday', two men died as a result of clashes between striking workers and the Royal Irish Constabulary.

During this time, women's suffrage was also a topic of lively debate, and on 17th June 1911, a march took place in London, just a week before the coronation of George V. Its purpose was to rally support for the proposed Conciliation Bill, which was scheduled for debate in Parliament. The march attracted a large attendance and united various women's advocacy groups in their call for female suffrage. Despite these efforts, the Conciliation Bill was ultimately defeated in the House of Commons. Nevertheless, working-class women now demanded improved pay and working conditions in their workplaces, and even Ben Evans & Co. Ltd, renowned for the excellent treatment of its staff, would feel the wind of change.

Britain enjoyed a brief period of relative stability before the Great War (1914-1918) disrupted the economy, and retail prices remained fairly steady with only modest inflation. The diversion of resources from peacetime economic activities to the war effort harmed productive capacity. Britain's financial position weakened as foreign assets were run down and government debts increased substantially to fund the war.

Retail Environment

The widespread introduction of mass production in Britain resulted in the increased availability of standardised, affordable goods. While small, independent shops continued to dominate high streets, particularly in smaller towns, larger establishments like Ben Evans gained prominence in Britain's urban centres. Concurrently, co-operative societies saw continued growth in popularity, and 'multiple' retailers such as Woolworths, Marks & Spencer, and Boots began expanding their operations nationwide. Competition intensified, aided by increased advertising in newspapers and magazines. Mail-order catalogues also gained traction, offering consumers the convenience of shopping from home.

The Great War significantly disrupted the retail sector. As men were called to military service, women stepped into their roles, including filling the vacant positions in retail. Many shops grappled with shortages of both goods and staff, leading to the introduction of rationing for certain foods and commodities. Luxury goods retailers faced particular challenges during the war years, though they experienced a resurgence during the brief post-war economic boom.

A Shooting Tragedy

One of the properties purchased by Ben Evans before street widening could be carried out was The Sporting Depot Company at Nos. 1 and 2 Castle Bailey Street, which featured a prominent figure known as 'The Sporting Farmer' positioned above the door of the store. When the new Ben Evans Castle Bailey Street building was opened, it did not include a sporting goods department, instead, Ben Evans relocated that business into premises he had bought directly opposite the main Castle Bailey St store entrance, relocating the figure of 'The Sporting Farmer' to a similar position above the new store. On the 25th of April 1910, the sporting goods store was the location of a horrific accident. (51)

At around 5.00 pm that evening, in an upstairs workshop, the store's gunsmith Mr J. Gaddish, an experienced and well-regarded employee, was conducting tests on a sporting rifle brought in for repairs by a customer. The rifle contained a bullet for testing the extractor mechanism. One of the store's assistants was facing Gaddish, a young man named Edward Davies, or 'Atkins' as he was known among colleagues, who was observing the proceedings.

As the gunsmith held the rifle in his hand, the bolt unexpectedly slipped, resulting in the discharge of the bullet that struck Davies squarely in the chest. 'Are you injured?' Gaddish asked anxiously. Davies, clutching his chest with one hand, replied with a broken voice, 'I fear I am', and staggered down the stairs of the store and into the shop, where he collapsed into a chair. Unaware of the severity of his condition, it was initially thought he was on the brink of fainting.

Medical help was urgently summoned, and Doctors Humphreys and Marks arrived promptly. Despite their efforts, Mr Davies was beyond saving as the bullet had lodged itself in his heart, and he had passed away before the ambulance dispatched to transport him to the hospital had arrived.

Ben Evans Performance 1910 - 1920

Year	March 1910-- Feb 1911	Net Profit	Net Profit
16		£14,976	£1,473,702 (2024)

At the company's Sixteenth AGM in April 1911, the Chairman Mr James Jackson D.L. J.P. acknowledged the general unrest 'that has afflicted trades throughout the year and which had not yet allayed', whilst noting that a prolonged illness had meant Mr Meredith, whilst attending the meeting, was absent from his position for much of 1910 and the early months of 1911. After welcoming Mr Meredith back to the company, the Chairman remarked that the local management had shown resilience during his absence. Under the leadership of the company Secretary, Mr G. W. Mayhew, they successfully concluded the year by achieving their financial objectives.

Mr Jackson informed the meeting that despite the problems caused by what he called the 'Dressmakers' Strike', the company were delighted that their customer base had stood by them through this unfortunate period, and that the firm had declined the request made by the Associated Trade Unions to take the striking workers back into employment as it would be tantamount to a betrayal of all those workers that had stood by the company.

The Dressmakers Strike

In February 1911, after the dismissal of a bodice worker at Ben Evans & Co. because of her poor standard of work, a walkout of 28 bodice workers followed, and accusations of breaching the Factories Act were soon made against the company. The 'slaves of the needle' (52) gained support over the following weeks as the strike went on, and several local meetings and rallies were held to highlight the plight of the striking workers.

On April 8th 1911, 'Swansea Labour Association' held a Mass Meeting in support of The Dressmakers' Strike at the Star Theatre, Wind Street, followed by a 'Procession & Demonstration'. (53) Amongst those present were ex-Labour leader and Merthyr Tydfil MP Keir Hardie, Miss Mary McArthur and Amy Dillwyn, novelist and female industrialist, daughter of Lewis Llewelyn Dillwyn, a local industrialist who had served as MP for Swansea for 37 years.

Over the following months, the company was subject to several unfounded accusations, including expecting apprentices to work without a wage and paying low wages to staff, accusations that were easily proven to be inaccurate. It was even accused of forcing a young girl into committing suicide because she was unhappy about her pay, something the girl's family and some of her co-workers strenuously denied. The company regularly highlighted its position in the local press and welcomed a third-party inspection of its books to refute the accusations made regarding non-payment and poor wages. It also indicated that legal action would be taken against the individual linking the company to the demise of the young woman.

Mr E. Meredith Thomas (Managing Director Sept. 1907 - Feb.1912)

After a long illness, Meredith Thomas passed away on Monday, 26th February 1912, aged 57 years old. Originally from Ystradgynlais in the Swansea Valley. Beginning his career at 'Waterloo House' in Merthyr, and later joined Ben Evans's enterprise in Swansea, reporting to John White. After a short period, he joined Messrs W. Tarn and Co. in London, where both Ben Evans and the late John White had previously worked.

Having recognised Mr Meredith Thomas's talent, it is unclear whether Ben Evans had sent him to London to gain further experience or if he had left of his own volition. However, having followed his progress at Tarn & Co., Ben Evans brought Meredith Thomas back to Swansea in 1880. Known among the firm's customers as 'Mr Meredith', he was the buyer for eight different departments within the business and had also established himself as a prominent figure in the markets of London, Paris, and Berlin. He had been with the company for nearly 33 years, and his appointment showed the foresight of both Ben Evans and the late John White in that the continuity of senior management of the company was also an important factor of their respective management legacies. His performance as Managing Director echoed that of Mr White, and the store continued to meet all targets set by its new owners, paying dividends to shareholders.

Year	March 1911-- Feb 1912	Net Profit	Net Profit
17		£11,141	£1,096,322 (2024)

Industrial unrest continued in South Wales and elsewhere in Britain throughout the year, leading to a substantial drop in profits for the trading period. At the May 1912 AGM, Chairman James Jackson lamented the passing of Meredith Thomas.

Mr G. W. Mayhew had taken charge of day-to-day business throughout Meredith Thomas's numerous stretches of illness and did so again following his death. However, this was not to be a permanent move, and in the following months, the board of directors, wanting a change of direction in how the firm was run, introduced a new General Manager to the staff in July later that year.

The company Chairman proclaimed that there were two indispensable requirements when searching for the right man: the prospective individual had to be Welsh and he had to 'excel as a top-tier draper'. The position was filled by Mr Richard G. Lewis.

Richard Lewis was a native of Pembrokeshire and educated at the old Greenhill Grammar School, Tenby. His previous employers included Messrs D. H. Evans, Peter Robinson, and John Barkers of Kensington, and he had also regularly played at three-quarter (at centre or wing) for London Welsh. Formerly an under-manager of William Whiteley Ltd in London, Mr Lewis played a crucial role in the murder case of Mr Whiteley, who was killed by a man named George Rayner. (54)

As the chief witness for the prosecution at Rayner's trial at the Old Bailey, Mr Lewis had just left Mr Whiteleys office when he heard gunshots. He rushed back to the room where he found Mr Whiteley dead.

Year 18	March 1912 -- Feb 1913	Net Profit £15,305	Net Profit £1,460,439 (2024)

At the company's Eighteenth AGM in April 1913, the Chairman informed shareholders of the company's founder's serious illness. He was sure that all would join him in recording their sympathy and very deep regret, and in sending a message of sympathy and goodwill.

He addressed the performance of the company over the previous trading period, commenting that a study of the figures of the accounts revealed the fact that, with scarcely an exception, every item showed an improvement on the corresponding figures of last year, although both stock and debt levels were areas of concern. Due to Easter falling much earlier than usual, the business's competitors began showcasing their spring goods sooner than expected. To avoid losing customers and falling behind in the market, the business felt compelled to make significant purchases of spring goods earlier than usual, even before their annual stocktaking. This was contrary to their usual practice and led to an increase in stock.

However, the subsequent sales were strong enough to manage the excess inventory effectively. Although sundry debtors (various customers who owe money) had been slightly reduced, the amount remained notable. However, given the nature and scale of the business, this amount was not as problematic as some critics suggested. Upon careful review, it was found that most of the debts were very short-term, meaning they were expected to be settled soon.

Typically, he said, it would be an arduous task for a newcomer to assume control of a company like Ben Evans, and success was attainable only for someone with extensive experience, a thorough understanding of the drapery trade, and adeptness in managing people. The new general manager had already changed the organisation's operations significantly through modern techniques and strategic adjustments. In what were regarded as the worst weather conditions known for half a century, in the nine months that Richard Lewis had been with the company there had been a material increase in profit, and the business generally showed a marked improvement under his leadership.

With the extensive construction of buildings and the opening of new shops in Swansea, the competition had become fiercer than ever. However, legitimate competition was welcomed, as it stimulated effort and promoted business. The more attractive and high-quality goods displayed in the windows or available within the drapery establishments of Swansea, the fewer customers felt the need to travel to London for their purchases.

The Death of Ben Evans

On Sunday, 4th May 1913, Ben Evans passed away at his home, Llanfair Grange, in Llandovery. Despite historic health issues, he had since enjoyed relatively good health.

In the early months of 1913, together with his wife, he had travelled to the South of France where he developed neuralgia, leading to sleep disturbances. Since returning to Llanfair Grange in April, he had been bedridden, and his London doctor was summoned to provide care. Despite receiving 'the finest medical attention', his condition steadily deteriorated, eventually leading to his passing at 74 years of age.

The many eulogies in the press across West and South Wales were in unison when addressing Ben Evans' business achievements, describing how over nearly thirty years, he had grown his business from two small shops on Temple Street to the imposing department store standing between Temple, Castle Bailey, Caer and Goat Streets, and praising him as a catalyst for change in the reshaping of the town's road widening schemes, one report calling the store 'The Whiteleys of Wales'. (55)

Despite his business success, he remained the same quiet and unassuming individual throughout his life, and the following comments would have likely meant far more to him personally, as they described Ben Evans the man, rather than Ben Evans the businessman. (56)

'Mr Evans was a pioneer in Wales in advocating for cooperation between employers and employees, and he remained deeply committed to the welfare of working men throughout his life.'

'As a compassionate leader in the business community, a humble and amiable individual in private life, and a devoted Christian philanthropist, Mr Evans will be sorely missed. His compassionate support for the unemployed during times of great distress in Swansea stands as a testament to his unwavering commitment to serving others.'

On Thursday, 8th May of 1913, the late Mr Benjamin Evans J.P., of Llanfair Grange, was laid to rest at Llandingat Church, near Llandovery, a very large and representative attendance that included 'members of county families, various public bodies, and leaders in the commercial world' was present.

His coffin bore a simple plaque that stated:

'Benjamin Evans. Died May 4th, 1913, age 74 years.'

A special service was held in Swansea at Capel Gomer, where the Reverend Dr Gomer Lewis fondly remembered Ben Evans 'the man'.

Acknowledging Mr Evans's support of countless deserving causes, he spoke of an individual who contributed £100 towards acquiring the freehold of the chapel, who had financed the purchase of a new organ, a person who for 18 consecutive years had provided £20 annually for blankets for the poor, and who had once even discreetly slipped an envelope containing six £5 notes when the doctor's fee was unexpectedly imposed upon him.

In August 1913, Ben Evans's will was read. (57) Having lost their only child in infancy, Ben and his wife Maria had no surviving offspring. The bulk of his estate was bequeathed to Maria, while the remaining assets were distributed among his extended family. Specifically, his nephew, the Reverend R.L. Rhys, and six nieces were named as beneficiaries of the residuary estate in equal shares; the shares of his nieces being 'retained upon trust for their benefit.'

The document also showed his benevolence continued even after his death, with the following charitable gifts allocated:

£900 to the Swansea Hospital.

£225 to the Deaf and Dumb Institution. Swansea.

£225 to the Institution for the Blind. Swansea.

£100 to the Orphan Home. Swansea.

£900 to George Muller Orphanage, Ashley Down. Bristol.

£200 to the W. Drapery.' Schools. Clerks.

£100 to the Earlswood Asylum.

£200 to the Commercial Travellers' Schools, Pinner.

£100 to the Vicar of Liansadwrn. Carmarthen, in trust for the poor of the parish, as long as the graves of the testator's family were well maintained in proper and decent condition, and should his family graves not be so maintained this legacy will revert to the Ecclesiastical Commissioners.

A life annuity of £ 52 to his servant, Lizzie Davies, and legacies of £50 each to her mother and her sister Maggie.

£200 to his cousin Rev George Edward Rees;

£500 to Mary, the sister of his said, cousin

A conditional legacy of £ 2.000 to his cousin, David Llewellin Evans, of Penarth;

£900 each to his wife's sister, Gwenllian Langman, and each of her sons, Harry Langman and Thomas Itheridge Langman

£400 each to David Walters, Rees, of Swansea and Edward Sidgwick;

£300 to the Rev Oscar T. Snelling, of Swansea

£250 to William Wyndham Powell "in recognition to many kindnesses" and £50 to his sister, Mrs Griffiths;

£250 to Benjamin Roberts, of Myrtle Hill, Llandilo;

£200 each to his cousin, Priscilla Chapman, and Mrs Morgan, of Llanwrda and £100 to Mrs John Lewis.

All the above legacies are free of duty and subject to these legacies and the payment of the duties thereon.

Ben Evans had also made provisions for his household staff at Llanfair Grange. All servants, both indoor and outdoor, employed at the time of his death were to receive a full year's wages. Furthermore, those who had served for more than four years were granted additional compensation, demonstrating Evans's appreciation for their long-term loyalty and service.

Year 19	March 1913 -- Feb 1914	Net Profit £15,197	Net Profit £1,464,930 (2024)

Maintenance of the store was ongoing. The wooden floors of the ground floor had been recently replaced, and in the early months of 1914, new windows were installed on the ground floor facing Castle Bailey Street, as well as those on the ground floor on Temple Street. Mr J. Penry Rowlands, the architect responsible for the design of the Castle Bailey Street building, was engaged to oversee the project on behalf of the store management. Works were carried out between 9th February and 14th March 1914 by Messrs Hoskins Bros. of Old Street, London, renowned shop-front decorators, who were 'subject to significant daily penalties' should the work take longer.

The comprehensive renovation plan included the conversion of the entrance on the Temple Street-Castle Street corner of the building into 24 feet of additional display space. This was not a straightforward replacement, and the company assured their customers that one of the windows fitted was the 'largest undivided window in Great Britain'.

At the April 1914 AGM, the effect that Richard Lewis had had on the business was visible to all. The volume of business was higher than any year previous, whilst profits, debt management and stock control were all in a far better position than had been projected a year earlier, all achieved with few changes made to the staff. Business in the Swansea area was growing, and meeting customer demands required expanding their reach. As a result, an additional motor vehicle was ordered.

The local roads were challenging due to rough surfaces and steep gradients which caused significant wear and tear on the motor vans. Although the two vans they currently had were still serviceable and performing well, the board considered that it might be more economical to replace them with new ones rather than continue investing in repairs, as the expanding customer base suggested that increasing their motor vehicle fleet might be a prudent strategy.

Addressing the previous year's business, Chairman James Jackson said that Ben Evans had remained steadfastly true to its long-established reputation for stability, and despite less-than-favourable conditions, there had been steady progress. The growth was not rapid or sudden but marked by a sure, if slow, advance. However, he recognised Richard Lewis's impact, stating:

'Our general manager, Mr Lewis, trained in a school that recognised that all other causes contributing to success were trifling compared with the one fundamental and permanent basis of selling cheaply and giving the best possible value, had reduced the gross profit even below that of previous years; so that, buying as they did most advantageously, and enjoying the fullest discounts obtainable from the wholesale houses, customers at Ben Evans get their wants supplied as cheaply or more cheaply than they could in any other drapery establishment in the United Kingdom.'

Early Closing on Saturdays
Mr Lewis had decided to alter the closing time of the store on Saturday nights from ten o'clock to nine, a change that allowed live-in employees to depart early enough to reach their family homes on Saturday nights rather than having to stay in town overnight and then travel on a Sunday morning.

Not only did this gain the appreciation of the staff, who could now spend all of Sunday with their families, but it also led to an increase in business on Saturday nights compared to before the earlier closing hours were adopted.

Half of the male live-in employees had moved out of the company accommodation, with the remaining men to soon follow, at which time the space made available would be turned into either retail or storage space.

The shareholders requested that Mr Lewis's position change from General Manager to Managing Director, but were told by the Chairman that this had not previously been considered by the board, and whilst this could not be confirmed at that time, there was no doubt that 'by the time they meet next year, it would be a practical question.' A few months later, Mr Lewis was formally promoted to the position of Managing Director.

TEMPLE A.F.C. (BEN. EVANS & Co., Ltd.) 1913-14.

With the kind permission of Dr. Ted Nield, whose grandfather William Holloway Bowen (bottom row, holding the ball) was captain of the team.

The Widening of Castle Street

After years of discussion about the widening of Castle Street, the Council had successfully acquired all the necessary properties for the first stage of this crucial improvement. It was hoped that after completion of the whole of Castle Street, the tramways would be continued from High Street through the widened Castle Street, and via Castle Bailey Street onto the Wind Street section. It was decided to initiate the widening immediately.

On Tuesday, 4th May 1909, demolition work began on the first buildings to be removed, starting from the corner extending from Masters' shop on Castle Street to Harris' fish shop on College Street, although the site for new business premises had yet to be leased. The ceremonial act of dislodging the first stone was carried out by the Mayor, Mr Morgan Tutton, the chosen location for this historic event being the top floor of the towering building previously occupied by Messrs Anderson and Cox, renowned rubber dealers.

The Mayor acknowledged that the town centre had been 'cumbered up with buildings not at all adapted to first-class business purposes' and lamented that the town had suffered because of this. He voiced his frustration as to the inability of the Council to yet secure any benefit from neighbouring premises; however, the Council had committed to clearing the current site within three weeks, promising that the people of Swansea would soon witness a significant enhancement to the street with the construction of the new building.

Following the opening of the impressive four-storey Castle Building on the corner of Castle Street and College Street in September 1910, the Council moved forward with a plan to demolish the eastern side of Castle Street to widen the street from 16 feet to 50 feet wide (although this was later amended to 60 feet) and erect a new structure that aligned with the frontages on both Castle Bailey Street and High Street.

In June of the following year, designs were approved for a new frontage that remains today, and the old buildings were demolished in 1912. During this period, footings of the original Swansea castle were found (not part of the current castle ruin, which is the second 'castle').

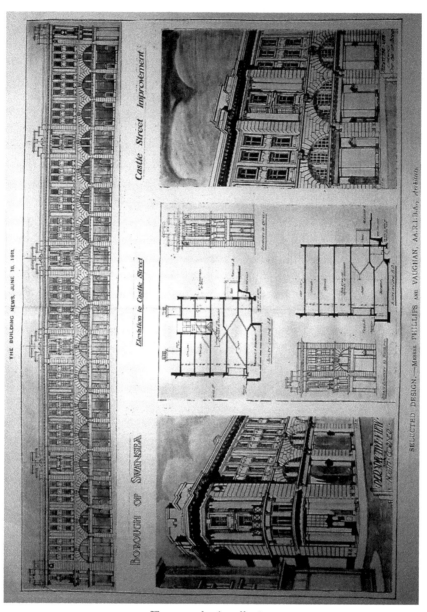

From author's collection

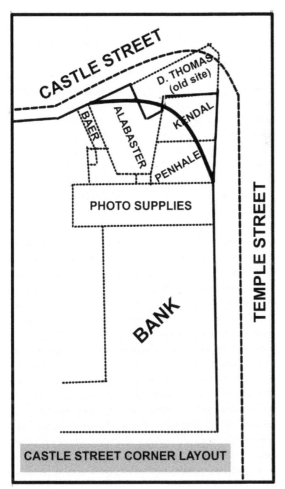

CASTLE STREET CORNER LAYOUT

The demolition of four properties on the western side of the street at the Temple Street - Castle Street corner was also part of the street-widening plan.

The Council could have carried out this work in 1878, but the option was allowed to lapse, however, the works were now required to accommodate the town's tram system.

Discussions rumbled on into 1915; the compulsory purchase of the relevant properties had been completed in principle, but the compensation negotiations between the Council and jeweller D. Thomas continued.

Demolition began on 'Alabasters' in March of that year and, in the following month, after the D. Thomas compensation discussions had come to an end, the remaining properties were demolished. (Mr Thomas had claimed £7000 but had received 'somewhere about as many hundreds'). In August 1915, Prudential Assurance opened a 'palatial' suite of offices on the Welcome Lane-Castle Street corner that had completed construction on the eastern side of the street.

Matters were further confused when an additional proposal was put forward to widen Temple Street to 60 feet to align with the frontage of Messrs Theophilus on the corner of Goat Street and Oxford Street as well as Castle Street. Such were the complications of this proposal that it was quickly abandoned.

The Great War

On 28th June 1914, in Sarajevo, Bosnia and Herzegovina, the assassination of Archduke Franz Ferdinand, heir presumptive to the Austro-Hungarian throne, and his wife, Sophie, Duchess of Hohenberg, was one of a series of events in Europe that, within a month, despite the efforts of many intermediaries, had resulted in a conflict that became known as The Great War, a global conflict between 'The Entente'—the allied forces of countries led by France, the United Kingdom, Russia, the United States, Italy, and Japan—and the 'Central Powers' (or 'Quadruple Alliance') made up of the German Empire, Austria-Hungary, the Ottoman Empire, and Bulgaria.

Despite talk of things 'being over by Christmas', the conflict resulted in an estimated 9 million soldiers dead and 23 million wounded, as well as an estimated 8 million civilian deaths, brought to an end by the signing of The Armistice of 11th November 1918 at Le Francport near Compiègne, in France, that ended fighting on land, at sea, and in the air.

Britain suffered 880,000 military fatalities, with more than double that number wounded. Nearly 275,000 Welshmen were under arms, representing over 21% of the male population of Wales at that time. Of these, roughly 35,000 Welsh soldiers were killed during the war, with particularly heavy losses at the battles of Mametz Wood on the Somme and Passchendaele.

Swansea's local press estimated that 15,000 Swansea men had served in the Great War, although in his book 'Swansea in the Great War', Bernard Lewis contended that these numbers are '...open to debate given the inadequacy of the recording systems at that time. What is known for certain is that almost 3,000 men with a strong link to Swansea were killed during the war.' (58)

The Great War officially ended when the Allied Powers and Germany signed the Treaty of Versailles on June 28, 1919.

Year 20	March 1914 -- Feb 1915	Net Profit £17,784	Net Profit £1,714,307 (2024)

In September 1914, Ben Evans and Co. secured several important Government contracts, including one for 15,000 blankets, whilst other contracts included thousands of shirts, trousers, vests, service caps, etc. for Britain's troops. The contracts were secured despite competition from several London and provincial retail suppliers, with the total order value being one of the largest ever secured in the Principality.

The April 1915 AGM was the company's twentieth, and it had once again celebrated another year of record trading. The meeting was different from any that had gone before, as Britain was now involved in the Great War, and many shareholders in attendance, like thousands of other parents across the country, had sons who were 'on the fighting line'. Over forty Ben Evans employees were currently serving. Upwards of 40 company men had enlisted, and it was noted that the married men employed by the company but now on military service received half-pay during their absence.

The volume of sales transactions exceeded that of any previous year, however, reduced prices meant reduced gross profits. In the face of keen competition, several Government contracts were secured which, carried out efficiently, led to further successes in that direction.

Speaking of the trade outlook, Chairman James Jackson said there had been a steady improvement, particularly in the last few months 'from the low-water mark of last August and September, and the returns of the Harbour Trust, a reliable barometer, marked 'Fair,' with a rising tendency.'

He did not believe the attempts of America to capture the Welsh tinplate trade would be successful, as when the war was over, the genius of the Welsh tinplate makers would reassert itself.

Year	March 1915 - Feb 1916	Net Profit	Net Profit
21		£18,498	£1,588,610 (2024)

Despite the war, the AGM of April 1915 shows that the company had had another record year, and exceeded levels of both sales transactions and profits, helped by the fact that the company had again fulfilled several government contracts.

There were now over 80 company men serving in the armed forces, their positions at Ben Evans had been filled by women or by men ineligible for service.

Year 22	March 1916 - Feb 1917	Net Profit £19,946	Net Profit £1,449,431 (2024)

In the AGM held in April 1917, shareholders were told that the company had had yet another record year. However, while the business continued to perform well, stock levels had risen considerably in the previous year. The supply of merchandise was very difficult, as manufacturers faced stringent restrictions, making it nearly impossible for retailers or distributors to purchase the products they needed when they wanted them. They had to accept whatever stock they could obtain and felt fortunate if they managed to get any at all. As a result, maintaining a larger inventory was essential to meet customer demands and retain their business.

Over 100 men had now left the company to join the war effort. In many cases, women had been employed to take their place and were proving themselves equal to the tasks given them, a case in point being in the counting-house, where this was proven by the low margin of book debts. One shareholder, without commenting on the abilities of individual board members, believed that shareholders in Swansea felt that local representation on the board of directors was inadequate. He urged the board to consider appointing a local individual to the board when the next vacancy arose, or by expanding the directorate. Furthermore, he proposed transferring the head office to Swansea. In response, the Chairman expressed appreciation for the local interest in the company's affairs but noted that, since the majority of shareholders were still based in London, he did not think it advisable to adopt either suggestion.

Year 23	March 1917 - Feb 1918	Net Profit £21,444	Net Profit £1,242,806 (2024

The following two years followed suit; despite the country being at war, the record profits shown in April 1916 were surpassed in 1917, and again in 1918. The company's own War Fund was started at the commencement of hostilities, had risen to over £300 in staff contributions, and had been distributed to various war charities. A Staff Benevolent Fund was set up in 1915 with £250 from the directors, with a further £250 added in 1917. An employee's request for assistance was handled strictly as a private matter.

By March 1918, 115 men in Ben Evans's employment were enlisted with either the Army or the Navy, and were 'fighting for King and Country', and four had lost their lives. The company's efforts to support the war effort were admirable and included regular fundraising concerts held in the town. In October of that year, Ben Evans and Co., Ltd. hosted a concert to raise funds for war charities. The event, chaired by Managing Director Mr Richard Lewis, showcased the town's finest artistic talents and demonstrated the company's commitment to supporting the war effort. During the event, it was revealed that Ben Evans and Co. had already contributed approximately £300 to war funds through staff subscriptions.

The concert marked the first in a series of events organised by the company to raise funds for war charities. Its resounding success promised even greater achievements in the future, with plans to secure a larger concert venue to accommodate the growing interest.

Year 24	March 1918 - Feb 1919	Net Profit £22,328	Net Profit £1,059,941 (2024)

Speaking at the AGM in April 1919, after the directors celebrated yet another record financial year, Managing Director Mr Richard Lewis focused on the hardships suffered by the people of Swansea through what he said was the darkest period in the world's history. The company had supplied 5,000 meals weekly in the previous year alone. He advised that when the majority of Ben Evans' men had returned from the war, he would form an advisory committee to decide how the staff Benevolent Fund, which had risen to a figure of £1,076, should best be allocated, given that it was set up for the benefit of the employees.

Year 25	March 1919 - Feb 1920	Net Profit £43,910	Net Profit £1,894,107 (2024)

At the AGM held in March 1920, the Chairman reported that the past year had been one of marked prosperity. It showed returns considerably above any previous year in the company's history, with profits nearly double that of 1919. During the early months of 1920, the business showed further expansion, but by mid-year the depression in trade evident since the previous autumn caused a sudden and immediate reaction. Chairman James Jackson commented that 'not even the meekest pessimist could at the last meeting have anticipated that the reaction from that period of inflated prosperity would have been so sudden and so marked as it had proved since.'

Fighting finally stopped after the signing of the Armistice on 11 November 1918 at Le Francport near Compiègne, in France, which ended the fighting on land, at sea, and in the air. The Great War officially ended when the Allied Powers and Germany signed the Treaty of Versailles on 28 June 1919.

Signed in the Hall of Mirrors at the Palace of Versailles exactly five years after the assassination of Archduke Franz Ferdinand, the Treaty established the League of Nations, from which Germany was initially excluded.

Under the terms of the Treaty, Germany was forced to accept full responsibility for starting World War I (the 'war guilt' clause, Article 231), whilst ceding land to France, Poland and Belgium, plus all of its overseas colonies. Germany's military capabilities were neutered, and it was required to pay heavy reparations to the Allied Powers.

To restore finances and transition to a peacetime economy, the British government cut spending by 75% between 1918 and 1920; however, this contributed to a lack of demand and stagnant economic growth.

While Ben Evans had thrived during the conflict, trade conditions were unfavourable for neighbouring store David Evans & Co., negatively impacting the company's operations and financial performance. In the aftermath of the war, Mr David Evans, Managing Director of the company bearing his name since its establishment, resigned from his position and divested his shareholdings in the business.

11 - Economic and Retail Challenges 1920 to 1930

Economic Conditions

In the decade before World War I, Britain's prominent global trading status was closely tied to the 'footprint' previously made by its Empire and accounted for 27% of the world's manufactured exports. However, the cost of war was high, and Britain had allocated well over 25% of its GDP to the war effort. Despite this, there was an albeit temporary postwar boom in Britain, led by the high demand for coal. However, this only served to camouflage the very real economic problems associated with Britain's loss of status as a prime manufacturing power. Findlay and O'Rourke (59) observed:

'World War I brought the liberal economic order of the late 19th century to an abrupt halt.'

After the initial boom period, unemployment rose sharply to over 10% and remained high throughout the 1920s, particularly impacting industries like coal, steel and shipbuilding. Factors like deflation, real wage unemployment due to falling prices, static wages, industrial unrest, and tight monetary policy exacerbated the economic malaise in the early 1920s.

Competition from the likes of Germany, Japan and the USA soon had a significant and detrimental effect on trade, and across Britain the decline of heavy industry in those areas that were once the engine room of the Empire was both rapid and devastating. By the end of 1921, the post-war boom had collapsed, and a prolonged economic recession followed. The South Wales coalfields experienced peak production in 1913 but faced a substantial downturn following the collapse of the post-war boom.

The high demand for coal quickly exhausted reserves, and after the business downturn, mine owners hesitated to invest in modernising their facilities and equipment. The Dawes Plan was implemented in 1924 to stabilise Germany's post-war economy. This led to the modernisation of their mining industry and their return to the international coal market, making it challenging for Britain to compete.

The decline severely impacted other industries such as steel, tinplate, slate, and agriculture, resulting in huge job losses. The diminishing presence of

South Wales's heavy industries prompted a significant movement of its population towards destinations such as London and the West Midlands as its key industries waned. The post-World War I landscape also saw a significant negative shift in the involvement of Welsh women in industrial employment as many women had stepped into new roles across industries such as munitions production, agriculture, transport, and other traditionally male-dominated fields to bolster the war effort while men were serving in the military. However, after the war ended, men returned and job opportunities dwindled.

Britain's economy grappled with challenges like the overvalued pound, deflation, and tight fiscal policies, compounded by a global downturn dampening the demand for exports. To strengthen the British economy, Chancellor of the Exchequer Winston Churchill pushed through The Gold Standard Act of 1925, which fixed the price at a level which restored the pre-war exchange rate of US$4.86 to £1 sterling. However, it had the opposite effect than intended, strengthening the British pound against other currencies, further hampering export competitiveness, whilst hurting industries like coal, iron, steel, shipbuilding and textiles, resulting in mass unemployment and deeper depression.

In the British mining industry, those who remained employed faced pay cuts and longer working hours. A 'General Strike', called by the Trades Union Congress and led by the miners, began on 4 May 1926; their mantra was 'Not a penny off the pay, not a minute on the day.' The strike, supported by many across the country who were not affiliated with the miners, lasted only nine days, at which point the TUC conceded defeat.

The Retail Environment

The economic environment remained in dire straits throughout 1922, and the extent and intensity of the trade depression in South Wales were without parallel, rendering the successful conduct of business extremely difficult. Stock management at 'Ben's' remained key to any success the company might glean from the year, and in the annual general meeting, the Chairman sympathised with their general manager 'who had to keep a sufficient and varied stock, whereas the inflation of prices might incur serious losses.' They had met their difficulties by selling at the lowest profit possible. The number of customers exceeded those of the previous year, but the total of their purchases had been less owing 'to heavy taxation and other causes'.

Whilst the high streets and shopping districts in Britain's towns and cities were packed with individual speciality shops, such as umbrella manufacturers, tea merchants, and other small businesses, all had felt the grip of the depression. Added to their woes was the rapid growth of mail order stores, check trading, co-operative societies and 'multiples'. Before the war, independent retailers made up nearly two-thirds of the market, whilst co-operatives and multiples made up nearly 30%, and department stores accounted for 2%; however, this mix would dramatically change over the next decade.

Britain's first mail-order business was set up in 1861 by Pryce Jones, a North Wales draper who distributed his flannels and clothing items via the nation's fledgling postal service. The 'Royal Welsh Warehouse' (later bought by John Lewis stores in 1938) boasted illustrious figures such as Queen Victoria and Florence Nightingale, along with several royal households across Europe amongst its clientele. By the 1920s, a competitive landscape had emerged in the UK's 'direct to consumer' mail-order sector, with companies like Freemans, Kays, Grattan, Empire Stores, and Universal Stores vying for market share, representing a burgeoning yet dynamic facet of British retail.

The advent of colour printing significantly elevated the profile of the mail-order sector, as in place of monochromatic hand-drawn depictions or uninspiring black and white photographs, vibrant colour photographs now showcased a gamut of offerings, spanning clothing, furniture, toys, and cutting-edge household technologies. Particularly appealing to customers with modest incomes was the option to settle purchases through manageable monthly instalments.

While the concept of buying on hire-purchase wasn't novel in British retail, having been pioneered by the Singer company in the 1860s to vend sewing machines to the working class, it became the modus operandi for mail-order firms. These companies facilitated payment plans through weekly or monthly instalments, managed by local agents. However, they retained the legal prerogative to repossess goods should purchasers default on payments, with items remaining on hire until the final instalment upon which ownership is transferred to the buyer.

Another avenue for obtaining goods upfront while deferring payment was through 'check trading,' utilising a 'Provident shopping check' or a similar offering from another company. Provident originated as a clothing club established by insurance salesman Joshua Waddilove in Yorkshire in 1880, aiming to assist local families in affording essential items like clothing, boots, and coal. By the 1920s, 'The Provident Clothing and Supply Company' had expanded its reach with 4,000 agents in 120 offices nationwide, a number that rose to 160 offices by 1930 and to 288 offices by 1951. The company forged agreements with over 14,000 retailers who, by 1930, accepted a promissory note known as a 'Provident check' as payment for goods sold, and a shopping guide was issued detailing the companies where these checks could be utilised. In a process similar to that used by the mail-order companies, a Provident agent collected weekly or monthly payments, albeit all orders had to be settled within twenty weeks.

Both mail-order and check trading sectors operated credit-checking systems, relying on data gathered from their agents to determine borrowing eligibility and assess debt risk. Customers were strongly advised against taking on more orders than they could afford to repay through regular weekly payments. Provident customers, in particular, were encouraged to obtain orders solely for their own and their families' use.

Although the Rochdale Equitable Pioneers Society of 1844 often serves as the focal point in the history of the cooperative movement in the UK, their origins can be traced to the dire poverty experienced by many during the 18th and 19th centuries, as well as the rapid urbanisation and escalating food prices resulting from a market-driven economy. Moreover, the lack of political representation for the working class during this era played a significant role. By 1860, over 200 cooperatives in the northwest of England were operating in a manner akin to the 'Rochdale Principles', and in 1863 these independent cooperative societies united to form The Co-operative Wholesale Society (CWS).

The CWS experienced rapid growth, supplying goods to cooperative stores throughout the country, and served over 500,000 society members in the North of England alone. However, this expansion fuelled intense competition for trade from non-cooperative wholesalers, prompting the CWS to set up manufacturing plants for products such as soap, boots, and biscuits, to improve their supply chain. By 1900, there were more than 1,400 cooperatives throughout the UK, many of which expanded further by opening additional stores or by merging with nearby societies.

Society members would inevitably be the customers of the society's trading locations, as the society would reward these members with a proportion of any profits, based on that member's spending with the society, via a dividend. This stirred resentment among private shopkeepers who viewed the dividend offered by cooperative stores as an unfair competitive edge. Consequently, some influential shopkeepers lobbied for wholesalers to cease supplying these emerging cooperative societies.

As both distributors and retailers, neither mail-order companies nor co-operatives needed to maintain large inventories of commodities, which would need to be devalued during economic downturns and as economic hardships drive more people to these lower-priced options, they typically sustained their turnover.

In a period marked by scarcity of products and widespread profiteering, cooperative societies worked tirelessly to guarantee that local communities could access foodstuffs like fresh bread, sugar, flour, rice, milk and other dairy products, often weighed out and measured by hand rather than pre-packaged, as well as preserved food, clothing, footwear, and dependable household items at equitable prices, while also addressing other community needs such as insurance, pharmacies, and funeral care. Additionally, these societies actively contributed to welfare initiatives and served as vibrant community hubs, organising social events, classes, and concerts, particularly in mining villages.

By the early 1920s, the cooperative movement in Wales had experienced steady growth with more than 80 independent cooperative societies spread across the country, affiliated with the national Co-operative Wholesale Society (CWS), and including seven societies in the South Wales valleys that had individually amassed annual trades surpassing £1 million. These were formidable local establishments operated by and for the benefit of community members. However, by the 1920s some smaller independent co-op societies faced growing competition from national supermarket 'multiples'.

Whilst mail-order stores, check trading, and co-operative societies all chipped away at the edges of the customer base of the department stores, it was the arrival of the 'multiples' - defined as a shop/store belonging to an individual or company with six or more shop premises, and better known today as 'chain stores' - that severely affected them, whilst at the same time radically changing the High Streets of Britain forever.

The 1920s marked a pivotal period in the proliferation and expansion of multiple stores across various sectors including news, groceries, furnishing, clothing and household goods, with numerous companies establishing locations nationwide. People's limited resources required them to shop where prices were lowest, and multiples, leveraging mass production and female labour, could offer goods at prices that smaller retailers could not hope to match.

Multiple stores enjoyed huge economies of scale in the procurement of goods and services, buying for many stores meant that they purchased items in volume and at the lowest prices, and thus had the option of either selling at a lower price than competitors and still making a profit, or else to sell at market prices and make a greater profit. If used tactically, they were able to use sales price management to put locally-owned competitors out of business.

In addition, they had some other key benefits that separated them from traditional local specialist stores as well as department stores, as the close monitoring of their stock and cash levels across the breadth of their stores allowed for:

- Centralised warehousing to support the various regional or countrywide stores
- Rotation of slow-moving stock from one store to another, reducing write-down stock levels as more stock was sold at the original, rather than a reduced, price
- Fast-moving items and/or product shortages to be quickly supported with stock from a central location or other company stores
- Opportunities for scaled introduction and monitoring of new products or sales formats across different markets to better understand market responses whilst controlling outlay costs should the introduction prove invalid
- The ability to hire specialised staff across a larger workforce, including the hiring of competitor's staff.

Woolworths, the renowned American five-and-dime store chain, accelerated its UK expansion during this decade and embarked on a rapid store-opening spree, driven by ambitious construction goals and streamlined building processes. Woolworths' stores boasted elaborate 'cinema front' designs in urban centres and hosted grand opening celebrations. British 'chain stores' followed across several retail sectors, using modern and improved merchandising and marketing methods, coupled with attractive pricing.

- W.H. Smith, founded in 1792, took advantage of the railway boom during the Industrial Revolution by opening newsstands at railway stations beginning in 1848, and by the 1920s, it had become a national retail chain with locations across the UK.
- Chain grocery store Home and Colonial Stores grew rapidly by acquiring and merging with other retailers like Maypole Dairies and Lipton's, and by 1931, Home and Colonial had over 3,000 branches across the country, becoming one of the UK's largest retail chains.
- Boots the Cash Chemist had 630 shops, extensive production facilities and 10,000 employees, and by 1933 had over 900 shops and numerous other production facilities.
- Marks & Spencer moved away from their 'Penny Bazaar' themed market stores and began building their chain stores in the mid-1920s (and had 234 stores by 1945).

A September 1927 Western Mail feature on Swansea's retail business highlighted the challenges to Swansea's traditional stores, noting that the town's business community was adapting to the evolving economic landscape and particularly to the rise of 'multiple shops' amidst increased competition --- 'New forms arise, and different views engage. Superfluous lags the veteran on the stage.' (60) The newly formed Chamber of Trade's proactive approach to attracting shoppers and improving facilities was already yielding results, with railway companies showing more consideration for Swansea.

Recognising that the influx of 'multiple shops' had transformed some of the town's main streets, such as the High Street, the report noted that the longstanding traders of Swansea had demonstrated resilience by continuing to operate their businesses successfully, even in the face of rising rents and modernisation. Some of the oldest Swansea traders 'preserve an unchanged and imperishable reputation, their ability to adapt and withstand competition speaks to their deep-rooted presence and commitment to the community.'

Ben Evans Performance 1920-1930

Year 26	March 1920 - Feb 1921	Net Profit £23,506	Net Profit £887,694 (2024)

Market prices dropped, and whilst companies of the size and nature of Ben Evans held substantial stock levels, prudent stock management was one of the keys to its success. Smaller competitors rapidly ran out of stock only to find that replacement stock was either difficult or impossible to find, and breakdowns in the supply chain further panicked the market. 'Ben's' was able to continue trading throughout the year, but whilst the level of stock turnover was higher than ever before, the profit percentage had been measurably less. The Chairman observed 'The sudden cutting of prices was of a feverish and spasmodic character to obtain ready money, and did no good whatsoever, but only led to want of confidence.'

He hoped that the upcoming opening of the Anglo-Persian Oil Works by the Prince of Wales, 'who brought luck to everything that he touched', would bring with it a change in prosperity sooner than any of them expected.

Year 27	March 1921 - Feb 1922	Net Profit £19,696	Net Profit £805,473 (2024)

Economic conditions persisted throughout 1921 without significant change, prompting Chairman Sir James Jackson to remark on the trying times and challenges faced by traders over the past two years. In the April 1922 AGM, it was reported that profits were nearly 17% below plan, and could have been much lower but for a mixture of reduced prices and a 'sufficient and varied stock'.

Addressing the shareholders, Sir James said that amid this uncertainty, forecasting the future trajectory of the country's general trade posed difficulties, and prospects for tax relief seemed bleak, with little indication of impending reductions, emphasising the importance of lowering the costs associated with freight transportation and postage, viewing such measures as highly desirable for the economic well-being of the nation.

Pressure on the company's management had been present throughout the year from local trade unions. Managing Director Richard Lewis assured shareholders that staff in all departments had been paid at least the minimum wage of the Trade Unions concerned, 'and the minimum was not the maximum in their establishment.'

Notes of the Red Triangle Committee at the YMCA from 1921 record the receipt of £15 for 'football boots for the boys' from Messrs Ben Evans and Co.

Year	March 1922 - Feb 1923	Net Profit	Net Profit
28		£22,074	£1,047,884 (2024)

In the AGM held in April 1923, it was stated that a slight upturn in market conditions meant that the company came close to matching its figures from two years prior. The board deemed these results satisfactory, considering the company's fortunes were tied to the industrial conditions of the district. Whilst a focus on stock management throughout 1922 resulted in the store's stock value decreasing to below £100,000 (equivalent to approximately £4,763,110 in 2024), it highlighted a real concern that too much money was tied up in the store's stock. While acknowledging the sporadic nature of the past year, the board expressed optimism that confidence in price stability would increase in the coming year, leading to more proactive buyer behaviour. Furthermore, they anticipated a gradual restoration of pre-war conditions. The issue of the company buying out the 'founder shares' was raised, and following further discussion, the matter was left for a further meeting.

In September of that year, an extraordinary meeting of shareholders was held, chaired by Walter J. Burt because of illness to Sir James Jackson, during which the Chairman's proposal to convert each founder's share into eight fully-paid second preference shares was accepted, and thus the matter was resolved to the satisfaction of all parties.

The company also opened a Paris Agency at No. 14, Faubourg-Poissonnière, the address appearing on company advertising from mid-1923.

Year 29	March 1923 - Feb 1924	Net Profit £25,834	Net Profit £1,305,074 (2024)

In May 1923, the Western Mail reported that Ben Evans & Co., 'one the most famous houses in the country' featured a special display in 'their huge block of premises' in conjunction with the visit of the Prince of Wales to the Bath and West of England Show held in Swansea. (61)

'The same care that has been exhibited by the Ben Evans experts in the beautiful period furnishings of the Prince of Wales' rooms at the showground is evident in all that the firm does, and this week the taste and style of the products are a perfect delight to the eye, whilst the prices are distinctly 'cut, a fact only made possible by the huge organisation and the specialising of buying by the huge emporium. All who have been privileged to view the quarters furnished for HRH the Prince during the visit, by Messrs Ben Evans & Co. of Swansea are in raptures over the work that has been done - its perfect taste, as a whole, and the charm of its individual pieces, being a theme on which the ladies in particular, find it easy to go into rhapsodies.'

As a result of his illness, Sir James Jackson, the company's Chairman for 16 years, stood down as Chairman and director Mr Walter J. Burt formerly replaced him.

Year 30	March 1924 - Feb 1925	Net Profit £25,195	Net Profit £1,279,636 (2024)

The thirtieth AGM convened in Swansea, with Mr Walter J. Burt presiding as Chairman. In his address, the Chairman referenced the published report and highlighted that whilst there was an increase in the number of customers compared to previous years, there was a slight decrease in the spending power of each customer.

Through careful cost control and thorough analysis of various expenditures, management produced a report showing results comparable to those of the previous year.

Year 31	March 1925 - Feb 1926	Net Profit £21,491	Net Profit £1,102,330 (2024)

South Wales continued to endure severe industrial depression over the previous year and at the AGM held in London in April 1926, Chairman Walter J. Burt remarked that despite the adverse conditions, company profits remained 'almost the same as the previous year,' although they had dropped by over 16%. However, the directors deemed it necessary to reduce the dividend by one per cent while maintaining the shareholders' accustomed returns.

Mr Burt expressed hope that the ongoing efforts of the Coal Commission would yield a solution beneficial to employers, miners, and the State, as while much work remained to restore the national coal industry to its former prosperity, there were nascent signs of returning economic health, and that a swift and progressive recovery in general trade would ensue.

Year 32	March 1926 - Feb 1927	Net Profit £18,358	Net Profit £937,430 (2024)

Walter Burt's optimism towards the renaissance of the coal industry proved widely misguided, as the General Strike of May 1926 ground the country to a halt. In the initial months of the financial year, returns indicated a promising improvement. However, as the year progressed, South Wales bore the brunt of the coal strike's repercussions, significantly impacting the company's operations across all branches.

South Wales endured the most severe consequences of the year's industrial strife compared to other regions in the country, and such a substantial decline in the spending power of the population due to the strike's effects had an inevitable impact on the company's business.

In the April 1927 AGM, the Chairman spoke with the shareholders stating that he and the directors felt that despite a drop in profit against the previous year's result, they were 'amply satisfied' with the results and suggested the shareholders be equally satisfied.

Year 33	March 1927 - Feb 1928	Net Profit £14,155	Net Profit £742,887 (2024)

At the company's thirty-third AGM, in preparing shareholders for a worse report than the one delivered a year earlier, Chairman Walter J. Burt said that it was evident to all observers that the firm had experienced hardships akin to the industries in the surrounding area, upon which the local population heavily relied.

Over the previous two or three years, concerted efforts were necessary to maintain the company's financial position. However, the preceding half-year had proved to be the most challenging period in the company's history, and it could be asserted that the past year had been unparalleled in the annals of South Wales.

Despite adversities, the company managed to sustain operations without incurring losses. In the initial six months, they were able to issue an interim dividend, albeit unable to declare a final one. In response to a letter received from a shareholder, the Chairman confirmed that there had been no external offers made for the acquisition of the business.

Year 34	March 1928 - Feb 1929	Net Profit £10,389	Net Profit £545,238 (2024)

The company's AGM, convened in London in May 1929, marked a sombre milestone in its history. Market conditions were so dire that Mr Burt conveyed profound regret over the unprecedented situation: for the first time, no dividend would be distributed to holders of ordinary shares, while net profits showed a significant decline, dropping to only £10,389.

The depth of industrial depression in South Wales, he reasoned, was unparalleled, making it a remarkable feat that any profit was realised at all under such circumstances.

Amidst this pervasive gloom, there was scant solace to be found. The prolonged depression in South Wales bore primary responsibility for this reduction in profits, precluding any possibility of dividends for ordinary shareholders. Despite faint indications of improvement on the horizon, every feasible measure of cost-cutting was being implemented, including the directors' decision to waive a significant portion of their fees until a resurgence of prosperity.

Year	March 1929 - Feb 1930	Net Profit	Net Profit
35		£10,522	£558,423 (2024)

The company's 35th AGM was almost a mirror-image of the previous year's figures, with net profit effectively stagnant at £10,522. No dividend was to be distributed to holders of ordinary shares for the second successive year. Nevertheless, Chairman Walter J. Burt, J.P. affirmed that despite the challenging economic climate the company had effectively preserved its robust financial standing.

The board recognised during the year that it would be imprudent to diminish the company's financial reserves for the sake of redeeming debentures, and they sought and obtained consent from debenture holders to postpone the commencement of redemption from January 1, 1930, to 1935. In exchange for this extension, the premium of 5 per cent due upon redemption was duly paid.

While the Chairman underscored that the company's financial position had strengthened compared to the previous year, a two-year balance sheet comparison was published in the financial press along with a five-year results comparison (see (e) in Appendices), likely aimed at quelling any rumours in the local stock market. Interestingly, despite the near-identical nature of the two balance sheets, the revelation that there was a substantial disparity in stock values across what were both challenging trading years was particularly noteworthy.

The board indicated that it had considered the possibility of appointing a locally-based director, though the reason for this was not specified to the shareholders.

In the following month, it was announced that Capt. J. Hubert Roberts, a prominent local businessman and owner of Messrs David Roberts and Son (Auctioneers, Estate Agents, Surveyors and Valuers) of 61 Wind Street, Swansea, had been appointed as a director of the company.

12 - Economic and Retail Challenges 1930 to 1940

Economic Conditions

The 1930s marked a tumultuous period for the UK economy triggered by the onset of the Great Depression that followed the Wall Street Crash of 1929. The post-war economic slump of the 1920s had already left Britain struggling with low growth, deflation and high unemployment even before the 1930s depression hit, as heavy war debts from WW1 led to a tight fiscal policy and the inability to stimulate the economy through government spending.

The collapse of the US banking system caused American lenders to recall loans from Britain, worsening the UK's economic crisis. In September 1931, after intense speculative attacks on its currency, where funds of over £200 million were withdrawn from London banks, the British government and the Bank of England, without prior consultation with other countries, suspended the operation of the Gold Standard Act of 1925, which had required the Bank of England to sell gold at a fixed price. A bill was swiftly passed through Parliament later that month to authorise this suspension.

Unemployment soared dramatically, surging from roughly 1 million in 1929 to over 2 million by 1930. By 1932-33, it peaked at around 3 million, encompassing 22% of the workforce. With unemployment rising and tax revenues falling, there was immense strain on public finances and services such as healthcare, education, and welfare benefits for the unemployed. There was a regional economic imbalance across the country, particularly hard-hit were industrial regions such as the North of England, Scotland, and Wales, where unemployment rates in some areas reached a staggering 70%.

The era was marred by widespread poverty and economic hardship, leaving many families struggling to afford necessities like food, clothing, and heating. Hunger marches highlighted the deprivation. Malnutrition and associated illnesses became prevalent, exacerbated by the government's meagre unemployment assistance and policies such as the unpopular Means Test, introduced in 1931, where officials visited families to assess whether they were entitled to help. Unemployment and economic hardship sparked widespread discontent, culminating in a massive demonstration on 3rd February 1935, when approximately 300,000 protesters took to the streets across South Wales.

In 1931, the Labour government of Ramsay MacDonald faced a severe budget deficit due to the Depression. MacDonald proposed spending cuts including reduced unemployment benefits, which caused a split in the Labour Party. MacDonald then formed a National Government coalition with the Conservatives, Liberals, and a faction of Labour, expelling those who opposed him from the party. Dominated by the Conservatives and their allies, the National Government won large majorities in the 1931 and 1935 elections, providing stability during the economic crisis. MacDonald resigned in 1935 and was replaced as Prime Minister by Stanley Baldwin who, in 1937, was in turn replaced by Neville Chamberlain. Under Chamberlain, the National Government pursued a policy of appeasing Nazi Germany.

Key policies included leaving the gold standard and imposing protectionist tariffs. The UK's exit from the gold standard in 1931 and the subsequent devaluation of the pound paved the way for a more expansionary monetary approach. This shift, coupled with interest rate reductions and controlled inflation from 1932 onwards, spurred a gradual economic rebound in the latter half of the decade. The late 1930s witnessed a boost in rearmament spending, injecting additional fiscal stimulus and driving down unemployment to approximately 1.5 million by 1937 as industrial output revived. However, full recovery remained elusive until the wartime economy took hold from 1939 onwards. The recovery, albeit moderate, was characterised by regional disparities, with a housing boom in London and the South East contrasting starkly with persistently high unemployment rates in other areas reliant on heavy industry such as South Wales.

The Treaty of Versailles was intended to establish a lasting peace after World War I. However, soon after Adolf Hitler became Chancellor of Germany in 1933, he began secretly rearming the country in violation of the treaty's restrictions on German military forces. In 1935, Hitler revealed he had built up a new air force. He also signed the Anglo-German Naval Agreement with Britain, which allowed Germany to expand its naval forces up to 35% of British tonnage. This violated the naval limits imposed at Versailles, angering France and Italy, who saw it as British appeasement of German rearmament.

One of the Versailles terms prohibited German military forces in the Rhineland, an industrial region abutting France seen as a natural defensive barrier. In 1936, Hitler marched 22,000 troops into the Rhineland, openly breaking the treaty. He offered a non-aggression pact to Britain and France, claiming Germany had no territorial demands in Europe. In 1938, amid public support, German troops entered Austria, annexing the nation in an event known as the 'Anschluss'.

At the Munich Conference in September 1938, Chamberlain secured an agreement allowing Hitler to annex the Sudetenland region of Czechoslovakia in exchange for promising no further territorial claims in Europe. Chamberlain declared this meant 'peace for our time'. Just six months later, in March 1939, Germany occupied the rest of Czechoslovakia. Chamberlain then made a defence pact with Poland. When German forces invaded Poland in September 1939, Britain declared war on Germany two days later.

Chamberlain remained Britain's Prime Minister until May 1940, when the National Government was replaced by a wartime coalition led by Winston Churchill, a critic of appeasement.

The Retail Environment

Smaller local shops like grocers, bakeries, butchers, and newsagents were common fixtures in villages and local neighbourhoods, and a range of mobile shops visited rural areas. Whilst individual speciality shops remained prevalent on British High Streets, the 1930s witnessed the monumental rise of major retail chains that catered to the growing working-class and lower-middle-class consumer market.

International chains such as C&A and F.W. Woolworth (with over 760 UK branches by the end of the 1930s) were present in most major towns and cities, alongside home-grown chains like British Home Stores (BHS), Burtons, Marks and Spencer, which attracted working-class and lower-middle-class clientele with their affordable ready-to-wear fashions, and Curry's, formed in 1888 and by 1927 had opened 134 shops selling bicycles, as well as the manufacture and sale of gramophones, wirelesses and other electrical goods.

Boots the Cash Chemist had a presence across the country, with some of their stores having a Boots 'Book Lovers' library in store, and in 1934 their main competitors Timothy Whites and Taylors Cash Chemists merged as 'Timothy Whites & Taylors' with 168 chemists and hardware stores across the country. Grocery chains also had a strong presence, with companies such as Home and Colonial, Sainsbury, and David Greig (who opened Britain's first self-service store in 1923 but closed it 8 months later), offering new convenience foods like sliced bread, frozen foods, and a variety of new confectionery and chocolate brands became increasingly popular. The growth of these retail chains provided new employment options for young working-class women.

By the end of the decade over 10,000 co-op stores were operating in England alone, highlighting the continued growth and prominence of the cooperative retail model during this decade, with new stores opening across both urban and rural areas to provide working-class communities with affordable goods and services. The stores functioned as general retailers, many with separate departments for drapery, groceries, and butchery, often located in different buildings. In industrial areas like South Wales, co-op stores were a significant presence.

The retail environment in Britain in the mid-1930s was very different to that which existed fifteen years earlier, and in 1936 Swansea had 10 department stores, 51 multiple stores, 13 cooperatives, and nearly 3000 individual stores (62) whilst the town's Indoor Market housed 415 small shops in the 2 acres covered by its roof.

Recognising the threat, mass meetings organised by the Council of Retail Distributors were held countrywide to rally independent traders against the 'Combines, Multiple and Chain Stores, Co-operative Societies and Bureaucracy' that 'Aim to Put You Out of Business'. On the 28th of June 1934 a meeting organised by 'Swansea and District Traders' and chaired by the Mayor of Swansea, Alderman William Harries JP, was supported by several Members of Parliament, and local and regional councillors. Inviting 'all retail traders', their clarion call was 'Organise or Perish!' (63)

The significant growth of multiple stores prompted many independent trader groups to express their concerns and many felt the Government needed to conduct an investigation, potentially through a Royal Commission, into the detrimental effects of multiple stores and co-operatives trading on the national life and prosperity of the country. In the annual meeting of Drapers and Allied Trades in May 1935, it was noted that a new Retail Trading Standards Association had been formed that would hopefully 'regulate the trade' (64) Vice-president Mr P. A. Best warned members:

'I sometimes think that too many merchants live in the past; in those days which, up to 30 years ago, had brought easy prosperity in comparison with the hard-earned meagre margins that are called net profits today. Social changes have taken the old autocratic authority from the employer, and unless he joins other employers in a strong combination, more and more authority, and with it even freedom to show initiative in development, will be taken away.'

When confronting the very real danger of multiple stores to traditional retail traders, Mr Best said:

'The multiple chain group speciality shops and the growth of large store units have made It necessary for the private trader to review his methods. The mere selling of low-priced articles is not sufficient to retain the support of your public, and the frantic efforts made by so many traders since the beginning of the slump to attract attention by stocking and advertising low-priced goods has had disastrous results.'

In October of that year at the autumn conference of the National Chamber of Trade in Cardiff, Mr Gilbert Shepherd emphasised the threat that multiple and chain stores posed to the best interests of towns and villages in his presidential address and highlighted how these stores displaced much of the individualism and personality that had driven public service. Mr Shepherd also called for electoral reform, both Parliamentary and municipal, to ensure that traders' wishes could be implemented through the ballot.

In February 1937, a Private Member's Bill to 'Protect independent retail shopkeepers against the uncontrolled establishment of centrally owned or administered multiple shops and co-operative trade societies' was introduced in the Houses of Parliament by Captain Balfour, Conservative MP for the Isle of Thanet. Aimed at controlling the growth of multiple shops and co-operative stores through a system of licensing, it faced swift defeat. When a count was challenged just after lunchtime, only 32 MPs—eight short of the quorum—were present, and consequently, the House was counted out, leading to the demise of the Bill. Dr Burgin, Parliamentary Secretary to the Board of Trade, had argued that the large growth of multiple stores had been driven by public demand for the kind of service they offered, and advised the House from the Front Bench to oppose the Bill, stating that the Government believed it was unnecessary and that its terms would not alleviate the issues it aimed to address.

At the annual conference of the Drapers' Chamber of Trade, in June of that year, the difficulty of trading as an independent in 1930s Britain was laid out in stark language by Mr J. K. Butler, who said that in many instances the terms offered for selling premises made it more profitable for them to sell or lease the premises rather than continue trading, particularly considering the challenges of increased costs and excessive competition.

Rent increases, closely followed by rates, were cited as major cost escalations that attributed to intense competition among multiple firms vying for prime positions in main shopping centres, and the cumulative effect of legislation, competition, and general difficulties was seen as stifling private enterprise. The private trader was vanishing.

A few months later, at a December meeting of the Rhyl Individual Traders Association in North Wales, (65) Councillor Edward Hughes described multiple stores as: 'the most insidious form of destruction our communal life has ever faced.' He warned that the private trader would be wiped out if multiple stores continued to grow. Hughes asserted that these stores take no interest in the town's welfare, stating, 'That is not good for our national life, but I believe before long action will be taken on this matter.'

Since the 1880s, the seemingly unplanned and somewhat reluctant approach taken to the development of Swansea's town centre meant that both retail and residential aspects of the town were entwined, and much if not all of the residential property in the town centre was over 100 years old and lacked modern sanitation. In the 1920s, Swansea Council took steps to clear the town of its 'courtyard' slum housing and relocate its residents to a new development above the town - 'The Town Hill Estate'. The town's Housing Committee had also authorised 'council housing' to be built in six other housing schemes to support local industry.

In total, over 2,500 houses had been built with a further 500 houses planned at Town Hill and Mayhill 2,000 (central relocation), Morriston 272 (for steel and tin works), Maesteg/Grenfell Park 280 (Port), Birchgrove 168 (Oil works), Llanerch 96 (Tawe east), Fforestfach 82 (Colliery district), and Cwmdu 10 (Colliery district). Swansea's 1933 slum clearance plan aimed to demolish a further 1,317 houses, a target it had met by June 1938. However, despite the growth in council accommodation, the retail centre still had a substantial residential footprint, given that many people lived above the businesses in the town.

Addressing a Swansea Council Sessional Meeting held on the 6th of March, 1931, regarding 'The Development of the Town Hill Estate', Ernest Morgan A.R.I.B.A., the Borough Architect, whilst reviewing the progress of the new council housing plans, highlighted the problems Swansea's retail centre faced in the coming years. (66)

'Swansea is hemmed in between the hills and the sea, and this, with the rapid growth of the population, has made the problem of housing and transport a matter of no small difficulty.

The main roads, all too narrow, follow the valleys and river beds, and the adjacent flat land has been developed for various industrial enterprises and houses for the workers, leaving the hills and steeper portions as a legacy to this and other generations. The result, moreover, is that the main arteries into the town are relatively long and expensive to widen because of the high value of the property or the flatter portions adjacent to them.

Like other towns with ancient history, little or no regard seems to have been paid in the past to ensure proper and easy access to the steeper portions; the development seems to have been haphazard and not according to pre-meditated plan; the forming of access roads and the development of the land is, therefore, a matter of expense and difficulty.'

Ernest Morgan's remarks highlighted the Council's recognition that revitalising the town necessitated clearing outdated properties to enhance residents' quality of life. However, this clearance also aimed to expand the town's retail offerings. He emphasised the essentiality of improved transportation links in and out of the town, coupled with wider roads to accommodate the growing number of motor vehicles.

Regrettably, this comprehensive modernisation endeavour carried a substantial financial burden that, given the present economic climate, was unlikely to be fully covered by the Council's resources.

Ben Evans Performance 1930 - 1940

All was not well at Ben Evans and Co. There had been divergent views between Managing Director Richard Lewis and other board members concerning the internal management of the business that had caused concerns for some years, a key point of contention being the certified value of the company's stock by Mr Lewis, profits had been in notable decline since the mid-1920s and a dividend had not been paid to shareholders since 1928.

Within weeks of the 1930 annual general meeting, the directors elected a locally-based director, Capt. J. Hubert Roberts of Swansea, to the board on 24th June that year. His nomination garnered support from holders of upwards of 30,000 shares. Given that the stock valuation was a real concern, consequently, the board sought independent counsel on the matter and engaged Mr Allan Hepworth, a respected business consultant and director within the distributive trade sector, who was brought in to assess their stock management concerns.

Mr Hepworth's report was received on 23rd January 1931 and revealed that 'in the vast majority of individual departments the stock was out of all proportion to the turnover, and that there was evidence of such a very unsatisfactory state of affairs as to demand immediate attention and drastic re-organisation.'

In a board meeting held three days later it was noted that: 'It is hardly necessary for the directors to refer to the continuance of the deplorable business conditions in South Wales which the company has had to face for so many years past, but they hope that by dealing with the position now disclosed on the lines indicated they may ensure, so far as possible, that the shareholders shall share in any improvement that may occur.'

Richard Lewis consented to step down from the position of Managing Director, and a compensation payment was made.

On the 28th May 1931, it was reported that for the first time in its history, the company's trading had resulted in a financial loss, due mainly to the drastic writing down of the stock-in-trade. (67)

Year 36	Feb 1930 - Jan 1931	Net Loss (£36,117)	Net Loss (£1,972,199) (2024)

The article also stated that Managing Director, Richard Lewis, had resigned from his office and directorship and that his son, Mr Philip G. Lewis, who had gained considerable experience in London, Paris and America, as well as Swansea, had been appointed general manager of the company. The board noted that it had received a notice of nomination in support of Richard Lewis, and one for another shareholder, Sir Percy Molyneux JP, nominated by Mr Lewis, for election as directors. The sitting directors advised company shareholders that neither nomination was endorsed or recommended by the board.

Following his resignation, Richard Lewis issued a circular to the press, stating that he, along with his wife, remains the largest shareholder of the company, and is also a trustee for the debenture holders, holding a total of 21,970 shares. He said that his stance on relocating the company head office to Swansea, proposals to appoint local directors, his views on director remuneration, and his efforts to achieve economies elsewhere, had led to a 'certain amount of friction and unpleasantness' between him and the rest of the board of directors. That said, he maintained that 'with strict economy and good and efficient management there is no reason why the prosperity of the company should not be fully restored and payments of dividends resumed.'

In the 36th AGM held on 18th June 1931, Chairman Walter J. Burt, JP, a director since April 1910 and Chairman since April 1924, announced during the meeting that due to his numerous commitments elsewhere, he would not be seeking re-election, whilst in the same meeting Capt. J. Hubert Roberts also stood down from the board. Elected to the board of directors were Mr George Wheatley, secretary of the company for the past eleven years, previous Managing Director Richard Lewis and Sir Percy Molyneux JP, Chairman of P. Molyneux Wholesale Fish Merchants of High Street, Swansea, and an ex-Mayor of the town.

The annual report and statement were adopted and resolutions reducing the value of the second preference and ordinary shares in the manner suggested were carried. The following month it was announced that Sir Percy had been appointed Chairman of the board and that the registered office of the company was to be transferred from London to Swansea.

The board implemented a comprehensive reorganisation of the store's operations based on Mr Hepworth's recommendations. This included taking decisive action to address the unrealistic levels of old stock, the implementation of a contemporary stock control system, and the adoption of the latest methods of merchandising.

The new general manager was instructed to urgently conduct a revaluation of the stock-in-trade as part of these efforts, and after accounting for writing off old, obsolete, and out-of-date stock, the certified value of the stock as of 14th February 1931 (and reflected in the balance sheet) was £43,731 7s. 10d. (£2,497,037 in 2024) in contrast to £77,376 12s. 8d. (£4,239,395 in 2024) the figure recorded in the previous year, a negative difference of over £28,000.

At this crucial time, whilst there is no evidence of a formalised reporting structure being introduced, there would have likely been a requirement for a monthly report that contained information on sales turnover, stock, credit, and debt levels, as well as non-financial measurements like the number of sales transactions and staff turnover. This report, completed by the Managing Director and likely sent to the board quarterly, would allow the board to comment and advise on corporate issues.

Johnson (68) emphasised the need for having such a regular interface noting, 'It shows a deep understanding that results (and problems) arise from and are explained by intricate processes and tangible relationships, rather than by abstract quantitative relationships that describe results in simple, linear terms.'

Year	Feb 1931 - Jan 1932	Net Profit	Net Profit
37		£13,384	£761,663 (2024)

In line with the stock adjustments, the board also took the opportunity to 'write down certain obsolete fixtures and fittings and to write off the balance of the debenture premium account' of £8,492, resulting in a total debt to the company's profit and loss account of £36,492 (the equivalent of £2.07 million in 2024).

It was proposed that the loss adjustment would be met by an immediate reduction of the nominal value of the 24,000 second-preference shares by 6d. per share, and of the 167,000 ordinary shares by 4s. per share, giving the stores' new management a real opportunity to make profits and thus the directors would then be able to pay dividends to the company's shareholders.

In the AGM held in Swansea, new Chairman Sir Percy Molyneux explained that whilst sales turnover was practically the same as the previous year, the company had made an impressive 52,640 more sales transactions, indicating a return of customers that had 'temporarily left us' as well as thousands of new customers; however, merchandise prices had fallen. Referring to the cost savings they achieved, he was assured the company could save an additional £1,300 without compromising the business's efficiency in any way. The company's property had been fully maintained, and the establishment now boasted an improved appearance.

The directors believed that trading would depend entirely on the prevailing conditions, but anticipated a much busier industrial period ahead, and as long as there were no further international complications, a successful year of trading lay ahead. The Chairman proclaimed, 'I can confidently say that Ben Evans and Company is still one of the most important stores in the provinces.' The company was happy to advertise the change in fortune of the business following the severe but necessary changes made in the previous year. Again, a two-year balance sheet comparison was published in the financial press along with a five-year results comparison chart to endorse the point that they were once again a company worth investing in. (see (f) in Appendices)

The Death of Walter John Burt

Later that year, it was reported that on 28th September 1931, ex-Chairman and director Walter John Burt JP, barrister and a director of several companies, was 'killed by falling in front of a train at Knightsbridge Tube Station, London'.

At his inquest held only days later, the Coroner said, 'This man was worried about everything — about his business, about the financial affairs of the country, and no doubt about his future. He was also suffering from sleeplessness and depression.'

A verdict of 'Suicide while of unsound mind' was recorded. (69)

Year 38	Feb 1932 - Jan 1933	Net Profit £11,031	Net Profit £643,258 (2024)

In March 1932, in a meeting of the Swansea Council Highways Committee, it was mentioned that a couple of interesting property improvements were planned for the town centre, one of which was for Messrs Ben Evans and Co.'s premises. Plans for extensive ground floor alterations to Messrs Ben Evans's premises were approved, with the Borough Surveyor noting that once completed, it would resemble a piece of Regent Street transplanted to Swansea.

The plans include no setbacks on Castle Bailey Street but propose constructing an arcade from Caer Street to Temple Street with suitable modifications to the existing entrances. On Caer Street, a colonnade will be built, expanding the narrow footpath by six feet, except where there are building support pillars. In Temple Street, modern shop fronts will be installed, as in other areas.

The thirty-eighth AGM was held at the company's premises in Swansea in April 1933, and Chairman Sir Percy Molyneux said that he felt compelled to highlight the notable increase in sales within the store. In the fiscal year 1931-32, there was an extraordinary rise in sales transactions compared to the previous year, and in 1932-33 there had been a further increase of 20,767 transactions.

Given the pressure to keep prices low to be competitive, the control and reduction of current and excessive overhead was vitally important given present-day trade conditions. However, he was confident that Swansea stores offer as good value as any part of the United Kingdom, and reiterated a slogan echoed by local traders: 'Buy in Swansea.'

He then revisited comments he had made a year earlier, when he had spent time discussing the prevailing economic conditions both locally and across the country. National and local taxation were hindering the anticipated recovery of the company's trading position, and the ongoing general depression, which occasionally lifts and offers false hope of improvement, has significantly impeded a return to a sound and profitable business.

Referring to the forthcoming planned alterations to their premises, he emphasised to the shareholders that the directors' policy was to ensure that shareholders received full value from their property, and was convinced the improvements would create a very fine modern shopping centre.

Nevertheless, he warned that as long as the current financial stringency persists, it interfered with customer purchasing power, which meant that he could not expect the company's trading position to improve satisfactorily.

The Mysterious Death of Capt. John Hubert Roberts

In October 1933, two years after Capt. Hubert Roberts had stepped down from his position as a board member of Ben Evans & Co. Ltd, he decided to take a well-earned vacation. (70) (71)

Flying from London to Baghdad, Iraq, he travelled on the Simplon Orient Express to the Syrian terminus, from where he then travelled by road to Beirut in Lebanon. From there he boarded a steamer to Alexandria in Egypt, from where he travelled by train to Cairo. He checked in to the Mena House Hotel on the 11th of October, but the following day he moved to The Continental Hotel.

He dined at the hotel on the night of the 15th of October, before settling his hotel bill, explaining he was catching the Alexandria train at 6.45 am the following morning from where he intended to board an ocean-going liner to London, leaving instructions for the hotel staff to wake him at 5.45 am. At 10 pm, he walked out of the hotel.

A staff member went to call him the next morning and found the room empty. The bed had not been slept in, and nothing had been packed. A passport and wallet containing £35 traveller's cheques and loose cash lay on the table, together with two photographs - one of a lady and the other of a child. The manager of the hotel immediately informed the police, and after allowing some time for his return, the authorities instructed all police posts to search for him.

On the 20th of October, the Mudir (Mayor) of Saftellaban near Giza informed the authorities that at six o'clock that evening, a body dressed in European clothes had been found in a canal off the River Nile under a bridge near the Pyramids road. On inspection of the body, it had a single revolver bullet wound in the right side of his back, and in the individual's jacket pockets was a first-class tram ticket to the Pyramids, some loose cash and seven bullet cartridges. No gun was found in the area, however, a new revolver was later found in Capt. Roberts' room, wrapped in a sock in a collar box.

Police were said to have 'scoured the nightclub quarter of Cairo', but had 'so far found no clue to the murderer'. However, a Dragoman (local interpreter) was arrested and his home was searched.

In Britain, a friend of Capt. Roberts received a letter from Capt. Roberts dated 15th of October, in which he explained that he had been pestered by local touts, and one man had upset him so much that he had 'almost knocked him down' after the man's verbal abuse 'insulted his ancestors, whereupon the man swore vengeance'.

An inquest was held, and two physicians, Dr Courtenay Pochin of the British Consulate and Dr Ismael Yusry, confirmed that whilst the body was in a decomposed state, using dental records it had been identified as Capt. Roberts, and in addition an initialled handkerchief was found on the body that matched that found in Capt. Roberts' personal belongings.

Both doctors also agreed that the fatal shot had been made 'from the closest range', and that it was 'most improbable' that the wound was self-inflicted.

A verdict that Capt. Roberts 'died of a bullet wound in the back inflicted by some person or persons unknown' was returned by the court conducting the inquest. The police informed the inquest they were continuing with the investigation, but had 'obtained no clues.'

In the same month, significant publicity surrounded the unveiling of the new Ben Evans 'Neon Illuminated Signs'. Signs were installed, one at the Temple Street - Castle Street corner of the building, and the other at the Caer Street - Castle Square corner of the building.

Supplied by Violite of London and installed by The Westward Electrical Company 1928 Ltd of St. Helens Road, Swansea, the signs ran off fourteen transformers that carried 42,000 volts.

The letters on the sign are 7 feet high, whilst the 'tail' under the letters is 27 feet long, making it 'the largest in the British Isles, and probably in Europe'. (72)

Author's collection

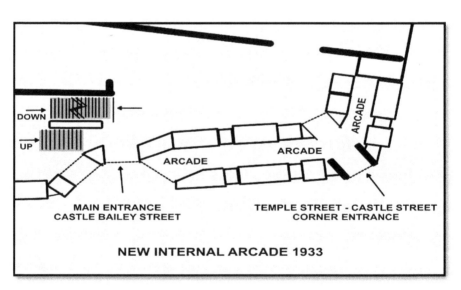

Modification work to the premises on Caer and Goat Streets was plagued by problems and delays, including disruption to working hours and damage to stock, and whilst an internal shopping arcade was also opened, it was not from Caer Street to Temple Street as planned, instead, it ran between the Temple Street and Castle Street corner entrances (see above).

Year 39	Feb 1933 - Jan 1934	Net Loss (£5,817)	Net Loss (£347,798) (2024)

In the 39th annual meeting held in April 1934, the Chairman said that 'the 11½ months' trading had been unsatisfactory', indicating that these issues had played a significant role in the poor results achieved, noting that the company had made a loss of £5,817.

Other factors also played a significant role in the company's poor performance, as whilst there was some progress towards recovery on a national level, the local economy remained sluggish, and the company's recovery aligned closely with the basic industries in Swansea and the immediate neighbourhood.

For the first time, Sir Percy acknowledged the threat posed by multiple stores to the shareholders. He said that their impact was significant on all retailers, and especially on the small traders, and blamed them for the closure of many independent stores. He noted that competition from specialist stores inevitably affected stores of Ben Evans' size. However, he did not dismiss the possibility of countering this competition and advised shareholders that since

Mr David Abel, previously Managing Director of wholesalers 'Vyse, Sons and Co.' of London, had joined the company on 1st February 1934, he had dedicated significant time to thoroughly examine every aspect of the store to best understand how to elevate every department to specialist standards. Philip G. Lewis retained his position as General Manager of the company.

Year 40	Feb 1934 - Jan 1935	Net Profit £7,923	Net Profit £473,716 (2024)

The 40th AGM of shareholders was held in April 1935, and the economic conditions had changed little in the previous twelve months. World conditions remained unstable, with no likelihood of any significant improvement in the basic industries that populated South Wales. The coal industry, apart from anthracite shipments to Canada, remained depressed, whilst shipping activity remained minimal, with little hope for a substantial improvement in exports until there was a significant change in import and exchange policies among Britain's continental neighbours. There was a noticeable improvement in the steel industry, and if it continued, there was some confidence that a new level of prosperity would soon be evident in its related industries.

Managing Director David Abel's input was immediate, and after working hard to maintain acceptable debt and stock levels, combined with increased sales transactions, he returned the company to profit.

After the issues caused by the structural changes to the premises in the previous fiscal year, the work was duly completed and has been deemed an unqualified success. The alterations and improvements made to the building now allowed the company to showcase goods in a marketable and attractive manner.

The colonnade on Caer Street allowed the company to display a wide variety of merchandise, and the additional and valuable window space has significantly boosted the visibility and appeal of goods, resulting in a significant increase in the volume of trade conducted in the store, indicating a steady rise in demand for high-quality merchandise.

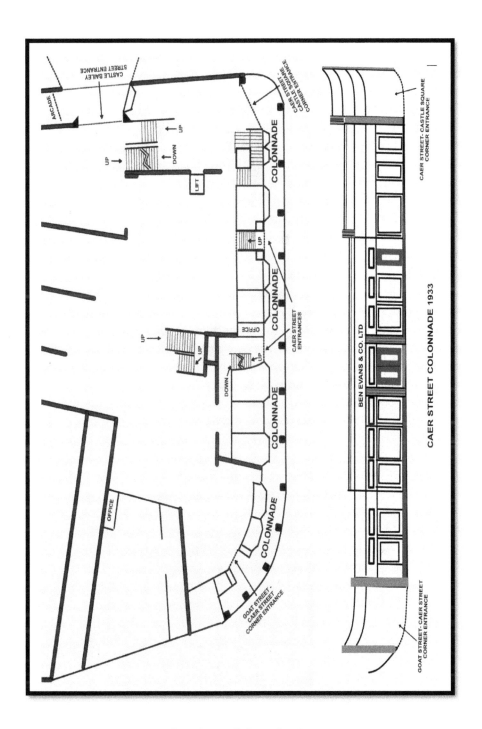

Caer Street Colonnade 1934

Year 41	Feb 1935 - Jan 1936	Net Profit £9,881	Net Profit £587,069 (2024)

South Wales had, more than any other part of the country, borne the brunt of the depression and had yet to see significant benefits from the overall economic revival. The retail business in Swansea remained heavily reliant on the basic industries of the area such as coal, steel, tin-plate, and shipping, and while the steel industry continued to show signs of recovery, other crucial sectors in this industrial district remained uncertain. Despite reports of considerable improvement in similar businesses in major English town centres, local trading conditions continued to pose challenges for Ben Evans and others.

Although, geographically, Swansea may not have been ideally positioned to accommodate what was commonly termed 'light industries', there was a genuine and sustained effort to attract them to the area, given the town's modern docks, suitable factory sites, comprehensive railway network, and road facilities capable of supporting any business complementary to the well-established heavy industries. Success in bringing these new businesses to the area would stabilise conditions and renew confidence in the trading area's industrial future, which in turn would stimulate retail growth.

In the AGM held in Swansea in April 1936, Sir Percy Molyneux reported that the new colonnade on Caer Street was proving to be a gratifying success. The window display that it provided the company was of inestimable value, and within the store, the general reorganisation and the increasing attractiveness of the newly arranged floor space were evident. Sir Percy felt that whilst the upgrade of the store was ongoing, when complete it would compare favourably with the best in the country.

'I feel certain that we are making a sure recovery, even if that recovery is a little slower than we would wish, but we are building on a sound foundation which I am hoping will lead us to a permanent dividend-paying position.... we shall not allow our efforts to slacken in bringing your store up-to-date and we hope to make it the most attractive shopping centre in the whole of Wales.'

Managing Director David Abel made clear to shareholders that keen competition made it impossible to increase the profit margins on merchandise, and that 'the small measure of success we have achieved is entirely due to the increase in turnover, the elimination of non-profitable departments, and a vigilant control of overhead expenses.'

Year 42	Feb 1936 - Jan 1937	Net Profit £10,052	Net Profit £593,496 (2024)

In the company's 42nd AGM, held at the company's premises in Swansea in April 1937, Sir Percy told shareholders that since the necessary re-adjustment to its accounts was made in 1931, he was confident that, barring any political upheaval in the coming year, the company would continue its progress towards a complete recovery.

Turning to the condition of the Ben Evans store, Sir Percy advised that special attention was being given to the store's departments that showed the greatest potential for expansion, ensuring they had the necessary space and amenities to display merchandise attractively. The importance of keeping the property in top condition was vitally important, and whilst the building was regularly maintained both inside and out, it had not had a complete overhaul since its construction. External cleaning, painting, and repairs were long overdue, and some stonework had become hazardous.

Whilst trading conditions in South Wales had still not yet seen the improvement evident in other areas of the UK, the steel and tinplate industries had made a noticeable improvement throughout 1936, which in turn improved shipping; however, the coal industry still lagged. Given that the state of local industry activity was a bellwether for changes in the retail environment, it was not a surprise that Sir Percy Molyneux voiced his optimism that it was 'the eve of an era of renewed activity and prosperity in South Wales.'

Sir Percy opined that he was optimistic that a lasting recovery in South Wales is closer than it has been in the past decade, but warned that whilst there was a drive to establish new enterprises in this area, efforts should focus on rebuilding the older industries on a solid economic foundation, noting that the likely change in fortune between management and workers of the coal trade would be 'the best news we have heard in a long time.'

He referred directly to an article in the 'Investors Chronicle' of 27th March

(73) on the prospects of the new agreement about to be entered upon by both sides of the coal trade of South Wales, which stated:

'The Wages Bill in 1920 (in South Wales and Monmouthshire) was £65,000,000 as against £14,000,000 last year so the proposed increase in wages should not be too onerous. One thing is certain, and that is the fixing of a new agreement six months before the old one was due to expire, marks a very welcome change in the procedure in negotiations, thus avoiding any prospects of trade dislocation. It is further understood that recent talks have given complete satisfaction to both sides and that the consummation of the agreement will lead to a far happier era in local industrial conditions.'

In November 1937, Sir Percy Molyneux JP, died at his home Gwern Einon, in Blackpill, Swansea after a long illness. Born in Grimsby in 1870, he had resided in Swansea for 45 years. Founder of the firm of P. Molyneux, Ltd. fish merchants, he was a prominent figure for many years In the public life of Swansea. A former Mayor of Swansea, he was a member of the Swansea Borough Council for 30 years. He became a Justice of the Peace in 1922 and was knighted in 1927 for his political and public services.

Year 43	Feb 1937 - Jan 1938	Net Profit £ 12,612	Net Profit £717,730 (2024)

The AGM held in April 1938 was led by the new Chairman Richard G. Lewis, J.P., who, after paying respects to his late predecessor Sir Percy Molyneux, reminded the shareholders of Sir Percy's words in the previous annual meeting, where he astutely predicted that the company's progress would soon resume, assuming no political upheaval. Given Sir Percy's position within local government, political and trade groups, his insights were based on a thorough understanding of the business and its prospects. Mr Lewis felt that the balance sheet and report presented to shareholders in the meeting stood as the best possible tribute to Sir Percy's wisdom and foresight.

The past year had seen a significant increase in sales turnover and also in the number of purchase transactions made throughout the store, and despite the increased turnover, stocks were maintained at close to the same level as the previous year. The gross profit rose by over 20%. The disposal of the company's removal and storage branch at Neath Road, Hafod reduced the property reserve account by £1,700, the amount received for the property. Under the watch of Managing Director David Abel, building renovations of the Ben Evans store were almost complete, and internally the business premises had been improved and renovated throughout.

In early November 1938, Ben Evans' Chairman Richard G. Lewis JP passed away, aged 69 years old. Born in Pembrokeshire and schooled in Tenby, at the age of 19 he left Wales for London where in 1889 he joined Whiteleys as a junior, later working for several prominent firms, before returning to Whiteleys as an under-manager.

He became a prominent figure in London's distributing trade, before joining Ben Evans in 1912 as general manager. Within a year he was appointed Managing Director and continued in that capacity until 1931, when he retired from the position, joining the board at the next annual general meeting, and subsequently became Chairman after the death of Sir Percy Molyneux JP in November 1937.

In the following month Alderman Edward Harris, a former Mayor of Swansea who joined the board in April 1934, was appointed the new Chairman of Ben Evans.

Year 44	Feb 1938 - Jan 1939	Net Profit £10,560	Net Profit £593,799 (2024)

Alderman Harris chaired the 44th AGM in April 1939, with Britain's involvement in international conflict a very real prospect.

After eulogising his predecessor Richard Lewis, Alderman Harris warned shareholders that Britain was once again in the midst of a crisis, and it was impossible to predict what lay ahead or what the impact would be on the country's trades in general. He hoped that with wise and calm guidance, the country would overcome these difficulties.

The increase in business that the company had enjoyed up to August 1938 was wiped out by the decreases in September, October, and November, which were directly attributed to the national crisis the country went through. Any hope for a recovery in December was thwarted by the inclement weather during those months, making it impossible to regain the lost ground, resulting in company profits back to 1936-37 fiscal year levels.

The directors believed that following the economies implemented in the company's departments and the improvements made, the trading results would continue to improve, and the company would persist in its course of recovery and improvement, with its prospects steadily advancing to a position satisfactory to all its shareholders. Managing Director David Abel pointed out that this setback was the first the company had experienced since the reorganisation five years before.

He concurred with the Chairman's remarks regarding the European troubles and was hopeful that matters would be resolved quickly and that peace would be secured, at which time Ben Evans would be ready to reclaim its place as the leading store in South Wales. The store, he said, was now well-equipped and prepared to handle any increase in demand, and although erected 45 years ago** it remained quite modern and 'houses a large and varied stock of up-to-date merchandise throughout the year, attractively displayed to appeal to even the most discerning customer.'

The selling space was regularly reviewed to ensure maximum profit, and a workroom measuring over 1,000 square feet and located at the rear of their fashion floor was being converted into a fur salon, which would open soon. This section of the business had steadily increased over the last three or four years and urgently needed the extra space for further expansion.

** The Castle Bailey building was erected and opened in 1894/95, not the whole store, much of which was over 50 years older.

Year 45	Feb 1939 - Jan 1940	Net Profit £11,773	Net Profit £642,874 (2024)

After Germany invaded Poland, Britain declared war on Germany on 3rd September 1939, honouring its pledge to defend Polish independence. This marked the beginning of Britain's involvement in World War Two. Following Britain's entry into the conflict, British Empire and Commonwealth allies such as Canada, Australia, New Zealand, South Africa, and India all joined Britain in declaring war on Germany in 1939.

In 1939, only around 30% of the food consumed in Britain was produced domestically, with the remaining 70% imported from abroad. However, the heavy dependence on imported food left Britain vulnerable to potential shortages if merchant shipping was disrupted by German attacks. To mitigate the risk of food shortages, the British government declared that rationing would be imposed as part of the national defence effort, and the public was instructed that the needs of the fighting forces took priority, necessitating rationing to ensure adequate supplies for the civilian population.

The 1939 Register, a survey of the civilian population, was used to devise a detailed rationing plan, and a system of ration books and coupons was utilised to ensure the population was kept healthy enough to maintain production on the home front. Each person was issued a ration book with coupons required to purchase rationed goods like food, clothes, and fuel. Rationing began with petrol in 1939, followed by bacon, butter, and sugar in January 1940, and meat in March 1940.

In May 1940, the 45th AGM of shareholders was held in Swansea under very different circumstances than the previous year. A state of war was declared in September 1939, and the business had to quickly adapt to the changed conditions and inconveniences caused by the war; additional insurance cover was put in place, as were A.R.P. services and related equipment required for the store. In addition, an A.R.P. shelter was also constructed at the company's freehold premises in St. Mary Square.

Chairman Harris reflected on the previous general meeting and said that at that time it was impossible to prophesy what lay ahead and therefore what the results would be upon the trade and business of the country, commenting that as a result of entering the War:

'The burden of taxation has already been increased and further burdens have already been indicated. Apart from the dislocation of trade and business which will inevitably follow, our ever-increasing national expenditure on the war and our preparation for a victorious issue will probably call for further sacrifices. these circumstances it would be unwise to venture any opinion as to our prospects. Whatever they may be we should not complain, but be prepared to pay and do all that is within our power, and to bear all sacrifices which may be necessary to achieve victory, without which all our prosperity is doomed.'

The Chairman highlighted a government act passed the day before the meeting, the Treachery Act 1940, that forcibly brought home to all the seriousness of the position the country was in, and the uncertainty of the future.

Speaking of the Managing Director, the Chairman advised shareholders that David Abel had been ill for several weeks, and was forbidden from attending the meeting. However, even throughout his period of illness he had made himself available, and at a time like this, his absence had been keenly felt across the business.

Despite the ominous economic conditions, the business was in good shape; whilst the war-related costs were acknowledged as necessary, profits were higher than the previous year, sales transactions were at an acceptable level, stock levels were under control, as were debt and credit levels.

In July of that year, after a long illness, David Abel passed away at his home in Mayals, Swansea, and the board appointed Company Secretary and board member Mr George Wheatley as the new Managing Director. Mr Wheatley had joined the company 25 years earlier and became a director in 1931. Mr William J. Richards was appointed as the new Company Secretary.

13 - Economic and Retail Challenges 1940 to 1950

Economic Conditions

In the spring of 1940, the Conservative leader resigned and the Tories invited the other main political parties into a coalition government. In May 1940, Winston Churchill became Prime Minister, forming a five-man war cabinet that included Labour leader Clement Attlee as his deputy. Within months, Nazi Germany began a sustained bombing campaign against the United Kingdom that lasted from September 1940 to May 1941, during which time millions of homes were damaged or destroyed, with London alone suffering around 2 million houses hit, and over 43,500 British civilians were killed by the bombings.

The Blitz, as it became known, represented one of the most intense bombing campaigns in history, inflicting immense destruction and loss of life across Britain, but ultimately failing to break the nation's will to continue the war against Nazi Germany.

London was bombed for 57 consecutive nights from September 1940, with the heaviest raid occurring on the night of 10th-11th May 1941, when over 500 German bombers dropped 711 tons of high explosives and nearly 2,400 incendiary bombs on London, killing 1,436 civilians. Over 700 acres were devastated, double the area destroyed in the Great Fire of London in 1666. While London was the primary target, the Blitz affected cities and towns across the UK, with few areas left untouched.

Other British cities like Coventry, Birmingham, Liverpool, Manchester, Portsmouth, Hull, Cardiff and Swansea were heavily bombed. Coventry suffered a devastating raid on 14th November 1940, with over 500 tons of explosives dropped, killing 568 people and destroying much of the city centre, whilst Liverpool and Merseyside were among the most bombed areas outside London, with over 1,900 killed in early May 1941 raids.

Wales faced devastating German air raids and bombings that left indelible scars on its towns and communities, the sustained aerial onslaught inflicted heavy casualties, widespread property destruction, and severe disruptions to daily life across urban centres like Swansea, Cardiff, and Newport. Retail shops, businesses and commercial districts in targeted areas bore the brunt of the bombings, with many establishments suffering irreparable damage or complete obliteration. The impact on the civilian population was equally severe, as families were forced to seek refuge in air raid shelters, cellars, and rural areas, fleeing the onslaught of high-explosive and incendiary bombs raining down on their communities.

Swansea in particular emerged as a legitimate strategic target for the Luftwaffe due to its vital role as a major port and dockyard, and the presence of a nearby oil refinery. The German bombing campaign aimed to cripple coal exports, a crucial resource for Britain's war effort, while simultaneously inflicting damage on critical infrastructure and demoralising civilians and emergency services. As a result of the air raids carried out between June 1940 and February 1943, a total of 387 people were killed, 412 people were seriously injured, and the lives of thousands of families were changed forever.

The Swansea Blitz, also known as the Three Nights' Blitz, was a devastating bombing campaign carried out by the German Luftwaffe that began around 7:30 pm on 19th February 1941 and continued for three consecutive nights, during which time an estimated 1,273 high explosive bombs and 56,000 incendiary bombs were dropped on Swansea's town centre as well as some of its residential areas, such as Brynhyfryd, Townhill, and Manselton, as well as Swansea's Eastside, which sits between Kilvey Hill and Swansea's docklands.

During the three nights of bombing, an area measuring approximately 41 acres was devastated in the town centre, with major landmarks like the Ben Evans department store and Swansea's Victorian Market reduced to rubble. In total, over 850 properties were destroyed and 11,000 damaged, whilst 230 civilians were killed, and 397 were injured.

The destruction wrought on the town centre left a profound impact on the town's landscape, and while some evidence of the bombing can still be found in the shape of shrapnel damage on certain buildings, the lack of older structures remaining in the town centre today tells a story of the wide devastation inflicted on the town.

The destruction of 'Ben Evans' - West Glamorgan Archives ref. D/D AWH 63

The 8th of May 1945 marked the end of World War II in Europe, but the conflict in the Asia-Pacific region continued until Japan's surrender in September 1945. British forces had fought across multiple fronts, including the Battle of the Atlantic against German U-boats, the North African campaign against Italian and German forces, and the invasion of Italy. By 1945, over 15 million Commonwealth and Imperial troops had served, fighting in campaigns from Europe to North Africa and Asia, and in doing so made vital contributions to the Allied war effort. Britain emerged from WWII victorious but economically devastated, and the aftermath of the war brought its own set of challenges for Britain and its people.

The war had caused immense damage to infrastructure, homes, and cities across Britain, and the country faced the daunting task of rebuilding what was lost during the conflict. This reconstruction effort required significant resources and careful planning, and as resources had been redirected from civilian needs to support the war effort, post-war Britain had to grapple with economic challenges that included shortages of goods, inflation, and high levels of unemployment. The return of millions of servicemen and women to civilian life also posed challenges. Demobilisation efforts needed to be managed effectively to reintegrate veterans into society provide support for those who had been injured or traumatised by the war and address the social and economic impact of their return.

Virtually all of Britain's foreign financial resources were depleted and it had built up massive sterling debt owed to other countries due to substantial WWII expenditures, including the lend-lease debt owed to the US which ended in 1945. The US Lend-Lease Act of 1941 allowed the US government to lend or lease (rather than sell) war supplies to any nation deemed 'vital to the defence of the United States' while remaining officially neutral in the conflict, allowing Britain to continue fighting against Germany on its own until the United States entered World War II late in 1941. By the late 1940s, the national debt peaked at over 230% of GDP, and Britain had to take out large loans from the U.S. ($3.75 billion) as well as from Canada (£1.2 billion) to pay for imports and necessities. This challenging economic situation made recovery difficult and contributed to unemployment in the immediate post-war years.

In May 1945, following the defeat of Germany, the coalition was dissolved when Clement Attlee withdrew the Labour Party from the coalition to prepare for a general election, and in July of that year, they took control of the government. Traditional heavy industries like coal mining, shipbuilding, and textiles were in disarray and suffered from a lack of investment, outdated technology, and rising foreign competition.

The loss of export markets and the inability to compete with cheaper imports resulted in job losses in these sectors. The transitioning of industries like manufacturing from a wartime to a peacetime economy had its difficulties, as a lack of investment and changing demand patterns posed obstacles.

The Labour Party had promised social reforms and a welfare state, and after they won a landslide victory in the 1945 general election, they rapidly nationalised major industries like railways, coal mines, road transport, electrical power production, and the Bank of England. In line with William Beveridge's 1942 report, they embraced his 'cradle to the grave' ideas, established the National Health Service and expanded the welfare state through programs like National Insurance.

The Retail Environment

The economic disruptions caused by World War II and the subsequent transition to a peacetime economy after 1945 had a profound impact on the retail sector, particularly in terms of consumer demand and spending patterns.

Wartime production and rationing measures severely limited the availability of consumer goods, forcing households to prioritise spending on essentials like food, clothing, and fuel over discretionary purchases. Rationing had been in place throughout the war years and continued for several years after the conflict ended to ensure equitable distribution of scarce resources, further restricting consumer choice and retail sales. Enemy attacks on merchant shipping and transportation infrastructure impacted the flow of goods and raw materials. Factories and production facilities were repurposed for military equipment and munitions, reducing the output of consumer products, and the demands of wartime production disrupted regular manufacturing and supply chains for consumer goods, leading to shortages and limiting retail inventory.

Disposable incomes declined throughout the war years, further constraining consumer spending power as well as the demand for non-essential retail goods and services. With resources scarce and the future uncertain, consumers adopted a more pragmatic and frugal mindset, focusing spending on necessities rather than indulgences, and prioritised saving over discretionary spending, further constraining retail sales during the war years.

Retailers experienced depressed sales volumes, and the buying power and low prices of both the multiples and cooperatives were a real concern to the very existence of independent stores, who, more than ever before, had to adapt their offerings and operations to the harsh economic realities of wartime, or else go out of business.

Rebuilding the Town Centre

From the turn of the 20th century, Swansea's town centre had undergone very little structural change. Its development had been essentially uncontrolled, and by the 1930s, it had evolved into a diverse blend of hotels, bars, restaurants, cinemas, theatres, department stores, independent retailers, multiples, and cooperatives populating the area from High Street southwards to Castle Street and then westwards to Oxford Street, where midway down its length stood the town's Victorian Market, a central hub for over 400 independent traders. However, the commercial heart of the town was shattered during the Three Nights' Blitz in February 1941. The bombing campaign wiped out 41 acres and over 850 properties, including major landmarks such as the Ben Evans department store and the town's Victorian market, leaving much of the town's commercial core in ruins.

In July 1941, the War Damage Commission authorised the Council to proceed with remedial works, including ground clearance and the allocation of temporary buildings, shops, and other facilities. However, it would take a year for the Council to take any action.

In 1943, after the passing of the Town and Country Planning Act, a newly formed Ministry of Town and Country Planning established an Advisory Panel on the Redevelopment of City Centres. The Panel identified eleven regions for consideration and selected seven 'test-case cities' that had suffered serious war damage, ultimately including Swansea, replacing Sheffield, which was originally listed. Key factors in the Ministry of Town and Country Planning's approach were the likelihood of encouraging new business to the test-case cities and ensuring that rebuilt towns and cities could handle future traffic needs – a problem inherent in old towns like

Swansea, with its disorganised road layouts.

However, the rebuilding of Swansea's town centre was a long, challenging process marked by conflicts between local ambitions and central government plans, as well as economic constraints. While other 'test cities' such as Plymouth and Hull employed third-party consultant town planners and architects, Swansea's reconstruction was placed in the hands of Borough Engineer J. Richard Heath.

When evaluating proposals to restore areas damaged during the war, it quickly became evident that a piecemeal approach would be unsatisfactory. The only viable solution was to devise a comprehensive redevelopment plan for the entire central town area. This comprehensive strategy would ensure that any major reconstruction projects undertaken in the initial years seamlessly integrated into the town's ultimate layout and design. A holistic vision was necessary to guide the rebuilding efforts and create a cohesive, well-planned urban environment from the remnants of war-torn destruction.

With some fine-tuning, Heath's plans were deemed acceptable to the Ministry of Town and Country Planning, but a month later he retired and was replaced by James Bennett, a Bristol-based planning officer who had never been to Swansea before.

By April 1944, Bennett had made little progress beyond Heath's initial plans, contributing to delays in the redevelopment process, and relations between Swansea Council and the Ministry were strained due to Bennett's perceived lack of capability, urgency, and self-centred approach. Political posturing within the Council and a perceived paternal attitude from the Ministry further exacerbated the tensions.

The Ministry had agreed on the rebuilding of 44 acres to accommodate the 41 acres lost to war plus the new roads and roundabouts envisaged, whilst the Council felt that 55 acres of land were required, and the Ministry suggested the Council put in a pre-approval Declaratory Order to speed up the procedure.

In August 1946, in line with the Town and Country Planning Act of 1944, Swansea Council put forward its Declaratory Order proposal for damaged areas and blighted land, a necessary step before Compulsory Purchase Orders could be requested, with property values based on 1939 levels.

The Council's proposal was met with a host of objections from the town's traders, including representatives of Ben Evans & Company, who wanted to rebuild on their original locations but objected to what they collectively recognised as an unacceptably high level of annual rates they were expected to pay for that privilege.

Nevertheless, in May 1947 the Compulsory Purchase Order was approved, followed two months later by the Declaratory Order which had been revised downwards to 134 acres. Construction of sorts began when in 1946 the Council began the building of twenty temporary structures for use as shops in the town centre. (74)

Disagreements between the Ministry of Town and Country Planning, the Ministry of Transport, and Swansea Council continued, and by May 1950 no new buildings had been constructed and only one new road.

Ben Evans Performance 1940 - 1950

Year 46	Feb 1940 - Jan 1941	Net Profit £ ----	Net Profit £ ---- (2024)

No report available

The bombing of Swansea by the Luftwaffe culminated in three nights of devastation on the 19th, 20th, and 21st of February 1941. The centre of Swansea was turned from bustling streets to a pile of rubble. The Ben Evans department store was lost on the last night of the bombing, the store's basement acting as a shelter for staff and customers alike.

The company's leaders took swift action and found temporary retail space on Walter Road, and five months after the destruction of Swansea's town centre, the 46th AGM was held at the company's premises, 24, Waiter Road, Swansea, on Thursday, July 31, 1941. Chairman Edward Harris addressed the board and the company shareholders:

'Ladies and Gentlemen, My board have decided it is desirable on this occasion that the Chairman's address to the shareholders should be printed and circulated with the notice convening the annual general meeting. In arriving at this decision, which follows the example of many other public companies, they were actuated by the knowledge that for the reasons disclosed in such address we are unable to present the usual reports and accounts, and by a sincere desire that the shareholders, and particularly those who may be unable to attend the meeting owing to difficulties in travelling, should in these circumstances be informed of the present position of the company and of its prospects for the future.

I sincerely regret that I am unable on this occasion to direct observations as Chairman to the balance sheet, accounts and profits of the company for the financial year ending 31st January 1941, as our splendid and important business premises were razed to the ground and all their contents completely destroyed by enemy action on the 21st February last. In one single night of savage devastation and havoc, the business of the company of which we were all so justly proud and which had flourished for over 74 years was swept out of existence. No greater misfortune could befall this or any other company.

It will take years of care, vigilance and toil to repair the losses we have suffered and to reconstruct our business and affairs on their former basis. The burden so suddenly thrust upon your directors is a heavy one. As they have already entered upon the task which confronts them, I propose to extend my observations so as to indicate in very brief terms what has already been done by them to preserve the assets and to maintain the valuable goodwill of the company. In July last we had the misfortune to lose the invaluable services of our Managing Director, Mr David Abel, whose death we all lament. He was seriously ill at the date of our last annual meeting, and inasmuch as I then referred in full terms to his illness and the part he had played in vitalizing and extending the interests of the company, there is no need for any amplification on this occasion.'

Edward Harris stated that shortly before David Abel's death, and with his full approval, the board had extended invitations to Sir Lewis Lougher, J.P., Mr David Williams, J.P., and Mr Ernest Dawson, one of their departmental managers, to join their board. Each of these gentlemen had long been associated with the company, and all of them accepted. It was, he said, a sad coincidence that they began their duties on the day of Mr Abel's death, after which the board appointed Mr George Wheatley, who had diligently served the company for 20 years as its secretary and 10 years as a director, to be Managing Director. He also expressed regret at the sudden death of Mr W. J. Richards, who had been appointed Company Secretary in August 1940.

The Chairman reported that the financial year ending on 31st January had been very satisfactory and had given the directors confidence that a dividend would be paid on the Ordinary shares, as per the previous year. However, the company's records had been destroyed before the accounts could be audited, which caused a delay in accurately determining the extent of the losses. Consequently, the accounts for the past year would be deferred until the next annual meeting, at which point the directors hoped to present a combined balance sheet and accounts for both the past and current financial years.

With this in mind, he advised the company's shareholders that it would be an opportune time to consider an appropriate scheme for reconstructing the company's capital fairly and equitably, whilst removing all distinctions between the three classes of shareholders. The company's Articles of Association might also need a complete revision. Given recent events, it was important for the company to have the freedom to decide how to use its profits and the right to retain and accumulate them as needed to support the company's financial position.

Immediately after the calamitous experience of February, steps were taken by the company to preserve its assets and given the value of the premises as well as the location of the site on which they were erected, the claim for compensation in respect of the company's freehold premises and fixtures had been swiftly lodged. However, the Government advised that this would not be dealt with until after the war. Stocks were fully insured against war risks, and a claim in respect of this had already been met.

Though several company ledgers were damaged, staff were able to arrive at the amounts due from most of the customers, and while many customers had already settled their accounts without needing reminders, it was hoped that all outstanding accounts would be settled by 31st January 1941.

With no town centre store remaining, the company's freehold premises at 111 St Mary's Square were modified to accommodate the ironmongery, furniture, and carpet departments, as well as to house reserve stock, and three well-situated freehold houses at Nos. 22, 23 and 24 Walter Road, Swansea, were acquired and converted into 'spacious and attractive shops' housing most of the company's departments.

In addition, three shops were also opened on Woodfield Street, Morriston, to meet the demands of customers in the northern suburbs of Swansea and throughout the Swansea Valley. Customary orders for new spring and summer stocks had been placed and accepted before the raid, and although the goods had not yet been delivered, the new premises were sufficiently stocked to be able to resume business.

Year 47	Feb 1940 - Jan 1942 **	Net Loss (£424)	Net Loss (£17,881) (2024)

** Report covers two years

Prompt action taken by the board, including the adaptation of the premises in St. Mary's Square and the acquisition of new premises, was instrumental in continuing the company's business. Trading at the Walter Road and the Morriston stores, however, was limited to eight months of the fiscal year as the company was obliged to incur 'unproductive expenses' that significantly impacted profits for the year. The steady growth and volume of business achieved since the opening of these new premises, despite numerous difficulties and restrictions, demonstrated that the company's goodwill was not merely speculative but extensive and well-founded, offering tangible value.

In response to the continuous requests from the store's patrons, a small, well-designed restaurant was opened at the Walter Road premises. The restaurant received strong patronage and was poised to contribute to the establishment of Walter Road as the new shopping hub for the town and its surrounding district.

In the forty-seventh AGM, held at the company's premises, 22 Walter Road, Swansea, on Thursday, 2nd July 1942, Chairman Edward Harris called attention to the consequences of the destruction of the company's town centre premises and indicated in very brief terms the measures already undertaken to surmount the difficulties that the business continued to confront. The company had endured the two most crucial years in its history, years in which 'severe losses were inflicted upon us and our whole fabric shattered seemingly beyond repair'. However, despite war conditions and the widespread restrictions upon trading, the company persevered, and whilst it was impossible to foretell how the claims under the War Damage Act would be finally adjusted, the consequence of the measures taken by the board as shown in the accounts presented was extremely satisfactory.

The accounts reported on covered the two years which ended on 31st January 1942, and after providing for renewals, repairs and doubtful debts and the amounts written off, the company had incurred a loss of £424 10s. 10d. for the two years under review, an amount far below the sum feared in the aftermath of the Blitz.

Year 48	Feb 1942 - Jan 1943	Net Profit £9,851	Net Profit £387,752 (2024)

The global conflict continued and, as a consequence, higher taxation and wartime restrictions such as the ration book system hampered businesses. At the company's 48th AGM held in May 1943, Chairman Edward Harris said that whilst trading was at a reasonable level and some suitable stocks were currently available, given that both the sourcing and timely supply of some goods were challenging, the prices of certain types of merchandise had risen considerably. The extremely satisfactory result would undoubtedly have been even better.

The company's War Damage Repairs claim was still under review.

Year 49	Feb 1943 - Jan 1944	Net Profit £8,421	Net Profit £320,773 (2024)

In February 1944, the Ben Evans board sent a scathing ten-page letter to the Swansea Borough Council highlighting the company's frustration with the council's proposed development scheme for the town centre, advocating the immediate abandonment of the proposals (75) (see (i) in Appendices).

The company's extensive critique characterised the proposals as collectively objectionable and unworkable, suggesting that the council should focus on a scheme that is reasonable, practical, and economical and one that can be financed and executed without delay. It advocated for a scheme that preserves existing social services, properties, and businesses, while also creating rather than destroying rateable value. The company emphasised the importance of securing all-round cooperation to achieve proposals suggested by officials that are both necessary and feasible.

The statement highlighted that owners have given notice of their intention to retain their leaseholds of freehold properties and argued that owners of war-damaged properties should be sought out and encouraged, rather than treated lightly and irresponsibly.

The company had paid £4,000 a year in rates for the site of 'Ben's', described as one of the town's most prominent and distinguished features, yet in the proposed redevelopment of the town centre, the site was earmarked to be an 'extensive open space' of dubious, if any, value to the town. The scheme, it argued, offers no comparable alternative site to either the company or to other prominent businesses, in terms of position, dimensions, potential, or value.

The letter stated that there was unparalleled potential for redevelopment on sound and moderate terms while encompassing some of the essential features advocated in modern town planning, yet the council's proposal seeks to 'augment the damage already done by acquiring and demolishing a vast number of other buildings.' That, together with the proposed use of large traffic islands, would mean 'the prosperity and destiny of the town are to be thrown into the melting pot for purposes that may, to some slight extent, regulate vehicular traffic and improve its appearance, but otherwise offer dubious benefit.'

In the AGM held in May at Walter Road, Chairman Harris highlighted the trading position, stating that despite 'the numerous restrictions currently in force, the additional burden imposed by supply limitations, quotas, purchase tax, and coupons, as well as the almost continuous issuance of orders and regulations', the profits of the company had been maintained and its financial position had improved. A steady volume of business had been maintained, highlighting the suitability of the Walter Road premises for properly displaying the merchandise of some of their departments. However, the company was prohibited from making much-needed structural alterations.

The Chairman advised the shareholders that the Swansea Borough Council had recently proposed a repayment scheme for the town planning and redevelopment of Swansea's trading centre that, if implemented, would deprive the company of the entire site of the former premises, which was widely recognised as one of the best and most centrally situated locations in the town. He said that whilst a scheme for the redevelopment of the shopping centre is immediately essential, there was no need, nor can there be any justification for one of such extravagant design that will involve huge capital expenditure, and will completely change the widths, positions and character of the town's streets, and would upset all prospects of rehabilitating the many who have directly and grievously suffered, and will needlessly and ruthlessly sacrifice valuable properties and rateable values.

If the business of the town is to be preserved, no time should be lost before proceeding with a well-considered scheme, which, without any strange or over-ambitious feature would achieve all that is necessary or desirable and command the cooperation and support of all interests concerned.

Year 50	Feb 1944 - Jan 1945	Net Profit £10,946	Net Profit £405,509 (2024)

A week after the War in Europe had ended, Alderman Edward Harris presided at the AGM on 16th May 1945 and remarked that it was the company's 50th meeting, making it a notable day in its history. The business was founded by the late Mr Ben Evans in 1862, and the limited liability company was formed in 1895. The company had always played a prominent role in the business affairs of Swansea, and its continued vitality and progress, despite the challenges it faced, testified to its stability.

This was the first meeting since peace had been declared, and the company had emerged triumphantly from a war unparalleled in world history. Despite war conditions and the consequent difficulties, trade had increased, profits rose, and the company's financial position further improved. In short, it was a very successful year.

He expressed hope that now that the war had ended, many of the restrictions imposed on businesses would be lifted, granting greater freedom to trade across all branches. He also anticipated that some of the wartime taxes, which had been accepted as necessary, would now be withdrawn. This would facilitate business expansion and better meet the needs of the people with an open market and no restrictions.

The Chairman was optimistic about the prospects for improved trade and conditions, and he hoped that the government would, amidst the multitude of State affairs requiring urgent attention, ensure that the restoration of the stricken towns receives special consideration and priority, as the current state of the town's buildings and premises was unattractive and did not draw visitors or business.

Swansea Town Council had approved a town development scheme which, although deemed by many as a distinct improvement over its initial proposal, still deprived Ben Evans & Co. of returning to its original location. The Council intended to create an open-air space in the town centre; however, no one had provided a solid justification for the proposal beyond claims that it is necessary to beautify the town, make it more attractive to visitors, and regulate street traffic. The Chairman felt that crucial factors such as property values, cost of works, losses, compensation, long-established associations, interference with existing ownerships and tenancies, public services and amenities, the just claims of traders for rehabilitation, and the importance of preserving the town's salient and noteworthy features had been either overlooked or disregarded.

Beyond approving preliminary plans and some site clearance, the town's traders felt that no tangible steps had been taken toward rebuilding the damaged trading centre of the town, and the impact of recent legislation on the proposals has yet to be considered, which may introduce unforeseen problems and difficulties. The preservation of trade and business within the town's limits has been left entirely to the traders and others who suffered directly.

The confusion generated considerable dissatisfaction among all interested parties, as the longer traders were compelled to operate from premises they moved to after the Blitz, the more they invested in what were intended to be temporary locations, and the greater their reluctance to face the sacrifices and risks of returning to what was rapidly becoming a disused and abandoned shopping centre. The Chairman opined, 'This, I believe, is a striking example of visionary and irresponsible planning.'

Government restrictions hindered the necessary property improvements to achieve the required capacity at Walter Road, and the company had purchased the freehold of No. 25 Walter Road, which was subject to a short-term tenancy. However, until a definitive decision was made on the fate of the original site, improvements on the Walter Road properties were on hold.

On 4th August 1945, Alderman Edward Harris, O.B.E., passed away at Haresfield, his home in Mumbles, Swansea. Born in Morriston in 1871, and a solicitor by profession, he had built up a large lay practice, and his professional colleagues recognised his standing by electing him president of what was then the Swansea and Neath Incorporated Law Society. He became a member of the Swansea Borough Council in 1918 and served as Mayor from 1933-34, the last mayor to officiate at the old Guildhall on the Burrows, before the Council's move to the Civic Centre. He had also served for many years as clerk to the Llwchwr Urban District Council and the Gowerton Bench Magistrates. He was awarded the O.B.E. for his work as Chairman of the West Glamorgan Advisory Assistance Board.

Year 51	Feb 1945 - Jan 1946	Net Profit £13,465	Net Profit £485,501 (2024)

The company's AGM was held at the Walter Road premises in May 1946, with Chairman David Williams presiding. The Chairman first spoke fondly of his personal friend and colleague, the late Edward Harris, who had served the company as both a director and a Chairman before his death.

He did not want to dwell on the frustrations concerning the council's proposal to rebuild the town other than to say that it would be quite some time before the rebuilding of the town's shopping centre began; objections to it were ongoing and decisions had still not been made. It was estimated that acquiring the necessary land for this purpose would take a year or more, and even then, residential buildings would undoubtedly take priority over business premises for the foreseeable future.

With this in mind, the Ben Evans board of directors could claim to have displayed initiative and foresight by acquiring the freehold premises in Walter Road. In the previous meeting, shareholders were advised that the company had acquired the freehold of the adjoining premises at No. 25 Walter Road, subject to a short-term tenancy.

The premises were now in company possession, and the necessary alterations and repairs were completed. The premises had been utilised by the business since February 1946. Walter Road had now developed into a popular and prosperous shopping centre, which the company's subsequent balance sheets had disclosed. Whilst costs were incurred in renovating No. 25, in the fiscal year ending in January 1946, sales turnover had continued to increase year on year, profits increased by nearly 19%, whilst stock, credit and debt remained at satisfactory levels.

In August 1946, a public inquiry was held at The Brangwyn Hall into Swansea Council's application to the British government for orders under the Town and Country Planning Act, and the intended Swansea Declaratory Area and Compulsory Purchase Orders for the blitzed area reconstruction scheme put forward in their proposals. Several companies had legal representation in the meeting, including Ben Evans & Co., the Chamber of Commerce, and Swansea Town FC.

Mr Harold B. Williams, representing Messrs Ben Evans as well as several breweries, questioning the legality of the proposals, asked why the Council felt it necessary to 'do more damage than the enemy did' and destroy 111 acres of currently occupied property.

He said that the foundation of the Council plan was a pre-war traffic problem, but laying out afresh an area to provide wide roads to deal with traffic problems was not covered by the government guidelines. There were powers under another section adequate to deal with road problems and warned the Council that legal challenges might follow.

He pointed out that any scheme which involved such 'damage' as the Council scheme did, showed a reckless disregard for the interests of the inhabitants. It appeared that there was no awareness of the cost involved, and the recovery of costs would fall to the private sector to pay in the rents subsequently charged.

Mr David Williams, Chairman of Ben Evans and Co. Ltd, testified that the company intended to return their business to its original site if possible. However, if they were required to pay a ground rent of approximately £7,500, they would need to relocate elsewhere.

Mr Gerwyn P. Thomas, representing the gas company, the Chamber of

Commerce, the Royal Metal Exchange, and various others, also objected. He stated that if the order were made, it would result in the sterilisation of a significant and extensive part of Swansea.

Mr Morris Morgan, representing Swansea Town FC, pointed out that there was no provision shown on the Council plan for a field to replace the Vetch Field, which was zoned partly for residential and partly for road purposes. Borough engineer Mr J. B. Bennett responded by pointing out that he thought they could find alternative sites for a football field within three miles of High Street station. Mr Haydn Green, secretary of the club, retorted that 'the club might as well go out of the town as have a ground three miles from the station.'

Morris Morgan argued that the lack of financial details regarding the Council's scheme rendered the inquiry pointless. The town clerk emphasised that there had been no refusal to disclose information; rather, the financial information was unavailable because they did not have the necessary data to prepare it. The inquiry was swiftly adjourned.

Year 52	Feb 1946 - Jan 1947	Net Profit £14,179	Net Profit £496,097 (2024)

In the 52nd AGM, Chairman David Williams informed shareholders of the Public Inquiry into the Swansea Declaratory Area and Compulsory Purchase Orders held in Swansea during the previous August. The inquiry lasted a week, and the company was represented by London counsel and a London architect with extensive knowledge and experience in town planning. The Ministry had yet to issue any orders, and he felt that it would be several years before the rebuilding of Swansea's town shopping centre began. Due to numerous wartime restrictions and an extreme shortage of supplies, the trading period under review had been very challenging, although profits had grown slightly on the previous year's figure.

In August of that year, the South Wales Evening Post had a front page sub-headline - "Ben Evans want their old site back.' (76)

Year 53	Feb 1947 - Jan 1948	Net Profit £12,672	Net Profit £414,221 (2024)

Addressing shareholders at the 53rd AGM on the 21st of May 1948, Chairman David Williams advised shareholders that the Minister of Town and Country Planning had now confirmed, with modifications, the order submitted by the Swansea Borough Council to compulsorily purchase approximately 26 acres of war-damaged land in the centre of the town.

It was highly improbable that substantial business buildings would be erected in the blitzed area for several years, and the company's property, destroyed by enemy action in February 1941, remained in the same condition as previously reported. No war damage compensation claim had been settled by or paid to the company.

Trading conditions had remained challenging throughout the last trading period, hampered by persistent vexatious wartime restrictions. Short supplies of merchandise handicapped every department of the company's business, and it was envisaged that those conditions would prevail for a considerable time. Despite strict monitoring of stock, credit and debt levels, profit for the year remained static.

In 1948, Mr James Graham Morgan, the men's department buyer at Ben Evans, concluded his remarkable 53-year career with the company.

Hailing from Llangendeirne, Carmarthen, he joined the firm in 1895 under the leadership of Managing Director John White. Upon his employment, he was bestowed the store name 'Mr Graham,' an appellation he retained until his retirement. (see Appendices (c))

A respected figure throughout the industry, Mr J.M. Morgan played a pivotal role in the company's success. His tenure spanned significant transformations since joining Ben Evans in the store's first year of incorporation, witnessing the evolution of the 'old' store to participating in the establishment and operation of the new premises on Walter Road. His extensive experience and industry knowledge made him an invaluable asset to Ben Evans, contributing to its reputation as a premier retail establishment in Swansea.

Year 54	Feb 1948 - Jan 1949	Net Profit £ 9548	Net Profit £283,132 (2024)

In May 1949, the AGM of Ben Evans & Co. Ltd. was held at the company's premises on Walter Road, Swansea, with Chairman David Williams presiding. The following is the Chairman's statement:

'It is my pleasure and privilege to submit to you the Balance Sheet and Accounts for the year ended on the 31st of January 1949. You will observe that this year the Accounts are drawn up to conform with the Companies Act 1948.

The Balance Sheet has changed in many ways and provides comparative figures for the previous year. This makes it unnecessary for me to go into the figures in detail. Purchase Tax is very troublesome and as the Board of Trade is unable to agree to any formula traders can be protected and compensated, any losses through changing conditions and uncertainties in connection with this tax must be regarded as a trading risk. Many other restrictions have outlived their uselessness and should be abolished.

Sales figures for the year were the highest since the Company suffered destruction in the blitz of February 1941. But the net profit, after provision for taxation, is slightly down. This is due to increased expenses, salaries etc,, and changes in Purchase Tax. There are undoubtedly many difficulties to be faced. But with the goodwill and confidence of our patrons and the loyal and efficient support of our staff, I am optimistic of our future prospects.

With reference to our blitz property in Temple-street etc, the authorities are still considering our claim for compensation, and it is hoped that a settlement will be reached in the near future.'

Year 55	Feb 1949 - Jan 1950	Net Profit £16,523	Net Profit £487,780 (2024)

It had been over nine years since the properties in Swansea's town centre were destroyed due to enemy action, and frustrations remained amongst the traders of Swansea as to the lack of concrete action taken towards the repair of the 'Blitz'-damaged town centre, the ambiguity causing significant dissatisfaction among all involved parties.

Forced to continue to operate from temporary premises around the town, many traders were investing in permanent modifications to these premises, and they would therefore be less inclined to return to a now-abandoned shopping centre, whilst at the same time the Swansea Borough Council was making strenuous efforts to ensure compulsory purchase of many of the properties lost in the bombing.

Ben Evans & Co. were in a similar position, and given the size of the original business, had acquired several Walter Road properties, and had to make a significant investment in them to maintain the standard expected of the original store, a recent and substantial expenditure being the installation of new and modern shop windows. In the early months of 1950, the company purchased the freehold of the adjacent property, No. 26 Walter Road, albeit with a short-term tenancy in place.

In March 1950, the company's Managing Director George Wheatley passed away at his home 'Elderado', Cockett Road, Sketty. He was 74 years old.

In the company's 55th AGM, held in May 1950 at 22 Walter Road, after Chairman David Williams had lamented the loss of Mr Wheatley, he advised those present that whilst Ben Evans & Co. went into 1950 having achieved their highest sales since moving to Walter Road, a combination of increased costs and restrictions, numerous consequential challenges, and fluctuations in Purchase Tax meant profits were down.

Mr Williams also advised that since the conclusion of their financial year (31st Jan) the company had received a communication from the authorities responsible for handling the compensation claim for the properties affected by the 'Blitz', and that 'following prolonged and challenging negotiations', a tentative agreement had been reached for the settlement of Ben Evans' compensation claim.

Castle Gardens (originally called 'The Rest Gardens', built on the site of the Ben Evans store (Author's collection)

14 - Economic and Retail Challenges 1950 to 1960

Economic Conditions

In 1950, Britain's post-World War II public debt was over 200% of GDP; however, the debt burden had declined rapidly to around 112% of GDP by 1959 as the economy expanded. Throughout the 1950s, Britain saw strong economic expansion that, coupled with rising incomes, resulted in significant improvements in living standards. GDP growth averaged around 3% annually throughout the decade, and real disposable household incomes rose by around 25% from 1950 to 1960.

The British government aimed to manipulate economic growth via a 'stop-go' methodology, using fiscal and monetary policies to try to manage the economy through alternating periods of stimulus ('go') and restraint ('stop') to help control inflation and balance international payments. Policy shifts contributed to volatility in areas like inflation and unemployment over the decade.

Prime Minister Harold Macmillan famously remarked in 1957 that 'most of our people have never had it so good', capturing the rising prosperity. Real wage gains were underpinned by productivity growth and a labour relations system that passed on gains to workers. Consumer goods like TVs and cars became more widespread, with just 1% of households owning a TV in 1950 rising to 25% by 1965.

New industries like electronics, engineering and chemicals were growing, but Britain remained heavily dependent on older staple industries like coal, steel and textiles. While still a manufacturing powerhouse, there were signs of the UK's relative industrial decline compared to rivals like Germany and the United States emerging, and there were also signs of emerging challenges like industrial shift, policy volatility, and relative economic decline setting in.

Retail Environment

In the early 1950s, the lack of adequate food storage facilities and constrained household budgets necessitated frequent trips to the market for most British families. A mere 15% of homes were equipped with refrigerators or freezers during this era, compelling housewives to embark on daily shopping excursions to procure fresh provisions, the majority of which took place at locally owned family-operated establishments. Bakeries, butcher shops, greengrocers, and fishmongers dotted the landscape, providing a personalised and community-oriented shopping experience, and it was common for vendors to deliver goods like groceries, vegetables, and milk directly to homes. Food rationing ended completely in Britain in 1954, allowing wider choice and availability. Canned and frozen foods became more prevalent as storage improved, and the decade saw the emergence of convenience foods.

The latter half of the decade saw the emergence of self-service stores and supermarkets selling a wider range of non-food consumer goods like appliances, clothing, and household items to meet pent-up demand. Hire-purchase restrictions were lifted in 1954, enabling purchases of durable goods, and consumer spending increased by 115% during the 1950s. As incomes rose and as electrification spread, sales of goods like vacuum cleaners, washing machines, refrigerators, electric cookers, televisions, and telephones grew rapidly.

Brands and packaging design became more important to guide consumers through the array of new product choices, and in the late 1950s self-service shopping took off, representing a major shift from the traditional small, over-the-counter shops that had dominated previously.

Large chain stores now dominated the high streets of Britain, with stores catering to demographic groups such as teenagers. Following the American model, Sainsbury's and Waitrose opened some of the first British self-service supermarkets selling non-food items in the late 1950s.

Ben Evans Performance 1950 to 1960

Year 56	Feb 1950 - Jan 1951	Net Profit £***	Net Profit £*** (2024)

*** Incomplete financial information published in the press.

Over the next trading year, the company continued to face challenging trading conditions and expected that the difficulties met were likely to persist for the foreseeable future. However, considering the circumstances, whilst sales figures had exceeded those of the previous year, the results for 1951 were deemed 'satisfactory'.

In the company's 56th Annual General Meeting, held in May 1951 at 22 Walter Road, shareholders were told that the company's Fixed Assets had changed dramatically since the previous meeting as a result of the removal of Freehold Property (lost in the bombing but remaining on the asset list) amounting to £147,507 and the Property Reserve Account to £15,485, a total of £162,992.

Only the company's freehold property on St. Mary's Street remained from property owned in that area as it was undamaged during the bombing.

The adjustments were required as the company had received full payment to cover the agreed valuation of the Temple Street freehold, as well as a payment from the War Damage Commission was received for the complete compensation settlement of the Temple Street freehold. Payment received also included the accumulated interest due for the period covering the nearly years of the war damage claim.

For the loss of the buildings that made up the ironic 'Ben Evans' store, the company received £29,630 from Swansea Borough Council for the Temple Street freehold site, which was subject to a compulsory purchase order. Additionally, £137,280 was received for the War Damage settlement for buildings on Temple Street, plus interest on the amount received from the War Damage claim, totalling £33,991 after deduction of tax, resulting in £200,910 total payments received (£5.326,436 in 2024).

A further £20,000 owed to the company by the Board of Trade as compensation for losses incurred due to enemy action on fixtures and fittings was still outstanding, however, this amount would be disbursed to the company upon providing proof to the Board of Trade that the same amount is necessary for fixtures and fittings utilised at the current (Walter Road) or other company-owned premises.

With full compensation received, and the fate of the Temple Street site now settled, the directors of the company could now focus on the direction of the company going forward, both financially and also concerning the location of the store. The Chairman advised shareholders that 'certain negotiations and discussions are even now taking place; it would not be appropriate for me at this stage to prejudice the discussions by giving any further information'. Shareholders emphasised that the store should stay at Walter Road.

Year 57	Feb 1951- Jan 1952	Net Profit £15,415	Net Profit £406,853 (2024)

The company faced significant challenges throughout 1951, operating under tough conditions, and witnessing a combination of a continual rise in operating expenses and a drop in sales, without an increase in profit margins.

Plans were initially submitted to the Swansea Council for significant additions across the Walter Road freehold site, however, after a prolonged delay, these plans were not approved. New plans were developed that included the remodelling of the rear portion of existing shop buildings at Nos. 23, 24 and 25 Walter Road, plus the ground, first floors and restaurant of No. 22 Walter Road, positioned on the first floor. The revised plans were approved by the Swansea Council, and planning consent was obtained. An estimated cost of £20,000 was agreed to complete the work, which included the installation of a 'modern lift'.

Subsequently, a building licence was applied for to carry out these alterations and additions, but at the time of the AGM in May 1952, the company had not been successful in obtaining such a licence from the Cardiff-based authorities. In the meeting, the Chairman expressed his frustration as to what he said was 'a very trying year' and said he was hopeful that national conditions would soon improve, allowing the company to proceed with the improvement work.

Despite the restrictive economic environment, in August 1952, the company acquired the freehold premises of No. 17 Walter Road, and after completing the necessary alterations on the ground and first floors, the furniture and carpet departments, which had been operating under challenging conditions at St. Mary's Square since the Blitz, were relocated to the new location, which was opened for business in early December.

In January 1953, the company was finally granted a licence by the Ministry of Works to proceed with the additions and alterations at the rear portion of the existing shop buildings of Nos. 22, 23, 24, and 25 Walter Road.

Year 58	Feb 1952- Jan 1953	Net Profit £9,883	Net Profit £239,229 (2024)

At the time of the 58th AGM held in June 1953, construction was underway with an expected completion by the end of October. Shareholders were informed that business conditions remained tough throughout 1952 and that the company was 'trading under great difficulties and conditions', its sales figures and profit margins down on the previous year.

The additions and alterations to the company's Walter Road properties were duly completed and on 12th April 1954, the fully furnished and outfitted two floors of the new extensions, a new and larger restaurant with brand-new furniture and fittings, including the installation of a first-class lift to the second floor, were inaugurated. The extensive work involved in these extensions and alterations disrupted business operations throughout the year, but the increased display and selling space and new amenities transformed the store.

Year	Feb 1953- Jan 1954	Net Profit	Net Profit
59		£1,494	£35,015 (2024)

The tone of the June 1954 AGM echoed the same negative aspects of the previous year's meeting, in that economic conditions were unchanged, and trading conditions remained 'difficult'. Sales figures were down yet again, whilst stock levels had increased substantially, likely due to a combination of slower sales and additional stock needed for the new extensions.

The £20,000 owed to the company by the Board of Trade as compensation for losses incurred due to enemy action on fixtures and fittings was finally received and added to the company's capital reserves, plus an additional amount of £6,371 that covered the accrued gross interest on the compensation payment received, added directly to the company's Profit & Loss account (£20,000 + £6,371 = £26,371, equivalent to £620,833 in 2024).

In response to Chairman David Williams' report and the company accounts, some shareholders, led by Mr Julian Hodge, advised that they were not happy with another year of poor returns, made accusations of mismanagement against three directors in particular suggesting they be removed, and strongly objected to the intended direction of the business being taken by the board of directors.

Within a week of the AGM, the following notice appeared in the Western Mail (77) on Wednesday, 23rd June, addressed to Ben Evans and Company shareholders and posted by 'Mr Julian Hodge of Windsor Place, Cardiff':

'The profit of £1494 on trading to January 31st, 1954, is very small in relation to the total capital employed in the business The trend of trading profit over the past few years has been downward. And I think there is little doubt that that is attributable to the fact that the centre of Swansea is being rapidly rebuilt and the trade is being drawn off more and more from Walter Road to the new shopping centre as building in the centre progresses further.

In these circumstances, no shareholder can view with equanimity the prospect of ultimately the whole of the investments of the company, which were valued at no less than £105,000 on January 31. 1954. Will be used for the development of the premises at Walter Road. I think that any prospect of expanding trade at rho present premises is doomed to failure. And that the result of the company over the past few years. Coupled with the extensive re-development of the town centre, cannot possibly justify the expenditure of further sums of money on the existing premises.

At the AGM of the company held in Swansea on Thursday, June 17, 1954, the Chairman stated that it was the intention of the Board ultimately to spend the whole of the company's investments on developing the property at Walter Road. In my view, the shareholders of the company should take immediate action to say that no part of the company's resources are needed at any time in the future upon such development. I am therefore wilting your support for the requisitioning to the directors of an extraordinary general meeting of the company with a view in appointing a shareholders' committee of inspection which will make recommendations at a later meeting of the members as to the future of this company.'

Over the following months, Mr Hodge issued several follow-up circulars requesting an extraordinary meeting to be called.

David Williams, who had been Chairman of the company for ten years, resigned his position in August but remained on the board, Mr E. Rhodri

Harris became Chairman, and on Friday 1st October 1954, the new chairman issued a response on behalf of the Ben Evans board pointing out that whilst there were several inaccuracies in Mr Hodge's utterances, he had also made several unsuccessful bids to buy the company on behalf of a third party, not mentioned in his circulars.

The response further noted that rather than request an extraordinary general meeting, Mr Hodge had privately requested an interview with the Chairman of the company, during which he inquired whether the directors would entertain an offer to purchase their shares. He was informed that the directors would be open to considering any offer, on the condition that the same offer was extended to all shareholders. Additionally, he inquired whether such an offer, if deemed insufficient by the directors, would be treated as confidential. He was assured that it would be handled as such. Subsequently, Mr Hodge presented an offer on behalf of an undisclosed principal, which was ultimately declined.

A further offer was made by Mr Hodge; with a condition that it must be accepted by at least 90% of the shareholders. However, as the directors themselves collectively held more than 10% of the shares, this condition could not be met, and the offer was once again unanimously rejected by the board of directors.

The meeting concluded, and whilst the board were not legally obliged to disclose the rejected offer to the shareholders, taking into account the value of the company's assets, they decided that the shareholders of 'a longstanding and reputable company like Ben Evans' have a right to be informed about potential buyers of their shares and who may potentially gain control of their company.

The Board unanimously agreed that Mr Hodge's latest offer fell short of their expectations, and advised all other shareholders to refrain from accepting it too. It was later made apparent to the board that the 'third party' interested in Ben Evans was 'Gwent and West of England Enterprises', and that Julian Hodge, was the interested party's Managing Director.

'Mr Hodge has tried in his letters to paint a picture to you of the insecurity of your investment, the dissipation by the directors of the assets and the poor trading figures of last year, but notwithstanding which he has clients who have sufficient confidence in the future of 'Bens' to endeavour to secure control of the company.

One reason why they want to acquire control could be that they see an immediate profit. The latest offer means that the purchasers will pay to you a purchase price of £172,700 In exchange for assets worth approximately £238,000 as shown in the last balance sheet.'

'Whilst it is the ease that the net profits for last year were disappointing it must be appreciated that the trading conditions were difficult owing to partial rebuilding and structural alterations being earned out. Since the end of the last financial year. However, turnover has shown and is showing a satisfactory increase. '

Concluding their public response, the board stated that the company had now acquired possession of the company's property at No. 26, Walter Road, Swansea, which was currently being integrated into their store, and on completion would further enhance the development of the business. With this expansion, the Board believed it would be timely to consider reorganising the management and financial resources of the company.

While acknowledging the company had faced challenges in the past, the response stated that the current financial position was robust, the outlook for the business was promising and that on completion of the works on No. 26 Walter Road, the board would take into account various factors including the geographical location of the business, the anticipated growth of Swansea, the potential return of capital not currently utilised, and most importantly, the best interests of the shareholders.

Julian Hodge was persistent, and issued another circular to the press within days (78), this time in the name of 'Gwent and West of England Enterprises', which stated:

To the Shareholders of Ben Evans & Co. Ltd.

Gwent and West of England Enterprises Ltd wish to announce that in pursuance of the power given to them in the Offer dated the 20th day of September 1954 to purchase the entire Issued Share Capital of Ben Evans & Co. Ltd., the date for receipt of Acceptance has been extended to the 30th November 1954.

The terms of the Offer are otherwise unaltered and are in accordance with the copy Agreement already passed to all Shareholders. Additional copies of the Form of Acceptance may be obtained on request from Gwent and West of England Enterprises Ltd., 31, Windsor Place, Cardiff.

S. E. TAYLOR, Secretary,
GWENT and WEST OF ENGLAND ENTERPRISES LTD.
21st October 1954

Despite the Board's advice to shareholders to refrain from accepting offers for their holdings, several shareholders decided to sell to 'Gwent and West', and on 24th December a follow-up circular was printed in the Western Mail, (79) maintaining Julian Hodge's aggressive stance:

To the Shareholders of Ben Evans & Company Ltd.:

Gwent and West of England Enterprises Ltd. Are pleased to announce that following the offer made on behalf of clients for the purchase of the entire Issued Share Capital of Ben Evans & Co. Ltd., they have received a number of Acceptances for the Ordinary and both classes of Preference Shares.

The prices offered were as follows:-
18/- for each 16/- Ordinary Share.
£1 for each First Preference Share.
15/- for each 2/- Second Preference Share.

Accordingly, the right reserved to accept this number of Shares has been exercised. The Offer has therefore become unconditional and transfers for execution will now be forwarded to those Shareholders who have so far accepted.

In the meantime, it has been decided to keep the offer open until further notice so as to give those Shareholders who have not yet accepted the offer a further opportunity of doing so.

Julian S. Hodge, Managing Director,
GWENT AND WEST OF ENGLAND ENTERPRISES LTD.
23rd December, 1954.

While hostile bids continued, possession of No. 26 Walter Road was acquired, a property that the company had bought four years prior, and the premises were merged with the main premises with minimal financial investment.

As a result of this expansion, the store's Furniture Department was relocated from No. 17 Walter Road to No. 26, thereby freeing up the entirety of No. 17 to be utilised exclusively by the Carpet and Linoleum Department.

The pressure on the Ben Evans board continued, but on 31st January 1955, the last day of the company's fiscal year, it was reported that they had once again rejected a bid from Julian Hodge's company.

The future of Ben Evans was the subject of much speculation throughout the early months of the year; the board feared a further aggressive approach from Julian Hodge's company but was also aware of interest from other parties and in particular Great Universal Stores.

Great Universal Stores was founded in Manchester in 1900 by the Rose brothers. By 1930, it was Britain's leading mail order company, and after the company's name was changed to Great Universal Stores Ltd in 1931, it went public.

In the same year, Isaac Wolfson joined the company as merchandise controller. Wolfson's contribution, initially voluntary in exchange for share options, proved pivotal despite the company's lacklustre stock market performance, and after leveraging funds from his father-in-law, Wolfson acquired a significant stake in the company, becoming joint Managing Director alongside George Rose in 1932.

In 1933 the company had made a loss of £55,000, but following Rose's resignation, Wolfson assumed sole leadership and his reorganisation of the company turned the 1933 loss into a profit of £330,000 the following year. In the twenty years that followed, in addition to consolidating and growing the company's mail-order catalogue interests, Mr Wolfson's business model involved buying up drapery and furniture store chains, clothing and department stores.

In 1955 his company was valued at £80,000,000, and in March that year, it was reported that Great Universal Stores were negotiating to buy Charles Baker & Co., an outfitter chain based in London with 15 stores, as well as the Belfast stores of Robertson Ledlie Ferguson & Company.

In June, an offer had been made to purchase Waring & Gillow, the famous Oxford Street, London, furnishers, and it was rumoured that Mr Wolfson eyed the Ben Evans store in Swansea as an appropriate addition to his business portfolio.

Year 60	Feb 1954- Jan 1955	Net Profit £3909	Net Profit £89,773 (2024)

Ben Evans & Co's 60th AGM was held in July 1955, and after another difficult trading year, a rise in expenses indicated a continuing negative trend. Although both cash and credit sales had seen an improvement when compared to the previous year, Chairman E. Rhodri Harris acknowledged that the results were 'unsatisfactory'.

Despite this, the net profit from trading totaled £3,909, surpassing the figures from the previous year. Additionally, inventory on hand was £45,400, which was a decrease of £1,900 compared to the inventory levels of the prior year. However, the company's current liabilities were £14,004. Although the Board considered this acceptable, although it was over four times the company's net profit.

'Ben Evans' had not performed well for several years but was now both cash and asset-rich. In addition to the total of £227,281 received in war-related payments over the previous two years, the company held Investments of £106,720 (made up of over £92,000 in Government Stocks plus others), whilst Current Assets of £87,459 were made up of over £50,000 worth of freehold property (17, 22, 23, 24 and 25 Walter Road) plus fixtures & fittings that included a 'modern lift.'

Openly angered by the pressure put on the business by Julian Hodge, the company's directors were primarily focused on thwarting 'Gwent and West's' persistent efforts, and decided that a capital reorganisation would make the company less attractive to prospective buyers, hostile or otherwise, and recommended that shareholders approve the proposal, reasoning that a portion of the company's substantial cash reserve should be distributed to its rightful owners, the shareholders.

The capital repayment scheme put forward by the directors to the shareholders proposed to:

'Write down each class of share by 37 ½%, which will mean that Ordinary holders will receive a cash payment of 6 shillings for each 16 shilling share, First Preference holders 7 shillings 6d for each £1 share and Second Preference holders 9d for each 2d share. All this will cost the company £53,503, but the directors consider capital resources will still be sufficient for all normal trading purposes, and future development will not be handicapped by any lack of resources. This capital return was foreshadowed by the Chairman last December when the board advised rejection of the offer from Gwent and West of England Enterprises.'

However, despite the board's recommendation, the capital reorganization proposal was roundly rejected by the company's shareholders, and on 28th July, Great Universal Stores made an offer for Ben Evans & Co. Ltd.

As reported in the press: (80)

An offer to purchase the whole of the share capital of Ben Evans and Co., Ltd. the Swansea drapers, has been made by Mr Wolfson's Great Universal Stores. The offer, which is conditional, is:

20s per share for the 20.000 six per cent shares, Cumulative Preference shares of £1 each, fully paid;

16s per share for the 24,000 non- Cumulative Second Preference shares of 2s each, fully paid:

2ls per share for the 167.000 Ordinary shares of 16s each, fully paid.

Ben Evans' directors made it clear that, from a personal perspective, they intended to accept the offer concerning their holdings, and in a letter dispatched to shareholders with further details, advised the company's other shareholders to follow suit.

The offer received was contingent upon being accepted by 22nd September 1955, and by a majority of not less than three-quarters of the holders (excluding the purchaser and its nominees) of each class of shareholding, comprising at least 90 per cent of the shares of each class not already held by the purchaser. Furthermore, if required to do so, the directors will resign from their positions without receiving any compensation for loss of office or any other payment from the purchaser.

On Friday the 29th of July 1955, the South Wales Evening Post reported 'Sale of Ben Evans to Great Universal' (81)

In October of that year, Great Universal Stores Ltd. boasted of 'Another Record Year', their circular showing a Net Profit of nearly £8 million. There was no mention of the companies they had bought and integrated into their own in the same trading period. (82)

A few months later, on Monday 30th January 1956, in a Western Mail article entitled 'The Year on the Stock Exchange,' (83) the passing of 90 years of business as Swansea's most famous retail company was summed up in one short and uninspiring line of text:

'The Swansea store of Ben Evans and Company Ltd. went over to Great Universal Stores Ltd.'

The store continued to function under the Ben Evans name, and in 1957 a new outlet opened at 105 Station Road in Port Talbot.

'Ben's' operated until approximately 1959, when the 'Ben Evans' name ultimately disappeared from Swansea's retail landscape, and there are no advertisements or telephone listings from that date.

15 - The Demise of Ben Evans & Co. Ltd

Under Mr Ben Evans' leadership, the store's success mirrored his entrepreneurial spirit during the rapid evolution of retail in Victorian Britain, securing its place in Swansea's history. After its incorporation in 1895, the business flourished under the leadership of Richard White and subsequently Meredith Thomas, both of whom had previously served as capable deputies to Ben Evans. The company's success was further enhanced by Swansea's status as a major industrial port in Britain.

After the death of Meredith Thomas in 1912, the board brought in Richard Lewis, a man experienced in the 'modern retail methods' used in London stores, initially as General Manager and by 1914, as Managing Director. Richard Lewis carried on where his predecessors had left off and, despite nationwide hardships, Ben Evans & Co. Ltd. performed well through the Great War (1914-1918), with year-on-year record profits.

Whilst many local retailers had limited or no stock, or else found it difficult to restock products, Ben Evans carried a huge and wide-ranging product inventory and was able to cater for its customers throughout the conflict. Its reputation amongst suppliers meant that its restock orders were promptly dealt with. However, following a brief post-war boom, the 1920s brought a prolonged economic recession, that abruptly halted over 50 years of continuous growth since the business's 1866 inception.

South Wales industries, particularly coal, tin, and steel declined, leading to deflation, wage stagnation, high unemployment, and social unrest. Money was tight, and people prioritised necessities like food and clothing over luxury purchases. The rise of mail-order companies and co-operatives, as well as the appearance of multiple stores on the High Streets across Britain, meant that by the decade's end, companies like Ben Evans operated in a retail landscape that was vastly different from its pre-war heyday.

The company's performance had plateaued throughout the early 1920s, but from the mid-1920s it saw a serious change in fortunes, that prompted the board of directors to scrutinise operations.

Richard Lewis's initial achievements and the confidence placed in him by the company likely contributed to his apparent autonomy in managing local operations. The geographical separation between Lewis and the board of directors may have further exacerbated this and allowed him to establish an unhealthy degree of independent control. The company's declining performance ultimately altered this arrangement.

In 1930, outside expertise was brought in to carry out a comprehensive assessment of the situation, and the recommendations made were swiftly implemented, resulting in the huge loss reported in early 1931. The store's vast stock levels, the very thing that carried the company through its glory years, was the same thing that caused the write-offs and financial adjustments needed to stabilise the company.

Britain's High Streets were full of new stores offering new products and services to a completely different type of customer, yet it appears that neither the company's local management nor its board of directors had the knowledge or the awareness that the retail world of the late-Victorian and early-Edwardian days had long disappeared and that companies like Ben Evans needed to continually evolve just to survive, let alone prosper, in the new retail world.

Resigning from his position, Richard Lewis remained the largest shareholder of the company, and within months he had managed to get himself elected to the company's board of directors. In the same meeting, the Chairman of the Board stood down.

With Richard Lewis now on the board, and his son Phillip appointed the General Manager the 1930s saw minimal growth, with the business neither proactive nor reactive to the ever-evolving retail environment. While funds were allocated to maintain and modernise the once-grand establishment, shareholders endured a second consecutive decade of underwhelming performance. Richard Lewis became Chairman in 1937 and held the position until his death a year later. After a few years without a Managing Director, David Abel was put in place in 1934, and he managed to steady what was essentially 'a sinking ship' until he died in 1940.

The February 1941 Blitz was devastating to Swansea, yet paradoxically, the destruction of the Ben Evans store presented its owners with an unexpected opportunity for financial recovery.

The company's financial performance had been lacklustre for two decades and in reality, shareholder returns had been provided through a combination of lower prices and various cost-control measures, rather than through genuine growth.

When viewed taking the effects of inflation in mind, annual profits made through the decades were drastically lower in real terms than those made in the pre-Great War 'glory days'.

The following example shows a comparison using the company's actual net profit figures adjusted for inflation (see also (g) and (h) in Appendices).

Date	Annual Net Profit	Annual Net Profit (adjusted 2024)
1895	£15,490	£1,701,524
1910	£14,967	£1,473,702
1927	£14,155	£742,887
1951	£15,415	£406,853

The lack of a coordinated and decisive approach between municipal and national authorities concerning Swansea's town centre rebuilding frustrated traders and townspeople alike, and it would take until 1948 for work on the first new town centre roads to commence (see (k) in Appendices).

Like other displaced traders, Ben Evans & Co. Ltd was compelled to secure or lease alternative locations to sustain their operations. Though initially considered a short-term solution, the move to Walter Road proved vital for the company's continued existence.

The company's directors expressed both privately and publicly their aspiration to eventually re-establish the business at its original location, as the company owned over 90% of the building in which the store once traded. However, the Blitz's devastation extended far beyond the bricks and mortar and encompassed significant losses in inventory, furnishings, equipment, fixtures and fittings.

A significant concern for displaced Swansea traders was the rumoured rateable values proposed by the Council for plots in the 'new' town centre. Sidney Heath Ladies Outfitters, originally at 7 and 8 College Street, Swansea, had also taken temporary accommodation on Walter Road but had decided to build a new store on a rebuilt Caer Street, while David Evans & Co. had decided to rebuild on their original site.

With a pre-Blitz rateable value of £2,333, an internal David Evans document from December 1955, held in the West Glamorgan Archives, states: (84) (see (j) in Appendices)

'Assuming the old Assessment to be £2,333, then the proposed new assessment of £13,000 shows an increase of 457% (that is 5.57 times the old Assessment).'

Applying the assessment mathematics used for the David Evans store to Ben Evans' 1939 payment, the 'new' rateable value would have been £22,280 per annum should the company have chosen to rebuild on their original plot. The pre-Blitz rateable value of the Ben Evans store was £4,000 per annum, with the company's directors stating they would not agree to a post-war payment exceeding £7,500 per annum.

Over the next ten years, the company attempted to maintain its status as Swansea's premier store by acquiring and developing several adjacent Walter Road properties, and by the end of the decade, the move to Walter Road was considered permanent.

After the company received compensation, including insurance payouts, war damage settlements, interest on payments, and eventually compulsory purchase compensation from the Council for the 'Temple Street freehold site', total compensation received by Ben Evans & Co. Ltd amounted to £227,281 (equivalent to £5,947,269 in June 2024), It also held investments of £106,720 (£2,512,430 in 2024), as well as over £50,000 (£1,177,113 in 2024) worth of freehold property on Walter Road.

It is good business practice for a company to invest in developing its facilities rather than keeping an unnecessarily high cash reserve, but even after factoring in the estimated costs of upgrading and maintaining the Walter Road store, after years of diminishing returns, the company faced a bleak future.

The company's brand value had significantly decreased since relinquishing its central town location, and Ben Evans & Co. Ltd was perceived as an underperforming company with strong assets, low debt, and substantial cash reserves, making it an attractive target for acquisition.

The board of directors had not anticipated this situation and had to deal with several hostile approaches to buy the company. Despite assurances to the contrary, the subsequent capital repayment scheme proposal put forward by the board appeared to have been instigated rapidly and under duress, rather than something that had been carefully planned, and shareholders swiftly rejected the proposal.

Within weeks, a new and successful offer was made to purchase Ben Evans & Co. Ltd, and like many other stores of its kind, it was absorbed by Isaac Wolfson's Great Universal Stores Ltd, a company known as the 'Glorious Gussies' by Britain's stockbrokers due to the significant volume of business it generated annually through acquisitions and sales.

In the late 1930s, Wolfson focused on acquiring companies with large hire purchase debts and property assets. Two of his earliest purchases were London House in Newport, originally owned and managed by Benjamin Evans Snr (see chapter 3 of this book) and 'Leslie's' in Cardiff, which subsequently began trading in Swansea at 37-38 High Street, previously the home of Great Universal Stores' local business.

Ben Evans & Co. Ltd traded for a few more years after its acquisition, with the Walter Road business finally closing around 1959. The Leslie's store on High Street, Swansea, continued to trade until the early 1970s.

By the early 1960s, the drapery businesses and department stores era was beginning to wane. Great Universal Stores Ltd set about selling, closing down, or repurposing many of the stores it had acquired over the previous 25 years. Nevertheless, by 1966, they owned 2,750 retail stores, mail order, and manufacturing concerns, with assets of over £197 million and trading profits of £32.25 million.

In 1866, the same year Ben Evans opened his store at 2 & 3 Temple Street, Lewis Lewis established his emporium on Swansea's High Street which continued to operate until it finally closed its doors in 1973. The David Evans store, which opened in 1900, remained in business until its final closure on the 15th of January, 2005.

REFERENCES

1. England, Bank of. Inflation Calculator. *Bank of England.* [Online] July 2024.https://www.bankofengland.co.uk/monetary-policy/inflation/inflation-calculator.

2. Wales, National Library of. NLW Online Newspapers. [Online] 2024. https://newspapers.library.wales.

3. Archives, British Newspaper. [Online] https://www.britishnewspaperarchive.co.uk .

4. Nixon, John. drawing 1923,0714.5. *British Museum.* [Online] https://www.britishmuseum.org/collection/object/P_1923-0714-5.

5. Gabb, Gerald. *Swansea and its History.* Swansea : Gerald Gabb , 2019. p. 1202.

6. Steinbach, Susie L. *Understanding the Victorians: Politics, Culture and Society in Nineteenth Century Britain.* s.l. : Routledge, 2012. p. 7.

7. Hosgood, Christopher P. *'Mercantile Monastries': Shops, Shop Assitants, and Shop Life in Late Victorian and Edwardian Britain.* 1999.

8. Hundred, The Elmbridge. The Elmbridge Hundred - William Whiteley. *The Elmbridge Hundred.* [Online] https://people.elmbridgehundred.org.uk/biographies/william-whiteley/.

9. Clunn, Harold P. *London Marches On.* s.l. : Caen Press, 1947. p. 191.

10. Ben Evans Snr Announcement. *Carmarthen Weekly Reporter.* 9 May 1913.

11. Partnership Dissolved. *Bankrupcy Gazette.* 7 July 1863.

12. The Fire in Temple St, Conclusion of the Inquest. *Swansea and Glamorgan Herald.* 19 May 1866.

13. Damaged by Fire and Water. *Swansea and Glamorgan Herald.* 16 May 1866.

14. The Gold Finders. *Swansea and Glamorgan Herald.* 25 May 1866.

15. Ben Evans Thank You to Patrons. *The Cambrian.* 31 January 1879.

16. Messrs B. Evans and Cos New Premises. *Western Mail.* 8 September 1886.

17. Business Enterprise at Swansea. *South Wales Daily News.* 4 September 1886.

18. Opening of Messrs B. Evans and Co.s New Premisies. *Swansea and Glamorgan Herald.* 1886.

19. Sutherst, Thomas. Shop Hours. [book auth.] T. Sutherst. *Death and Desease Behind the Counter.* 1894.

20. Parliament. Working Hours for Children. *apl.parliament.uk.* [Online] 1886. https://api.parliament.uk/historic-hansard/commons/1892/feb/24/shop-hours-bill-no-26.

21. Richardson, Dr Benjamin Ward. Female Health. [book auth.] S. Webb & H. Cox. *The Eight Hour Day.* 1886.

22. Tait, Lawson. Women's Health. [book auth.] S. Webb & H. Cox. *The Eight Hour Day.* 1886.

23. Shorter Hours Movement Meeting. *Swansea and Glamorgan Herald.* 25 August 1886.

24. South Wales Notes, Early Closing at Swansea. *South Wales Daily News.* 7 October 1886.

25. HoW. Early Closing at Swansea, Action by Local Tradesman. *Swansea and Glamorgan Herald.* 10 September 1890.

26. Clare, Peter. The Cambrian. *B. Evans and Cos. Model Stables.* 12 September 1890.

27. A Walk Through... *The Cambrian.* 28 November 1890.

28. B. Evans Refurbishment. *South Wales Daaily News.* 28 November 1890.

29. The Widening of Castle Bailey St. *The Cambrian.* 17 February 1893.

30. An agrrement arrived... *The Cambrian.* 29 September 1893.

31. Newsletter, YMCA. *Ben Evans Rugby XV.* Swansea Museum. Swansea : s.n., 1894.

32. Sudden Death of Lord Swansea. *The Cambrian.* 30 November 1894.

33. New Castle Bailey St Building. *The South Wales Daily Post.* 24 November 1894.

34. Swansea Town Improvement. *The Cambrian.* 24 November 1894.

35. Illness of Mr B. Evans. *The Cambrian.* 31 July 1891.

36. Ben Evans and Co. Ltd offered. *The Sketch.* 13 February 1895.

37. Another Public Company. *Llanelli Mercury.* 14 March 1895.

38. Convertion into Joint Stock Company. *Western Mail.* 13 February 1895.

39. The Floating of B. Evans & Co. *The South Wales Daily Post.* 15 February 1895.

40. Largly Oversubscribed. *Star of Gwent.* March 1895.

41. Public Subscriptions. *The Sketch.* 20 February 1895.

42. Following BE. *South Wales Daily Post.* 23 February 1895.

43. Ben Evans & Co. Ltd - First AGM. *South Wales Weekly Argus and Monmouthshire.* 6 July 1895.

44. Electric Light at Messrs Ben Evans and Co... *The Cambrian.* 11 January 1895.

45. Balchin, WGV. *Swansea and its Region.* s.l. : University College of Swansea, 1971. p. 322.

46. New Heating Ssystem. *The Cambrian.* 27 March 1896.

47. Grand Opening of Ben Evans & Co's New Premises. *The Cambrian.* 6 May 1898.

48. Ben Evans & Co..s New Premises. *South Wales daily Post.* 7 May 1898.

49. Notes, YMCA. *May Committee Notes.* 1902.

50. Ben Evans Big Mourning Order. *The Cambrian.* 23 July 1909.

51. Shooting at Ben Evans. *The Cambrian.* 29 April 1910.

52. Miss Dillwyn and the Dressmakers. *The Cambrian Daily Leader.* 13 March 1911.

53. Keir Hardie at Swansea. *The Cambrian Daily Leader.* 10 Aprill 1911.

54. Horace George Raynor. *Black Kalendar.* [Online] http://www.blackkalendar.nl/c/2866/Horace%20George%20Rayner.

55. Death of Ben Evans J.P. *The Carmarthen Journal.* 9 May 1913.

56. Ben Evans J.P. *Cambria Daily Leader.* 5 May 1913.

57. Will of Ben Evans. *The Carmarthen weekly Reporter.* 22 August 1913.

58. Lewis, Bernard. *Swansea in The Great War.* s.l. : Pen & Sword Military, 2014.

59. O'Rourke, R. Findlay and K. *Power and Plenty.* s.l. : Princeton University Press, 2007. p. 407.

60. Moore, W. Walford. Swansea's Famous Stores. *Western Mail.* 30 Septeeber 1927.

61. Bath and Wst of England Show. *Western Mail.* 18 May 1923.

62. Heath, J.R., Borough Engibber. *Notes Relating to the County Bourogh of Swansea prepared for the Mimstry of Town and Country Planning.* County Borough of Swansea. s.l. : West Glamorgan Archive Services, 1943.

63. Swansea and District Traders Mass Meeting. *Western mail.* 26 June 1934.

64. Custom Campaign - Alarm at Co-Operative Societies' Programme. *Western Morning News* . 29 May 1935.

65. Rhyl Inependent Traders Association. *Welsh Gazette.* December 1937.

66. Morgan, Ernest. *The Development of the Town Hill Estate, Swansea.* Swansea : s.n., 1931.

67. Ben Evans Report: Copany's First Loss. *Western Mail.* 28 May 1931.

68. Johnson, H.T. Lean Dilemmas. *Lean Accounting: a living systems approach to lean management and learning.* 2006.

69. Killed By Train. *The Strait Times.* 3 October 1931.

70. Wslshman Believed Victim of Nile Tragedy. *Western Mail.* 20 Ocober 1933.

71. Shot Swansea Caapatin, Vengeance Threat. *Western Mail.* 8 November 1933.

72. "Coup" for Swansea. *Porthcawl Guardian.* 13 October 1933.

73. Wales Wages Bill Increase. *Investors Chronicle.* 27 March 1937.

74. Report on Inquiry Proceedings. *South Wales Evening Post.* 7 August 1946.

75. Directors, BE Board of. *Town Planning of Swansea and Redevelopment of its Shopping Centre.* West Gamorgan Arcihves . 1944. p. 10, GB 216 D 268/5.

76. 'Five-Point Plan'. *South Wales Evening Post.* August 1946.

77. Julian Hodge Notice. *Western Mail.* 23 June 1953.

78. Annoucement to the Shareholders of Ben Evans & Co. Ltd. *Western Mail.* 22 October 1954.

79. Announcement. *Western Mail.* 24 December 1954.

80. Bid for Swansea Draper. *Western Mail.* 29 January 1955.

81. 'Sale of Ben Evans to Great Universal'. *South Wales Evening Post.* 29 July 1954.

82. Great Universal Stores Record Year. *Western Mail.* October 1955.

83. Great Universal Stores Ben Evans went over. *Westerb Mail.* 30 January 1956.

84. note, David Evans internal. WGA website. [Online] December 1955.

86. England, Bank of. Bank of England Inflation Caalculator. [Online] 2024. https://www.bankofengland.co.uk/monetary-policy/inflation/inflation-calculator.

APPENDICES

a) Ben Evans - Chairmen and Managing Directors

b) Ben Evans Advertising

c) Ben Evans Ordinary Share Certificate 1937

d) Ben Evans & Co. Ltd - Report and Balance Sheet, 27th February 1896

e) Balance Sheet Comparison 1929 and 1930

f) Balance Sheet Comparison 1931 and 1932

g) Ben Evans & Co. Ltd Net Profit 1895-1954 (adjusted for inflation June 2024)

h) Ben Evans & Co. Ltd Net Profit 1895-1954 inclusive (figures used based on ?? 2024 conversion rates)

i) Ben Evans & Co. Ltd Directors letter to the Mayor, Aldermen and Councillors of the County Borough of Swansea, February 1944 (D 268/5 in West Glamorgan Archives)

j) David Evans internal Document Relating to the old David Evans Store, December 1955 (D/D DEC/1/2 in West Glamorgan Archives

k) 'Redevelopment of Central Town Area, 31st December 1959 - Internal Council Document (DD/RMD 1/66/8 in West Glamorgan Archives)

(a) Ben Evans - Chairmen and Managing Directors

CHAIRMEN

Ben Evans (owner)	June 1866 - July 1895
Sir Joseph Renals	July 1895 - November 1907
James Jackson DL JP	November 1907 - April 1923
Walter J. Burt	April 1923 - June 1931
Sir Percy Molyneux	June 1931 - November 1937
Richard Lewis	November 1937 - November 1938
Edward Harris	November 1938 - August 1945
David Williams	August 1945 - August 1954
E. Rhodri Harris	October 1954 until sale of company

MANAGING DIRECTORS

Richard White	July 1895 - August 1907
Meredith Thomas	September 1907 - February 1912
Richard Lewis	July 1912 (as GM) then MD from September 1914 - January 1931
David Abel	February 1934 - July 1940
George Wheatley	July 1940 - March 1950

(b) Ben Evans - Advertising

Known over the years as 'B. Evans & Co.', 'Ben Evans & Co.', 'Ben Evans & Co. Ltd', 'Ben Evans', or simply just 'Ben's', from its earliest days, the Ben Evans store embraced newspaper advertising as a cornerstone of its marketing strategy. The company consistently promoted its offerings in local publications while also leveraging regional press to keep its customer base across South Wales and beyond informed of the latest deals. In Swansea, the Mumbles Train and the town's tram service were frequently adorned with eye-catching advertisements for the Ben Evans store.

The company became known for its elaborate fashion shows, often used to unveil a new product range or department. Seasonal sales, which could last for weeks, evolved into eagerly anticipated events on Swansea's shopping calendar. Benjamin Evans' engagement with various charitable causes served a dual purpose: it provided financial support to worthy initiatives while simultaneously enhancing the company's public image.

This multifaceted approach to advertising, which included print media, public transport, fashion events, and philanthropic activities, continued even after the company's incorporation. The strategy not only promoted specific products but also solidified Ben Evans' reputation as a pillar of Swansea's retail landscape. 'Ben's' maintained this comprehensive marketing approach throughout its history, ensuring its prominence in the local and regional retail scene.

For many years regarded as 'the finest store in Wales and the West of England', by 1900 it had 26 departments, in 1920 it boasted 35 departments, and by 1940 it had 42 departments over its five floors, but did not use the term 'department store' in its advertising until the 1930s, instead officially describing itself as a 'General Drapers and Complete Home Furnishers'.

Over the decades, Ben Evans was the self-proclaimed 'Premier Fashion and Furnishing House of Wales and the West', 'The South Wales Shopping Centre' and by 1933 'The Shopping Centre of Wales'; however, in the years following the Blitz the company's directors, perhaps aware of the stores diminishing relevance, was content to use the terms 'Swansea's Premier Store' and even 'Swansea's Finest Gift Shop.'

(From author's collection)

B. EVANS & COMPANY,
SWANSEA.

(From author's collection)

BEN EVANS

& Co., Ltd.,

"The House for Quality,"

SWANSEA.

THE HOUSE OF
BEN. EVANS & Co.
SWANSEA.
THE HOUSE WITH OVER 80 YEARS' TRADING REPUTATION.

BEN EVANS & Co. Ltd.
SWANSEA'S PREMIER STORE

BEN EVANS

SWANSEA'S FINEST
GIFT SHOP.

FIVE FLOORS &
"EVERY FLOOR
A GIFT FLOOR"!

BEN EVANS & CO., LTD., SWANSEA

With the kind permission of **Brian (MCN Studios)**

BEN EVANS & Company Ltd.
17, 22, 23, 24, 25 & 26, WALTER ROAD, SWANSEA   Telephone 56191

(c) Ben Evans Ordinary Share Certificate 1937

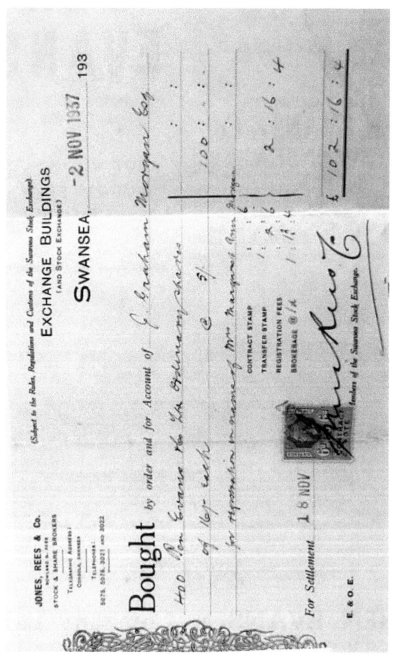

With the kind permission of Steve Maddock

(d) Ben Evans & Co. Ltd - Report and Balance Sheet, 27th February 1896

The following report and balance sheet were taken as read:

The Directors beg to submit to the shareholders their first annual report, profit and loss account, and balance sheet. The accounts cover the period from January 1st, 1895 (the date at which the business was taken over as a going concern), to February 27tb, 1896, viz., 11 months.

During this time the trading profit made has been £15,359 12s. 5d., from which has to be deducted interest on debentures and other fixed charges, leaving a balance of £8,251 5s. 4d. Of this sum, £1,22. 16s, 6d. has been written off the item of 'Formation Expenses, leaving £7,025. 8s. 10d. available for dividend.

The directors recommend that a dividend at the rate of 7 per cent. Per annum be paid on the ordinary shares for the period commencing March 1st, 1855 (the date on which the capital of the company was subscribed), and ending February 27th 1896, less the interim dividend paid on the 7th October 1895.

The buildings, fixtures and fittings have been maintained in a state of good repair out of revenue. Notwithstanding the great depression of trade in the staple industries of the district viz., the coal and tin-plate trades), the directors are able to report that the sales have been in excess of any previous year. The retiring director (Mr James Jackson), being eligible, offers himself for re-election.

The shareholders will be asked to confirm the appointment of Messrs Percy Mason and Co., chartered accountants, as auditors of the company, and to fix their remuneration.

BALANCE SHEET - 27TH FEBRUARY, 1896	£ s d	£ s d
Capital -		
100,000 Ordinary Shares of £1 each, fully paid	100,000 0 0	
3,000 Founders Shares of £1 each, fully paid	3,000 0 0	
		103,000 0 0
Debenture Stock		75,000 0 0
Do. Two months interest		625 6 0
Premium on Issue of Debentures		3,750 0 0
Sundry Creditors		9,183 0 0
Profit and Loss Account - Balance	8,251 5 4	
Less amount written off - Formation Expenses	1,225 16 6	
	7,025 8 10	
Less Interim Dividend of 3 ½% paid October 7th 1895, on Ordinary Shares	3,500 0 7	
		3,525 8 3
		195,083 18 2
Freehold and Leasehold Property, Machinery, Plant, Fixtures, Fittings, Horses and Carts, Goodwill, etc, etc	133,750 0 0	
Add amount expended	1,411 15 0	
	135,161 15 0	
Less amount written off	361 15 0	
		134,800 0 0
Stock		33,527 17 0
Sundry Debtors		15,250 12 9
Cash at Bankers	5,851 5 3	
Do. In Hand	107 4 4	
		5,958 9 7
Rebate on Insurance		443 12 0
Formation Expenses	6,329 2 6	
Less amount written off	1,225 16 6	
		5,103 6 0
		195,083 18 2

PROFIT AND LOSS ACCOUNT - 27TH FEBRUARY, 1896	£ s d
Dr.	
To Interest paid on Purchase Money	1,448 19 7
To Interest paid on Debentures	4,375 0 0
Directors & Trustees Fees	1,053 7 6
Amount Written off, Leaseholds, Fixtures, etc.	361 5 4
Profit to Balance Sheet	8,251 5 4
	15,490 7 6
Cr.	
By Trading Profit after paying general expenses, repairs, and writing off bad debts from 1st January 1895	15,359 12 5
Transfer Fees	130 7 5
	15,490 7 6

We have examined the books and accounts of Messrs Ben Evans and Co. Limited and we hereby certify the above Balance Sheet and Profit and Loss Account to be correct. Dated this 19th March 1896

PERCY MASON & Co., Chartered Accountants, 64, Gresham Street, London, E.C.

Founder Shares: It would take 28 years for the 3,000 Founders Shares to be removed from the Balance Sheet when, in September 1922 an extraordinary meeting of shareholders was held, chaired by Walter J. Burt during which the Chairman's proposal to convert each founder's share into eight fully-paid second preference shares was accepted, and thus the matter was resolved to the satisfaction of all parties.

(e) Balance Sheet Comparison 1929 and 1930

BALANCE SHEET COMPARISON 1929 and 1930		
Capital and Liabilities	February 1929	February 1930
Preference Shares	£20,000	£20,000
Second Preferences	3,000	3,000
Ordinary Shares	167,000	167,000
Debentures	85,531	85,531
Creditors	13,026	12,614
Reserve	8,000	8,000
Debenture Premiums	2,017	1,463
Unclaimed Dividends	952	
Property Reserve	20,306	20,306
Assets		
Properties etc.	136,850***	136,503
Fixture etc.	19,058***	19,043
War Loan	19,987	19,987
Stocks	32,023	77,377
Debtors etc.	41,272***	41,357
Cash	17,489	22,427
Prepaid Rates etc.	1,395	1,327
Debenture premiums	--------	2,127
Total Assets	£321,076	£321,076

*** After providing for amounts written off

5-YEAR RESULTS COMPARISON 1926-1930 INCLUSIVE				
Year Ending	Profits £	Written Off etc. £	Carry Forward £	Ordinary Dividend %
Feb. 1926	21,491	2,190	149	6
Feb. 1927	18,358	2,416	281	4
Feb. 1928	14,155	2,212***	302	2 1/2
Feb. 1929	10,389	1,741	316	NIL
Feb. 1930	10,522	2,000	225	NIL

*** From reserve

(f) Balance Sheet Comparison 1931 and 1932

BALANCE SHEET COMPARISON 1931 and 1932		
Capital and Liabilities	February 1931	February 1933
Preference Shares	£20,000	£20,000
Second Preferences	3,000	2,400
Ordinary Shares	167,000	133,600
Debentures	85,531	85,531
Creditors	12,507	12,221
Reserve	8,000	5,508
Property Reserve	20,306	20,306
Unclaimed Interest etc.	1,410	973
Assets		
Properties etc ***	136,335	136,078
Plant etc.***	16,049	15,970
War Loan	19,987	19,987
Stocks	43,731	47,012
Debtors etc.	37,301	40,731
Cash	25,701	24,813
Amounts Prepaid	1,256	1,267
Loan	1,000	---------
Debit Balance	36,492	---------
Total Assets	£317,863	£285,858

*** After deducting amounts written off, etc.

Appending is a comparison of the results of the last five years:

5-YEAR RESULTS COMPARISON 1928-1932 INCLUSIVE				
Year Ending	Profits £	Reserve etc. £	Carry Forward £	Ordinary Dividend %
Feb. 1928	14,166	2,212***	802	2 1/2
Feb. 1929	10,389	1,741	316	NIL
Feb. 1930	10,522	2,000	225	NIL
Feb. 1931	(36,117)	33,687	36,498 ##	NIL
Feb. 1932	13,384	2,304	157	2% §§

*** From reserve ## Debit balance §§ On reduced capital

(g) Ben Evans & Co. Ltd Net Profit 1895-1954

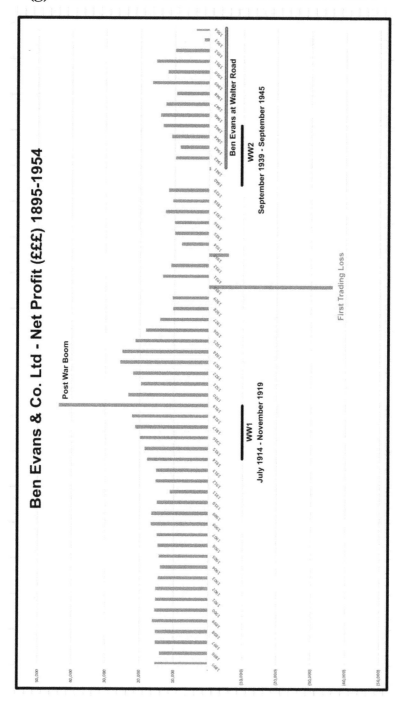

(h) Ben Evans & Co. Ltd Net Profit 1895-1954
(adjusted for inflation June 2024)

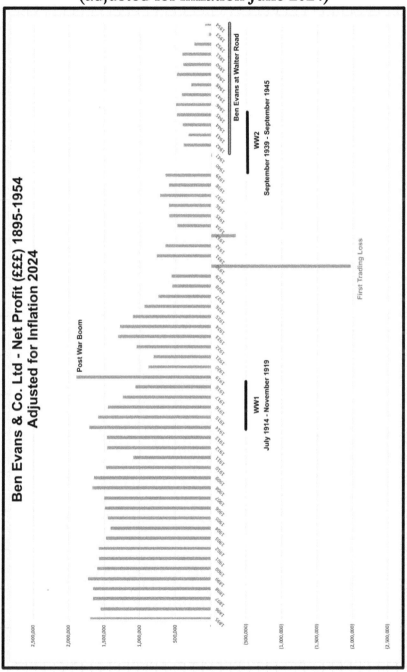

(i) Ben Evans & Co. Ltd Directors letter to the Mayor, Aldermen and Councillors of the County Borough of Swansea, February 1944

(Original document GB 216 D 268/5 in West Glamorgan Archives, Swansea)

BEN EVANS & CO., LTD. GENERAL DRAPERS
12 ST. MARY'S SQUARE, SWANSEA
Secretary's Office, Feb. 22nd, 1944

To the Mayor, Aldermen and Councillors of the County Borough of Swansea
LADIES AND GENTLEMEN, TOWN PLANNING OF SWANSEA
    AND REDEVELOPMENT OF ITS SHOPPING CENTRE

Prior to an enemy air raid in February 1941, the business of Ben Evans & Company, Limited, one of the largest of its kind in South Wales, had been in existence for over 70 years and contributed largely to the popularity and attractiveness of Swansea as a Shopping Centre. The premises of our Company were amongst the most conspicuous and stately features of the Town. Their importance and value were in some measure reflected by the fact that we annually paid over £4,000 0. 0. in rates into the coffers of the Town. The total rateable value of the block of buildings of which they formed part was £6,357 0 0. The scheme now under consideration by you proposes that our valuable building should not be restored, but the site of the whole of the said block used as part of an extensive open space of doubtful if any value to the Town. So far as the scheme goes no alternative site comparable as to position, dimensions, potentialities, or value, is to be offered us by way of exchange or compensation so that (subject to any conditions which may be imposed by the War Damage Commission) we are not only to lose our property, but to be put out of business as well. What applies to us will apply to many other well-known firms throughout the Town.

The only reasons put forward for such interference with so many well-established and foremost businesses of the town, and for the sacrifice of so many valuable properties, with their high rateable values, is that traffic will be expedited and better controlled and the Town beautified, the dubious inference being that the attainment of these objectives will then both create and new businesses. This is a reversal of the old but common sense beliefs that it was businesses which created traffic, and that traffic should be so controlled as to serve, and increase, rather than interfere with or destroy, business.

It is obvious that it the scheme is adopted by you the interference imposed upon our activities and the losses we shall inevitably suffer will be of such magnitude and consequence that our future will be imperilled and this through no act, failure or omission on our own part. Not only, therefore, are we directly concerned with your proposals, but entitled to place our views frankly and fully before you for your consideration before you commit ourselves to the acceptance or proposals which we respectfully venture to think are misconceived and opposed to the true interests of the town.

It will not be inconsistent with growing public opinion to suggest that the preparation of post-war plans and schemes of all kinds and descriptions is almost becoming a pastime, and particularly so where the contemplated expenditure would be borne out of public funds.

The task of preparing a Town Planning Scheme is comparatively an easy one. The probabilities are that everyone who has viewed the devastations at Swansea and has some passing acquaintance with the Town, has his own ideas of what such a scheme should be. The problem of estimating at their proper worth all the essential factors and conditions to be taken into account and upon which alone can a fair, reasonable and acceptable scheme be based, is a far different and far more difficult task. Greed of power. overzealousness, and ill-founded optimism, as for example that the population of Swansea, though at present declining, can within a given number of years be expected to be in the neighbourhood of 250,000, inevitably lead to strange and visionary ideas and far-fetched proposals.

There are really two matters involved in the scheme, namely, the restoration of that portion of the central and oldest area of the borough which by long usage, constant development, and service, had become universally recognized as the Shopping Centre, and which has been so completely devastated by enemy air raids, and as complementary thereto the Town Planning and Re-development of the whole of such central area.

Whatever views there may be as to the merits or demerits of the combined Scheme prepared by the Borough Engineer and Surveyor for this, and even a much larger and more ambitious, area, there are some aspects of the situation upon which there be common agreement, namely:

(a) That a scheme for the reconstruction of the Shopping Centre should be the first to demand attention.

(b) That owing to the concentration of the devastation and the close proximity to each other of such a large number of buildings which have been either completely demolished or rendered unusable in the central part of Swansea, an unrivalled opportunity has been presented for carrying out a scheme for its re-development on sound and moderate lines, but embracing so far as they e necessary and economically possible, some of the features represented as essential in modern Town Planning.

(c) That though due regard should be had to the indeterminate advantages of re-development, yet as the prosperity of the Town is being imperilled and its community prejudiced by the loss of its shopping and business facilities, the more immediate need is for reconstruction or its Shopping Centre.

(d) That the demand for reconstruction is so urgent and the consequences or delay so urgent and the many that no time should be lost in waiting for an ambitious scheme of re-development which may prove unattainable for very many if at all because of extravagance of design, or cost. or indifference as to its extent and merits. Or suggestions which have been made as to demolition of many properties not damaged or within the precincts of Centre, at a time when there is already an acute shortage of housing and the inevitable difficulties as to the acquisition of these other properties and the provision of alternative accommodation tor persons displaced. Etc, etc.

When considering the need for urgency it should also be borne in mind that as the result of the War Damage Amendment Act, 1943, now incorporated in the consolidated War Damage Act, 1943, a large number of the owners of war-damaged properties situated within the Shopping Centre have been officially informed that instead of their properties being considered total losses, for which value payments would be appropriate, they will only be able to claim cost of works payments after they have made good the damage done to the respective premises providing they comply with licensing and other requirements.

Obviously, these owners await and must be afforded the opportunity of proceeding with their several claims in the only manner thus open to them. Moreover, the investment in the re-building and restoration of their respective premises of all the monies which will become payable to the owners of war-damaged premises should reduce all or any of your anxieties and worries as to finance and materially contribute towards bringing any approved scheme to full fruition. Your Estate Agent, who has a shrewd knowledge of the value of properties in Swansea, should be in a position to advise you as to the total sum of the amounts which can reasonably he expected from these sources, or which in certain events may be expended directly by the War Damage Commission.

After the said raid we were compelled to acquire other and much smaller premises at a considerable distance from our former sphere of operations in order to preserve the goodwill of our business. The patronage and generous support extended to our Walter Road and other scattered premises convince us that our return to larger and more commodious premises of our old site would be greatly welcomed by the public at large. At the same time, such support would not, without serious trepidation, warrant us in embarking upon any doubtful or hazardous venture of a permanent character in a part of the town other than on the which was our own freehold, and the advantages of which were created and proved or us and are therefore already known to us.

As an indication of the desire of other owners to restore their premises, it may be stated that but very few of their number have availed themselves of the opportunities given them by Parliament of terminating their labilities under the leases held by them, but on the contrary that nearly all of them gave given notices to their freeholders of intention to retain their leases. The cooperation of all owners of war-damaged properties should therefore be sought and encouraged and not lightly and irresponsibly treated as a matter of no account. From whatever angle the position is examined no just cause can be advanced for any avoidable delay in proceeding with reconstruction which is so vital therefore to the persons immediately affected, as well as to the Town at large.

Though it can be admitted that the planning of Swansea as it existed before the War was not free from objection, the streets in its central part were surprisingly symmetrical in their ultimate layout. It must not be inferred that its detects were either serious or irremovable by process of time, and this without the haphazard upheaval of business or ownership of property, especially if reasonable allowances are made for its exceptional position and confines, and the natural and therefore age-old hindrances to any wider and more ambitious layout which, though there was no need or demand for same, would have anticipated what are today loftily described as the intricate problems arising out of modern ideas and practice.

Even the most ardent and prodigal of our planners, who would condemn the past and seek to improve upon it at any cost, must admit that as compared with other large towns and districts which have adopted or are contemplating the adoption of town planning schemes on a large or comprehensive scale, there is not a large extent of land in Swansea suitable for the easy and inexpensive construction or streets possessed of all the questionable advantages of modernity or in a manner stable as the groundwork for a layout in accordance the principles and practices clamantly advocated by them. It can be asserted that whilst Swansea had defects peculiar to its position, it also had merits and attractiveness of its own which at all times conduced to its prosperity and steadily attracted and fostered business. In this respect, we respectfully submit that our own experience, fortified by that of others, is of far greater value and far more reliable for your future guidance than the theoretical assumptions of our planners.

The narrowness of some of its streets, and the bends turnings in others were the tenacious relics of an old town founded and expanded long before Building Bye-laws were in vogue. They were inconspicuous memorials of its antiquity, growth and history, 'summoned up remembrances of things past,' and therefore had their niche in the traditions of the town. as well as in the affections of its inhabitants They were not inconvenient for business, were not a hindrance to the prosperity of the town. and there was no reason to suppose that they did not adequately serve their several purposes, or were bereft of innumerable advantages erroneously represented as not obtainable except in modern planning.

Their long continuance in the very centre of Swansea. not-withstanding the many and important improvements which have from time to time, and particularly within the last 50 or 60 years, been carried out both by the Swansea Council and by private enterprise, of themselves indicate that they not a bar to the business and progress of the Town. Improvements such as the construction of Alexandra Road. the widening of Castle Bailey Street (carried out by us, and for which we claim and should be given credit) and Castle Street, and the demolition of all the horrible slum cottages in the four very narrow streets which surrounded St Mary's

Church, and were thereby widened and now constitute, the present-day St. Mary's Square, undoubtedly removed the most serious defects in the ancient streets of the Town. Other defects could gradually have been affected by the erection of new buildings in conformity with the revised Building Bye-laws of the Town. But for unfortunate differences as to the compensation payable, it can be safely stated that the improvements consequent upon the construction of new buildings would have been more numerous.

The power now vested in or obtainable by the Council are such as will enable them to overcome most of the difficulties experienced in the past without embarking upon any scheme which by reason of its magnitude and cost will only delay progress.

Long straight and wide streets intersecting each other at regular intervals with their many spacious and dignified squares and blocks of property, which have no regard to the past and its traditions customs, even to existing conditions and habits but abounding with diverse architectural and decorative features and with facilities for both slow and fast vehicular traffic as general rule commend themselves to the Engineer and Architect, and even to those who regard these matters merely from the point of view of the distant, but entirely uncertain, future. We venture to believe that a careful and unbiased examination of the present layout of the streets in the centre of Swansea will disclose that in large measure they conform to the general pattern already referred to, and that any deficiencies appearing could be sufficiently altered or improved to meet all reasonable requirements in any scheme for reconstruction. Save at a fabulous and totally unwarranted expenditure of public moneys the complete requirements of such a general pattern are only feasible in virgin or slightly occupied country. Without drastic and unnecessary alterations and demolitions, complete disregard for existing properties, public services, amenities, conditions and rights, and a complete upheaval, they are not feasible at Swansea. Neither are they needed. Even if and where feasible they may not be picturesque or artistic in their setting, and, which is of greater significance to any Shopping Centre, may not afford acceptable inducements to business, It is easy to construct a centre for new business. but it is an entirely different matter to attract business to it.

In an old town tradition and custom play their part and cannot be ignored. Care is, therefore, necessary to ensure that in the re-development of the Shopping Centre the interests and goodwill of its business people are preserved and that there shall not be so many changes as will offer them no reasonable opportunities for trading on a remunerative basis, or will cause so much turmoil, discontent, and apprehension as to drive them elsewhere tor existence.

As the damaged portion of the centre of Swansea does not offer the opportunities to be found in virgin or sparsely occupied localities for planning on a grand scale, it is now proposed to augment the damage already done by acquiring and demolishing a vast number of other buildings. According to the report made by your Borough Estate Agent, it is proposed to demolish at least 178 Dwelling-houses, 59 Shops, 12 Public Houses, 53 other business premises and 3 Schools and Institutions. These striking figures speak for themselves and indicate beyond fear of contradiction that the town has to be further desolated to fit in with the plans, instead of the plans being prepared so as to fit in with the town, and its needs and financial resources.

In other words the prosperity and destinies of the town are to be thrown into the melting pot for purposes which may to some slight extent serve to regulate its vehicular traffic and improve its appearance but are otherwise of dubious benefit.

Though not actually designed for the modern-day form of vehicular transport which creates so many dangers and difficulties, in its regulation and control as to require special consideration in any scheme of redevelopment, the streets of Swansea have not the past hampered or restricted this form of traffic to any unusual or marked extent. This is probably due to several causes. Because of the surrounding hills and its exceptional position between these hills and the seafront, Swansea has been out of the direct line of any considerable volume of through or town to town traffic. It cannot be compared with Newport, Cardiff and Neath or even Llanelly, in this respect. So far as the centre of the Town is concerned it's through traffic has been largely limited to that proceeding to the Mumbles, or to the beauty spots of the Gower Peninsula. In addition, there is of course, the traffic from other towns destined for Swansea itself and not proceeding beyond.

The traffic for Mumbles and Gower can be dealt with without any great changes to the streets of the town. Its volume and character are such that there can be no justification for the preparation of very grandiose schemes or the expenditure of vast sums of public money for facilitating or controlling its movement.

The traffic mainly to be considered is that between Swansea and its suburbs, and between its adjoining townships, most of which is of a business character, but all of which is needful to the town and contributes so materially towards making it a business centre. In dealing with this there should be proper regard for the requirements and convenience of the town's own community, as well as for those of its visitors, and so far the shopping centre is concerned, for its full maintenance and growth and the development of its business. This form of public transport should therefore continue to pass through the streets of the shopping centre, which should be wide enough to allow this to be done. It should not be confined to any street or streets encircling the shopping centre, or distant therefrom.

Public transport which caters for local needs, and of necessity requires frequent stopping places, as well as pedestrian crossings, cannot be truly described as fast-moving traffic, so that there is no special need for a large number of traffic islands of colossal and almost unprecedented dimensions for control or guidance. We are advised that the proposed traffic island on the site of Castle and Castle Bailey Streets, and on the sites of the numerous buildings formerly adjoining or adjacent to these streets, with its green sward surrounds, will be about 4 1/2 times the size of Piccadilly Circus, one of the busiest traffic centres in the world. It is regretted that. save to experts, the plans do not sufficiently come close to this almost incredible proposal.

If in catering for focal needs on sound economic and practical lines the town can at the same time he beautified or if the through traffic for Mumbles and Gower can be so dealt with not to interfere in the least degree with the streets within the shopping centre, and therefore with business, so much the better To radically alter the town at the risk of sacrificing its business, and its facilities for new business, or the sake of imaginary. doubtful or unsubstantial benefits would be an unpardonable blunder.

The exhortation to plan boldly cannot mean, neither can it justify planning extravagantly, or beyond the needs which exist or can reasonably be expected to arise. Neither does it justify planning on prodigal or uneconomical, which, when the total expenditure is known would straightaway hold up the scheme to ridicule on all sides.

The provision of a large number of vast traffic islands, even if trees be planted thereon, or they are gaily decorated with shrubs and flowers, is not going to beautify the town to such an extent as to justify the huge expense involved in the acquisition and sterilization of these expensive sites The loss of rateable value alone would be tremendous, whilst the effect of these traffic islands upon adjoining or adjacent premises would not attach much business or conduce to that end.

The suggestion made in some quarters that the rateable values would not be lost. but transferred elsewhere, is plausible on the face of it. but it presumes so much as to be utterly fallacious.

Experience has taught us in Swansea that fairly narrow streets with shopping facilities on both sides are generally far better for business than a very wide one. Experience in other towns also demonstrates that they are more favoured and patronized than any wide or grand, but entirely one-sided street, devoid of business attraction on the other side. There may be noticeable exceptions to the latter proposition as, for example, Princess Street, Edinburgh, with its magnificent and historical setting, but these are few and far between.

It is also generally found that the wider the road the greater the number of motor cars which can be parked therein. It is highly desirable that motorists should be given reasonable opportunities for the transaction of business and for shopping. parking in the streets for other purposes should not be permitted at the cost of either curtailing business or obstructing recess to business premises, or in any other manner interfering unfairly with legitimate business. Instead, ample facilities should be given for parking at selected sites convenient to the shopping centre.

As business may result from the visit of the casual visitor and even from that of the pleasure seeker, the car parks should be at such locations as will not prevent or hinder resort to the shopping centre. We would however stress that dark spots or spaces not developed for business purposes generally diminish the values of all neighbouring premises, so that great care should be exercised in selecting the sites for all car parks. The number and location of the car parks proposed in your scheme will require careful consideration.

Though the present proposals have avowedly been designed to beautify the town for visitors, it would seem that sight has been lost of the town's almost unrivalled foreshore and sands, or the beauty and attractiveness of its suburbs, and surrounding countryside, and the number, situation and charm of its numerous parks and open spaces.

If beautifying Swansea for business and commercial purposes, and so as to attract new business is the main consideration, it is strange that no constructive proposal has been submitted for the clearance and utilization of the sites of the many ugly tips and derelict works at Landore and alongside the main entrance to the town, or falling this tor concealing by any other means their hideousness and thus alleviating the spirit of despondency which they create,

It is also almost equally strange that no proposal has been made for restoring to the public, and particularly visitors to the town, the unrivalled view across the docks and seawards across the Bay towards Port Talbot and Porthcawl, and the heights beyond them, which would always be obtainable from High Street or Worcester Place if there were no buildings on some part or the eastern side thereof. If the situation of a few of these buildings could be suitably arranged, or it new road in the nature of a promenade constructed at their rear from the G. W.R Station as say, King Street, a vista would be opened up without any excessive cost, which would give our visitors some idea of the importance of the town and its shipping, as well as of the beauty or its surroundings.

There are many other and equally important objections to the present proposals. As it is impossible in the space at our command to call attention to all of them, we must content ourselves by referring in brief terms to just a few. They are:

(1) That no information has been afforded as to the extent to which the cost will be borne by the Government and the town respectively, or whether the scheme will (as there is good reason to believe, and in fact has been indicated by Sir William Jowett K.C.) have to be self-supporting.

(2) That no estimate has yet been prepared of the scheme as a whole.
We readily acknowledge that as it is impossible to state what the cost of labour and materials will be after the war and no forecast can be made as to the financial assistance which may be forthcoming, it is probably impossible to prepare any accurate estimate but such difficulties should not prevent an estimate of the cost being given, which would be subject

to all or any financial adjustments which might be disclosed at a later stage, this would afford a rough idea of what the rate-payers, and its businessmen in particular, are asked to commit themselves to.

In this respect, though the questions of compensation for loss of business or other disturbances may be intricate and require special consideration, there is nothing to prevent an estimate being made of the 1939 values of the many undamaged properties already referred to which is proposed to incorporate into the scheme for demolition.

We venture to believe that the financial implications of the scheme should be fully ascertained and disclosed before any steps are taken to bring it into being.

(3) That the greater the cost the greater will be the ultimate burden to the tradesmen either in the way of acquiring sites and erecting or acquiring new premises, or in the way of rent, and therefore the remoter the possibility of carrying on business on a remunerative basis.

(4) That the acquisition and sterilization of the very many valuable sites proposed. with the consequent disuse or abandonment of long lengths of sewers, water mains, electric cables,
etc. and the substitution of new and expensive services of the like kinds. is totally unnecessary and unjustifiable and nothing less than reckless expenditure and waste of public money.

(5) That but little endeavour seems to have been made to retain or otherwise render available to property owners and the businessmen of the town the sites of the premises owned by them, or in which they formerly carried on business.

(6) That the proposed location of the General Market and of the Wholesalers Market or Centre, are entirely wrong. both from the point of view of ready access, business, and vallecular traffic. It is not too much to say that the locations now proposed would definitely increase instead of lessen the traffic difficulties which the scheme purports to remove.
(7) That the scheme has apparently been designed on the assumption that nearly all the main traffic into the centre of Swansea will be from the North, whereas it can reasonably be expected that after the construction by the Ministry of Transport or Glamorgan County Council, of the proposed by-pass from Briton Ferry to Lonlas, most of the Eastern traffic

which is not of a through character, but destined for Swansea alone, and which now comes in through Llansamlet and Morriston, will come in via Port Tennant Road, which will also require considerable widening and adaptation.

(8) That no one has yet had the temerity to state the period in which the scheme can reasonably be expected to be carried out. Some there are who claim that fifteen to twenty years will see its completion but there are others who assert in positive terms that it will not be completed within the next fifty to a hundred years, if then. All the information yet given is that the scheme can be proceeded with piecemeal, which at best is unsatisfactory. All this uncertainty is very disturbing and especially to those of us who are anxious, if the opportunities are favourable, to resume business on our own sites, and this on the lines and to the extent in force before the war.

Lastly and in general support of our observations and objections, may we pray in aid the statement contained in Memorandum B issued by the Ministry of Town and Country Planning to all local authorities on the 3rd November 1945, wherein it is said 'Before detailed planning proposals can be prepared on a well-considered basis, planning authorities will need adequately informed of the factors affecting their district, etc, etc.

Of late years the population of Swansea and District has decreased, many of the local industries have been permanently closed, the prospects for continuance of all the tinplate works are as dismal as they can be, and the prospects of obtaining new industries into the area are to say the least vague, it is not indeed remote. We appreciate that you are gravely concerned as to these matters and have taken steps to promote and further the claims of the town tor consideration of the location of new industries.

Nevertheless, we cannot ignore the fact that so many public authorities are strenuously submitting demands for consideration that the position has become a more or less chaotic scramble teeming with difficulties as to fulfilment and with embarrassing consequences. Neither can we, when estimating the chances of a favourable response to your efforts ignore the steadily increasing discontent with the continuance of Government control of Industry, from which West Wales, and the Tinplate Trade, in particular, have already suffered so heavily. It is highly probable that in all the circumstances Government assistance may be both negligible and tardy, and that our hopes for a certain solution to our industrial difficulties and a full return to commercial prosperity should in the future, as in the past, be based upon individual initiative. This brings us back to our previous statements that your scheme should be an economical one and that the practical cooperation of the property owners and businessmen of the town is absolutely necessary to its success.

Until there is more definite knowledge as to our future prospects, the time is not opportune for any considerable expenditure unless this is proved beyond doubt to be absolutely necessary. It must be borne in mind that entirely apart from these planning proposals your Council has a heavy programme of improvements and therefore many heavy commitments in respect of works designed to meet post-war conditions. In all the foregoing circumstances we trust it will not be deemed an impertinence if we remind you that the question of Rates is one which usually is taken into careful consideration by all persons intending to found new industries. We are informed that housing is to have the first call on labour and materials in the post-war period. It seems inevitable, therefore, that there should be serious delay in carrying out whatever plans or schemes may be decided upon and also that the more extravagant, ambitious and uneconomic such plans or schemes may be the greater will be the delay.

It is self-evident that no time should be lost before abandoning the present proposals, which collectively are objectionable and unworkable, and, instead, concentrating upon a scheme that is reasonable, practical and economical, which can be financed and carried out without any avoidable and unnecessary delay, will preserve existing public services as well as properties and businesses, will create rather than destroy rateable value, and will secure all-round co-operation in achieving those of the proposals suggested by your officials which are really needful and possible.

Yours faithfully,
For and on behalf of Ben Evans & Co., Ltd.
GEO. WHEATLEY, Managing Director.
B.C. MILLARD, Secretary.

(j) Figures Relating to the old David Evans Store, December 1955.

Original document GB 216 D/D DEC/1/2 in West Glamorgan Archives, Swansea

War Damage Settlement.

Agreed Site Value - **Total: £32,000**

Divided up as follows:

I0/II Castle Street.	10,400 (equal to 32½% of the whole)
11 Temple Street	4,500
I0 Temple St. and 30/35 Goat St	17,100
	£32,000

Basic Valuation for Building: £50,000

Basing the value of the building on the above:

Taking 4% of the Site Value. equals	£1280 p.a.
Taking 5% of the Site Value. equals	£2525 p.a.
On this basis, a fair valuation for the whole would be	£3805 p.a.

The old building was larger than the new as it had an extra floor, as well as an extension to Castle Street, with a frontage of about 30 feet. This Castle Street frontage also gave us a Ground Floor entrance to the First Floor Showroom on the main block.

When we were negotiating through Messrs Hales & partners, for a Finance Company to build the new building, and to let the 1st part of the Ground Flour to us, with all the upper floors, it was agreed that the following rental should be paid to the Finance Company:

For the part Ground Floor with all the upper floors.	£5750
Plus, if we took an extra lock-up shop.	£1350

Old Store.

Rates paid by David Evans. & Co. for:

| Year ending February 19/39 | £1911. 15s. 10d. Rate though to be 16/4 |
| Year ending February 19/40 | £1982. 11s. 05d. Rate though to be 17/- |

On these figures, it would appear that our rateable value was about £2333, but this probably included Rates paid on the Garage.

Assuming the old assessment to be **£2333**, then the proposed new assessment of **£13,000** shows an **increase of 457%** (that is **5.57 times the old assessment**).

(k) Redevelopment of Central Town Area
(Internal Swansea Council Document)

Original document DD/RMD 1/66/8 in West Glamorgan Archives, Swansea

RMD/EMR   31st December,1959

As a University town Swansea, with its
extensive docks, covering a deep water
area of 270 acres, is the nearest large
Bristol Channel port to the Atlantic
Ocean.

It is also an important industrial centre,
being the fifth-largest County borough   162,000 (1959)
in the Kingdom with a population of
serving a Regional population of   400,000

The area of the Borough (including 24,241 acres
foreshore)
The area of the Borough (excluding 21,600 acres
foreshore)

Rateable Value of Swansea (December £2, 286,962
1959)

During the war the town suffered from
Extensive air raids, particularly on three
successive nights of concentrated attacks. In
February 1941, when of the main business
and shopping centre 44 acres were
devastated with considerable damage over
an area of   280 acres

Of the 38,260 houses in the Borough -
were completely destroyed: 802
were seriously damaged   1,300
the number requiring first aid repairs   20,000

ANALYSIS OF BUILDINGS DESTROYED OR BADLY DAMAGED

	Town Centre	Whole Borough
Shops (one third of main shopping area)	350	450
Hotels and Public Houses	33	45
Industrial Buildings	42	60
Office Buildings	40	40
Wholesale Warehouses	39	39
Places of Worship	13	18
Public Buildings (Clinics, BBC. etc.)	6	6
Schools	6	20
Clubs and Boarding Houses	5	4
Cinemas and Dance Halls	4	5

Before the end of the war plans were prepared for the rebuilding of the Town Centre on modern lines and an Application to the Ministry for a Declaratory Order was made on	17th April 1946
which was followed by a Public Inquiry on	7th to 15th August 1946
A Declaratory Area of 134 acres was confirmed by the Ministry on	25th July 1947
Work on the First Stage Roadworks commenced on	1st November 1948
The Kingsway was opened by Princess Margaret on	1st November 1950
Work on the Second Stage Roadworks commenced on	1st January 1951
Work on the Third Stage Roadworks commenced on	April 1958
Loss of rateable value in town centre due to enemy action	£121,682 (1941value)

Work on the first permanent shop started on the 18th of December 1950. Up to the 31st December 1959, the following new buildings have been completed.

New Shops including Public Houses	146
Castle Street Shops (Re-built after war-damage)	13
Warehouses	10
Light Industry	6
B•B.C. Studios	1
Flats at New Street	44
Castle Gardens in Town Centre	
Office	5
2 Car Parks	2
Merchant Navy Hotel	1

PUBLIC BUILDINGS COMPLETED
New Central Fire Station
Repeater Station
Telegraph Office
St. Mary's Parish Church

UNDER CONSTRUCTION

Shops including Public Houses	2
Warehouses	51
Residential Hotels	2
Office Block	2
Light Industry	1

APPROVED SITES

Motor Showroom and Garage	
Shops/stores - East of Dragon Hotel	
Warehouses	1
Clinic	1
Arcades	2

DRAFT PROPOSALS

Occupational Centre	1
Wholesale Fruit Warehouses	1

PROPOSED FLATS

At Dyfatty	Approx. 237
At Brynmelin	Approx. 190